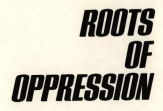

ROOTS
OF
OPPRESSION

**INTERNATIONAL PUBLISHERS
NEW YORK**

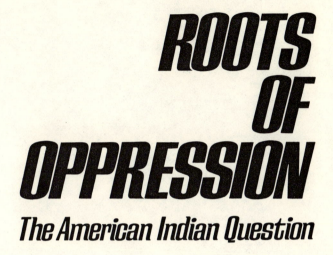

ROOTS OF OPPRESSION

The American Indian Question

by Steve Talbot

Copyright © 1981 by International Publishers
All rights reserved
First edition 1981
Manufactured in the United States of America

Library of Congress Cataloging in Publication Data

Talbot, Steve.
   Roots of oppression.

   Based on author's thesis (Ph.D.)—University of
California, Berkeley.
   Bibliography: p. 195.
   Includes index.
   1. Indians of North America—Government relations.
I. Title.
E93.T2   1981   305.8'97   81-6521
ISBN 0-7178-0591-3   AACR2
ISBN 0-7178-0583-2 (pbk.)

CONTENTS

ILLUSTRATIONS

TABLES

PREFACE

This is the first of a projected two-volume study of the Native American question in the United States. The present work introduces the Indian movement and describes the political economy of struggle. The second volume will deal primarily with social and cultural genocide and the Indian resistance to it. Both volumes present contemporary events in their historical perspective, the methodology of historical materialism.

This work reflects my Ph.D. thesis in anthropology, written at the University of California, Berkeley, in 1974, when I was teaching in the Native American Studies Program. Although it has been extensively revised, I nevertheless owe the "Berkeley Indians" a considerable debt for the support I received in undertaking the initial research, including release time from teaching duties. This book is respectfully dedicated to them.

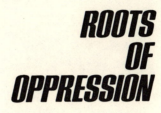

No one shall be arbitrarily deprived of his nationality nor denied the right to change his nationality.

The Universal Declaration of
Human Rights, Article XV

1

THE SO-CALLED
INDIAN PROBLEM

It is usual to refer to the depressed state of Native American life as "the plight of the American Indian" or simply as "the Indian problem." Native American activists, on the other hand, deny they have either a plight or a problem: instead they have injustice (see *Akwesasne Notes* 1974a:41).

Injustice means a lack of justice, a wrong, a violation of a person's or a people's rights. Plight, however, connotes not only a bad state or condition, but also a predicament or dilemma—in other words, "a difficult situation usually offering no satisfactory solution" (Webster's *New Collegiate Dictionary,* 1967 edition). To characterize the Native American situation as a plight is to say that theirs is a sad and tragic condition, but, unfortunately, one to which there is no solution.

Plight means that it was the destiny of "primitive" peoples to "retire" from the pages of history and become the "vanishing Redmen," in order to make way for U.S. capitalism and its supposedly superior Yankee culture. Plight is therefore part of the racist and national chauvinistic baggage of world colonialism and imperialism, the rationale for the genocide of the indigenous peoples and the seizure of their lands.

The term "Indian problem" appears to have had a more recent origin. Once Native Americans, the less than ten percent who survived, were confined to reservations as conquered peoples by the close of the nine-teenth century, it became the concern of the federal government to find an effective means for colonial management and control. To speak of an Indian problem, therefore, is to shift the burden of responsibility from capitalism to Native Americans, from the oppressor to the oppressed.

Despite this obfuscation, the Native American situation in the United States is a critical social issue and thus should be termed, as is common in the literature of political struggle, *the Native American question*! This is the case because, in the first place, the majority of Native Americans have similar problems arising out of their common oppression, problems not only shared with the working class generally, but special problems—the continuing theft of their lands and resources by Big Business, astronomi-cal rates of unemployment and low income, racism of a kind directed toward indigenous peoples, neo-colonial management by the U.S. gov-ernment of the reservations, and the suppression of the Native Ameri-cans' rich and varied histories, languages, traditions and life-ways.

In the second place, non-Indians—Black, Brown, White and Yellow—also have a vested interest in this question, because state monopoly capitalism in its theft of Native American land and resources is at the same time "ripping off" the public domain; it is threatening the environ-ment for all citizens and causing energy rates to soar, food prices to rise, because of the link between the energy corporations and agribusiness. The corporations also employ the "Indian differential" in the wages paid to Indian workers, thereby threatening union wages for other workers in the nation as well. This theft and exploitation is not in the public interest anymore than it is in the interest of the Native American peoples. The difference to Native Americans is that their struggle is one for survival!

The trouble is that bourgeois apologists define the issue differently than do Native Americans, and certainly differently than those who would base their analysis on an anti-monopoly perspective.

Bias in Anthropology

Anthropologists, whether they realize it or not, are among the chief apologists for the Establishment when it comes to the Native American question. For anthropologists, the root of the problem lay with indigenous *culture*—traditions, language, religion and values, kinship obligations, and social structure. Native Americans are said to have a "cultural" or "value conflict," a "cultural crisis," because they "live between two worlds." Anthropological analysis implies that the cultural factor is responsible for Indian poverty. Murray Wax (1971:195), for example, a proponent of cultural pluralism, believes that in order for Indians to maintain their ethnicity, they must in the main accept poverty "since poverty is an integral part of the U.S. socio-economic system."

Following this line of reasoning, one can say that poverty, racial discrimination, inadequate education, reservation undevelopment, etc., are caused by the oppressed rather than the oppressor. There is the underlying assumption that ethnic rights are incompatible with social and economic development, the latter being seen as synonymous with capitalism. No alternative social policy is envisioned, such as found in socialist states which are multi-national, where the "cultural in form, socialist in content" formula allows for economic development and a rising standard of living at the same time there is a flowering of culture.

To illustrate further this point concerning anthropological bias, we will discuss an article by Nagel which appeared in a special issue of *Current History* (1974). We will see that while Nagel is justly critical of anthropological treatment of the Native American situation, he at the same time naively reiterates its erroneous philosophical assumptions.

Nevertheless, Nagel gives useful information on dollar income, unemployment, poverty and ill health, and the poor living conditions found on U.S. Indian reservations. Since over 60 percent of all Native Americans, according to his analysis of the 1970 Census, still reside on or near reservations, it is obvious that these are important areas of inquiry if one is to get a basic understanding of the question. Yet these are the very topics usually neglected by anthropologists in their studies.

Nagel justly criticizes anthropologists for their neglect of the statistical method and economic data. He cites the experience of another researcher, Stephen Lagone, who examined 12 drawers of file cards in The Library of Congress under the heading, "Indians of North America" (Lagone 1969a).

Lagone found twelve drawers in all containing approximately 18,000 file cards, but only 16 cards dealt with "statistics" and 11 with "census." On the other hand, under the subheadings "pottery" and "legends" there were 103 for the former and 314 for the latter. Under "population" and "income" there were no cards at all. The facts speak for themselves: anthropologists, upon whom others rely for expert information, have collected data primarily on pre-Columbian life, on the more esoteric and less politically strategic areas of culture, i.e., "primitive" religion, "primitive" art, folklore, material culture and technique, kinship and linguistics. We may therefore turn to Nagel, an instructor of English, for a relevant economic description.

Living Standards of Reservation Indians

An introductory knowledge of the Native American question can be gained by following Nagel's presentation on contemporary living standards found on reservations.

Dollar income. Three-fourths of reservation Indians in 1968 had a per capita cash income of below $900, below one-third of the national average for that year. Median family income in 1969 was $5,832, "compared to $9,590 for the general population, and $6,191 for all minorities" (Nagel 1974:246).

Even the populations of resource-rich reservations are poor. For example, the Northern Cheyenne of Montana had an average family income of only $2,600, and the Salt River people in Arizona, $2,325. It is hardly surprising, therefore, to find that Native Americans are forced to rely on government programs for one-third of their income, compared to 15 percent nationally. Nagel (1974:246) concludes: "Reviewing such figures, the United States Commission on Civil Rights noted in 1973 that the Indian was the poorest American; and a prominent journal for Blacks said the Indian 'is the most forgotten and mistreated minority in the United States.'"

Unemployment. Nagel found the unemployment rate for reservation Indians triple that of the work force living nearby. In 1968 the Bureau of Indian Affairs reported an overall unemployment rate of 42 percent. A number of reservations had even higher unemployment: 86.1 percent for the Choctaws in Mississippi, 77 percent for the Pueblo Indian villagers of New Mexico, 72.5 percent among the Blackfeet of Montana, and 55 percent for the "Five Civilized Tribes" (Choctaw, Chickasaw, Creek, Cherokee and Seminole) of Oklahoma. The various peoples of the Dakotas were mostly unemployed, the worst off being the Pine Ridge Oglala Sioux.

Furthermore, in a study of 19,000 Oklahoma Indians, it was found that of the 47.5 percent who were unemployed, well over half received no unemployment or other welfare insurance.

Of those reservation Indians able to find work, farmers were found to be the major private employers, providing 64.35 percent of the jobs. But farm work is seasonal and low paying, many farmers discriminating against Indian employees in workforce reductions and providing few fringe benefits.

In 1968 only 4,000 Indian workers out of a reservation labor force of 120,000 (about 3 percent) held industrial jobs. Thus we find that, next to farm labor, the government itself is the largest single employer for reservation Indian workers. For example, on the Papago Reservation in Arizona, 30 percent of the permanently employed work for the BIA and 17 percent work at the Public Health Service hospital. As of November 30, 1969, the BIA employed altogether 8,250 Indians fulltime, the Indian Health Service 3,200, and the Office of Economic Opportunity and other federal units on reservations, several hundred. However, points out Nagel, the jobs Indian workers hold in government agencies usually pay little. In fact, most Native Americans in government employment are in the lower grades. They are seldom promoted to the higher grades, the higher positions being held as a general rule by whites.

Poverty and ill health. Indian life expectancy overall is only 44 years, and on some reservations it is much lower. The death rate for children under 14 is almost two and one half times that for all other citizens, and in every category of medical illness, Native Americans in 1970 had a higher death rate. Ill health, Nagel notes, is directly related to poverty and squalid living conditions. ". . . Of 4,335 Indian admissions in a five-year study, 616 suffered from malnutrition, 44 had incurred kwashiorkor or marasmus, and 572 were small for their age. And [in the Navajo Nation] 20 percent of the Indian children hospitalized evidenced malnutrition and 10 percent of those under four suffered iron deficiency anemia" (Nagel 1974:248).

Twenty-five percent of Indians suffer from mental illness, according to Nagel's information, ranging from major psychoses to personality disorders and alcoholism, this last being a sign of emotional stress.

Despite recent improvements in the incidence of tuberculosis, trachoma and other diseases endemic to Native American communities, the fact remains that disease still assumes major proportions relative to the rate of improvement for the rest of the country. In fact, Nagel concludes, some Indian health care is more typical of underdeveloped than advanced industrialized countries.

Poor living conditions. Nagel (1974:248) also describes current living conditions found on reservations. Eighty to 95 percent of housing is dilapidated, makeshift, unsanitary and crowded, whereas only 8 percent of houses in the general population fit these categories. Most Indian homes have only one or two rooms, and construction is a tar paper shack, a dirt hut, an adobe mud hogan, or a grass wickiup. More than half of all reservation Indians have no indoor bathrooms; forty-five percent of the outdoor toilets have been found inadequate by sanitation officials

Most Native Americans have no running water on their premises, and a survey by the Public Health Service of 42,506 Indians in 11 western states found that 81.6 percent had to haul their water for a mile or more. "The water is drawn from ponds, ditches, creeks and wells, and 77.8 percent of the water tested was found to be contaminated" (Nagel 1974:249).

Cultural Determinism or Oppression?

Thus Nagel points out the bias of anthropology which has led to a lack of statistical data on contemporary Native American communities, and he seeks to correct this in his article on reservation Indian economics. Yet in his conclusions he resorts to a curious line of reasoning: he devotes a full page to the proposition that "the Indian's progress has also been limited in part by his own character, value system, and philosophy" (1974:249). He states further that

> Indian values include nepotism and factionalism. Indian beliefs include the Image of Limited Good, that holds that the world's quantity of goods is established and that if any individual acquires too much, he deprives others of their fair share. The Indian's concept of man's inviolable harmony with nature has led him to reject mechanization, and even to refuse special fertilizers and improved seeds. . . (1974:249).

And again: "The Indian is aware of the inherent conflict between his character, values, beliefs and attitudes, and the character of non-Indians who live in comparative splendor. . ." (1974:249).

The sweeping generalization that non-Indians "live in comparative splendor" ignores the millions of Black and Chicano poor, let alone the even more numerous poor white, or even the working class in general, whose real income is plummeting. Even more important, however, are the conceptual fallacies, such as the Image of Limited Good. This theory was formulated by applied anthropologist George Foster to "explain" the so-called lack of progress by Mexican peasants. It has since been widely employed by academic colonialists to blame the victim rather than the victimizer.

The informed and perceptive reader will be able to detect the half-truths and racist apologetics in such theories, but it is, of course, impossible to say whether Nagel himself is aware that his conclusions to an otherwise informative article incorporate shopworn anthropological clichés, which cause the greatest possible bias and harm to the Native American cause. In fact, Nagel subscribes to the notion of *cultural determinism,* a form of philosophical idealism, the same sterile explanation used by anthropology. After describing the problem more-or-less in economic terms, Nagel asserts that the cause of reservation poverty, unemployment, ill health, and poor housing is due to Native American "culture" (character, values, etc.), at least "in part." He states, in effect, that reservation Indians are the cause of much of their own oppression.

It must also be pointed out that the idea of cultural determinism has been picked up and used by government agencies in their official delimitation of the so-called Indian problem, as a rationalization for the failure of governmental programs and policies. Government spokespersons assert that it is the "Indian culture" or "reservation subculture" that impedes economic development, resulting in joblessness and poverty. For example, in a compendium on economic development by a Joint Committee of the U.S. Congress in 1969, the Bureau of Indian Affairs stated that "these handicaps [relating to poverty] are aggravated by geographical isolation and a set of values" (Bureau of Indian Affairs 1969:331); and again (BIA, 1969: 333), that a lack of education, lack of resource development, inadequate credit, poor housing, health problems, etc., "have their roots in the basic cultural differences" between White and Indian. But this line of reasoning sets the problem on its head! The cause, in reality, is not the cultural patterns of Indian societies, but, rather, the economic imperatives of capitalism.

In the same report, to illustrate our point further, the Economic Development Administration (1969: 356) states:

> Perhaps the greatest single element impeding the development of solutions to the problems facing the American Indian has been the evolution of a reservation subculture which transcends individual tribal lines. This subculture has produced individuals who are apathetic, have low self-images, tend to be failure oriented, and feel that they have little or no control over the future. Bare subsistence is accepted as the normal condition of reservation life; poverty is a self-fulfilling prophecy.

We must take sharp issue with these examples of a non-materialist line of reasoning, these tautologous arguments. On the contrary, Native Americans are poor not because they are ethnically inferior or genetically flawed, but because their lands and resources are expropriated by non-Indian operators and large corporations, because they are rendered powerless as indigenous nationalities, and because their labor is grossly underpaid or else shunted aside entirely.

Transnational oil corporations have seized the oil treasure belonging to the Alaskan Eskimos; timber companies have expropriated Klamath and Menominee forests; corporate farmers and ranchers have tied up millions of acres of land belonging to the impoverished Plains Indians; giant coal concerns affiliated with copper and oil multinationals intend to strip mine at cheap rates huge portions of the Crow, Northern Cheyenne, Hopi reservations and the Navajo Nation; electric power utilities in league with agricultural interests and the government itself are stealing Indian water. (These facts are documented extensively in various issues of *Akwesasne Notes* and *Wassaja,* both national Indian newspapers.)

Native Americans are powerless because the government through the Bureau of Indian Affairs (BIA) controls reservation life, rendering the indigenous peoples helpless to halt their exploitation despite Indian ''self-government'' under the 1934 Indian Reorganization Act. The U.S. government thus betrays its trust responsibility for Native American lands and resources. In fact, the BIA, along with the agencies of Reclamation, Mines, Commerical Fisheries, Land Management, Army Corps of Engineers, and more recently, the Department of Energy, do not act in the Native American interest in land, resource and water transactions, but rather in the interest of the corporations and multinationals to whom they are in fact beholden (Cahn 1969:157–162).

Given this picture, whose fault is it that reservation Indians are ''ripped off,'' their lands and resources unfairly expropriated or exploited, with little economic or job returns to the reservation peoples?

Most Native Americans cannot find work on the reservations or in their villages, and a growing number have been driven into the cities in search of it, often failing even then to find steady jobs at fair pay. California, for example, has not only a high number of Indian workers, but also a highly skilled and self-motivated Native American workforce (Jorgensen 1971:73–80). Yet Native American workers are at the bottom of the employment and income pyramids in that state.

With chronic unemployment in the United States between 5 and 7 percent officially, and about 10 percent in reality, and with racism in employment an established fact so that much higher proportions of the minorities are without work, whose fault is it that most Native Americans cannot find steady jobs? Theirs or the system's?

In summary, Nagel employs anthropologically-derived assumptions about supposedly strategic aspects of Native American culture determining the present depressed state of reservation life. His ''scientific'' procedure is to boldly assert this reputed cause of poverty in juxtaposition to a description of these problems in statistical terms. But this is scientism, not science. It is an exercise in fallacious reasoning, to say nothing of racial bias, which is common to most works by bourgeois writers on the so-called Indian problem.

It is hardly surprising, therefore, to find the contemporary Indian movement redefining the Native American condition as injustice rather than as "a problem." The movement is no longer willing to let the so-called experts—the academicians and government officials—delineate the Native American question for them.

The Indian Movement

Since the late 1950s there has been a marked upsurge in the tempo of political action among Native Americans, for land, cultural rights, and social justice. Termed the "new Indian" movement, it was sparked by events in the international arena, such as the socialist revolution in Cuba, and the civil rights movement at home, to say nothing of the Native Americans' own history of protest (see *Chronicles of American Indian Protest*, Council for Interracial Books For Children, 1971).

The National Indian Youth Council, the first all-Indian youth protest group, was formed in 1960 (see Steiner, 1968). Day, in his informative article on Indian activism, (1972:507–532), contends that the NIYC was born out of frustration with the paternalism of the Bureau of Indian Affairs and with the limited goals and cautious tactics of the National Congress of American Indians (NCAI). The NCAI, founded in 1944, represents the federally-chartered tribal councils and is therefore under the thumb of the government to a considerable degree.

In 1964 the NIYC helped lead the fishing rights struggle in the state of Washington in a series of "fish-ins" when the state supreme court, in a racist decision, nullified Indian treaty rights to fish. This led to the founding of the militant Survival of American Indians Association in the same year.

The Alaska Federation of Natives, responding to Eskimo, Aleut and Indian regional political agitation, was organized in 1966. Its purpose was to act as an umbrella organization in opposition to the land and resource grab by the new state of Alaska and to pursue a blanket land claim for Alaska Natives.

The increasing activism included the "Resolution of the Thirty Tribes" against the government's omnibus bill, which called instead for a "foreign aid program'' for Indian people. It included also actions such as the chief of the Iroquois League demanding the return of a number of sacred wampum belts from the state of New York, and also the participation of 300 Indian demonstrators in the Poor Peoples' Campaign.

In 1968 the American Indian Movement was organized in Minnesota. Originally founded to combat urban racism and to organize Indian survival schools, it soon established chapters in many states and led demonstrations, culminating in what is probably its best known demonstration, the 1973 "occupation" of Wounded Knee in defense of Oglala Sioux civil rights.

Also in 1968 Mohawk Indians at St. Regis blocked the international bridge to protest customs duty charges in violation of the 1794 Jay Treaty. Their use of direct action inspired the "Indians of All Tribes" in the 1969 take-over of Alcatraz. The occupation of the former prison island in San Francisco Bay signalled the beginning of a series of land occupations—Ft. Lawton, Mt. Rushmore, Stanley and Ellis Islands, to name the better known ones.

These were among the forerunners in the new level of Native American political activity. Self-determination and self-help were the watchwords of the new organizations. Red Power was defined by Vine Deloria, Jr. (Day 1972:507) as "power over our own lives. . . We simply want the power, the political and economic power, to run our own lives in our own way."

The high points in the growing protest movement have been the Trail of Broken Treaties Caravan in 1972, on the eve of the national elections, with its occupation of the BIA offices in Washington and presentation of a program of reform, the "Twenty Points"; the 1973 Wounded Knee demonstration on the Pine Ridge Reservation in South Dakota on the issue of self-government; the formation of the grassroots coalition, the International Indian Treaty Council in 1974, and its recognition in 1977 as a non-governmental organization of the United Nations; and the 1977 United Nations-related international Conference on Discrimination Against Indigenous Populations in the Americas, held in Geneva, Switzerland.

Recently, the Council of Energy Rich Tribes (CERT) was formed. Termed the "Indian OPEC," it represents an amalgam of class, nationality and political forces with the purpose of raising royalty rates and getting a better deal from the energy monopolies. Another significant development is the founding of Women of All Red Nations (WARN), a militant Indian women's organization.

These developments show that there has been steady progress toward greater unity in action and in a common set of demands. The Geneva Conference enabled the movement to bring the Native American question to the attention of progressive international forces and enlist their support, which shows that Native Americans see their struggle as part of the world revolutionary struggle.

The upsurge in political activity, however, has been met by increased repression from the State. The American Indian Movement in particular has been targeted for attack. In South Dakota hundreds of activists have been murdered, jailed as political prisoners, have simply disappeared, or their deaths listed as "accidental" by the officials. The Oglala people at Pine Ridge have filed more than 6,000 written complaints concerning violations of their civil rights, but to no avail.

The view fostered by the Establishment, however, that Native American political militancy is a new phenomenon, that there is a "new Indian" who has been influenced by "outside agitators," is erroneous. Vine Deloria, Jr., touches on this point in *God Is Red* (1973:41):

> For generations it has been traditional that all historical literature on Indians be a recital of tribal histories from the pre-Discovery culture through the first encounter with the white man to about the year 1890. At that point the tribe seems to fade gently into history, with its famous war chief riding down the canyon into the sunset. . . A mystical Hiawatha, a saddened Chief Joseph, a scowling Sitting Bull, a sullen Geronimo; all symbolize not living people but the historic fate of a nation overwhelmed by the inevitability of history.

In fact, there is a continuity between the struggles of the past and those of today. Those of past centuries have continued into the twentieth, but the strategy and tactics have necessarily changed. The principal issues, on the other hand, have remained much the same, namely, the struggle for a land base, self-government and cultural rights.

This continuity can be illustrated by selecting instances of political resistance and organization since the final defeat of the western Indians by the U.S. military in the last century (see Forbes 1972:20–22). The 1890 massacre of unarmed Indians at Wounded Knee has come to signalize the closing of the western frontier, the dispossession of the last Indians and their confinement to reservations as colonized peoples. The Wounded Knee Massacre followed on the heels of the 1871 unilateral action by Congress to end the treaty-making process and the 1887 Indian Allotment Act, this last, as Teddy Roosevelt saw it, "to break up the tribal mass."

1911—The Seneca Nation presses for the collection of back rent due them from white residents of Salamanca, New York, a town which "just grew up" on reservation land. The Society for American Indians is founded in the same year. The Society is a "town meeting" for educated, English-speaking Indians who press for citizenship (not conferred by the federal government until 1924).

1912—The Alaska Native Brotherhood is formed. Cherokees continue to resist allotment in Oklahoma, and armed posses are sent to arrest the "dissidents."

1913—There is a Navajo "war" in New Mexico.

1915—There is a Paiute "war" in Colorado.

1917—Frank Little, the Indian organizer for the IWW union and a member of its executive board, is taken from his hotel, where he was suffering from a broken leg, and hanged by a mob from the trestle of a railroad bridge.

1920s—The Society of Northern California Indians and the Mission Indian Federation are founded. The Chickahominy Tribe and the Six Nations Council (Iroquois) are reconstituted.

1922—An all-Pueblo Indian Council is formed to oppose white squatters, to press for Pueblo religious freedom and other matters.

1922—The Cayuga chief, Deskaheh, goes to Geneva, Switzerland, to the League of Nations to seek recognition of his people's sovereign rights, but his two-year mission fails.

1925—The Indian Defense League is organized by Clinton Rickard of the Tuscaroras.

1937—The Navajo organize the Eastern Boundary Association to obtain land for 7,000 landless Navajos living on the public domain, actually traditional Indian land.

1939—The Pyramid Lake Paiute launch new legal efforts to oust white squatters. The Seneca Nation at Tonawanda issue a "Declaration of Independence" to the State of New York.

1940–41—Traditional Indians, in an effort to preserve their respective nationalities, resist U.S. selective service laws. A number of Papago, Ute, Seminole, Hopi and Iroquois go to jail as draft resisters.

1942—The Six Nations (Iroquois) independently declare war on the Axis powers.

1944—The National Congress of American Indians is founded by the Indian employees of the Bureau of Indian Affairs.

1949—Twenty-six Hopi traditional leaders send a letter to President Truman in which they assert the sovereign rights of the "Hopi Indian Empire," including their refusal to lease lands for oil exploration.

1950s—Traditional Indians are active, working through the Indian Defense League and the League of North American Indians. Many Indian organizations, from the traditionals to the NCAI, oppose the government's termination policy of doing away with tribal status and the attack by state governments on land, water, hunting and fishing rights.

1957—The Tuscarora fight the New York Power Authority. The Seneca oppose Kinzua Dam. The Mohawk re-occupy land which had been taken from them by white squatters.

1958—Tuscarora resistance stiffens and the Miccosukee of Florida fight the Everglades Reclamation Project. Traditional Indian "nations" recognize the new revolutionary government of Cuba. Fidel Castro invites them to send a delegation to Cuba and they accept. They want Cuba to intercede for them in the United Nations, to obtain UN standing as independent nations. The Pit River "nation" of California re-establishes its traditional land claim, which by 1970 brings this small people into direct confrontation with the largest private utility company in the world, Pacific Gas and Electric.

1959—Traditional Indians demonstrate in Washington, D.C., where they attempt to arrest the Commissioner of Indian Affairs. A delegation of Hopi leaders visits the United Nations to confer with UNO officials. The traditional Indian movement spreads to other parts of the United States and Canada.

1960s—The U.S. public finally awakens to the realization that Native Americans are organizing and demonstrating. The stereotype of the passive Indian begins to crack and by 1969 crumbles altogether. New protest organizations spring up, not only those already mentioned above, but others as well. A number are formed by Indian students who are beginning to force their way into colleges and universities.

In summary, the notion that the Indian protest movement is entirely new is simply not true! As Forbes, from whom much of the above chronology of events is drawn, tells us (1972:22):

> It is clear that Native American resistance to colonialism and oppression is becoming more intense with each month that passes. But it is equally clear that there are no "new Indians" as such, and clear the "Indian revolt" was not

born in the 1960s. More people of Native American background have come to identify with the resistance movement, that is true, but its roots go back deep into the past.

Peoples and Nationalities

The key fact in the Native American struggle is that it is being waged by diverse, but related indigenous nationalities. An understanding of this major aspect of the question can be gained by examining the Native American population and its distribution.

Government officials and bourgeois social scientists have been running a numbers game on Native Americans. By "numbers game" is meant the manipulation of population and demographic facts, whether willful or unconscious, to cover up the genocide of the Indians, orchestrated by the U.S. ruling class in its quest for profits. Take, for example, the fact that we are taught in school that the aboriginal population of North America was about one million. Yet the one million figure, when traced to its original source, turns out to have been a "guesstimate" by early investigators and later "carved in stone" by Kroeber who was a leading figure in U.S. anthropology.

Estimates have ranged from a low of half a million to a high of one and one-half million Indians. In 1928 the ethnologist, James Mooney, estimated that the original population of North America north of Mexico, including Greenland, was 1,153,000 with 849,000 for the United States proper. Since these figures are close to recent census counts of surviving Indians, the implication is that the European conquest and later U.S. expansion was not too destructive of the indigenous nationalities. This, however, is far from the truth of the matter and covers up the extent of the genocide.

Studies by the anthropologist Dobyns (1966), based on modern scientific techniques and current data, give a figure of 10.5 to 12.6 million for the aboriginal population of North America instead of one million. Dobyns's studies are noteworthy because, given the higher population figure, the extent of the genocide would be considerably larger than if the lower figure were used. Wax, in a recent work (1971:32), finds the Indian population in 1800 for the United States to be about 600,000. A decline from an original population of one million to 600,000 is one thing, but from 10 million to 600,000 is quite another! The latter ratio would make the genocide for the United States 94 percent, which is as tragic as the

case in South America where, using Dobyns's aboriginal estimate of
about 100 million persons, the genocide was over 90 percent.

Many introductory works on Native Americans start with the rhetorical
question, "Who is an Indian?" Various conflicting definitions—
historical, legal, racial, cultural—are then paraded before the reader who
is finally left in helpless confusion by the failure to give a definitive
answer that could lead to an understanding of the Indian question. "The
federal government, state governments, and the Census Bureau all have
different criteria for identifying a person as an 'Indian.' Federal criteria
are inconsistent from one agency to another" (Ayres 1978:24). Nowhere
is this confusion greater than in the U.S. Census data, as the following
table will illustrate.

TABLE 1.

AMERICAN INDIAN POPULATION
OF THE UNITED STATES

Year	Population	Percent Difference
1900	237,196	
1910	276,927	16.8%
1920	244,437	−11.7%
1930	343,352	40.5%
1940	345,252	0.6%
1950	357,499	3.5%
1960	523,591	46.5%
1970	792,730	51.4%

SOURCE: U.S. Dept. of Commerce 1973:xi.

Changes in the numbers of the Indian population may have actually
resulted from racial bias and mistaken notions about ethnicity, leading to
different definitions and procedures used to eliminate persons of mixed
racial descent and those living off reservations, rather than from actual
growth or decline. In censuses prior to 1950, persons of mixed Indian and
Black or white descent were variously classified, sometimes as Indian
and sometimes as Negro. In 1910 and 1930 a special effort was made to
include all persons of mixed Indian and white descent as Indian. In 1960,
persons of mixed Indian and white descent were included if they were on

a tribal or agency role, and those of mixed Indian and Black descent "only if the Indian ancestry predominated or if they were regarded as Indians in the community." In the 1970 Census, however, the definition was broadened further, and persons of mixed descent were asked to report the "race" with which they identified themselves. Thus self-classification was used rather than observation by census enumerators.

The term "Indian" is a historical convention used to lump descendants of the original populations of North America, no matter how dissimilar the various peoples are to one another in terms of genetic makeup, physical appearance, language, religion or economy. It is curious, then, that those indigenous peoples known as "Eskimos" are termed separately, but such is the colonial legacy. The term "Alaska Native," signifying Eskimos, Aleuts and Indians of Alaska, is in the same category. Thus the term Native American will be used in this work to mean indigenous peoples or nationalities.

The present-day Native American population, when Alaska Natives (Eskimo and Aleut) are added, is 827,091 (Faherty 1974:243), or about 0.4 percent of the total U.S. population. Actually the total figure for Native Americans is probably higher. Taking into consideration that the official undercount for Blacks in the 1970 Census was seven percent, it is reasonable due to a number of factors to consider a 10 percent undercount for Native Americans. All things considered, a figure of one million is probably close to the truth of the matter, although one must keep an open mind until greater conceptual clarity is brought to the question and better statistical information is available.

Ethnicity

The one million figure is for self-identified Native Americans, which is in reality more of an ethnic or national (the two terms are used interchangeably here) identification than it is a racial one. On the other hand, estimates range from three to as high as 15 million people for those of Indian ancestry. But there is a big difference between having an Indian ancestor, i.e., being an Indian-American (like Italian-American, or Irish-American), and being an American Indian or Alaska Native. The former persons are not Native American in the sense of belonging to an Indian or Eskimo community, speaking a Native American tongue, or living a Native American way-of-life. Chicanos alone, for example, number 12 million, their racial stock being a mixture of Caucasian and Moor from

Spain and various American Indian peoples, but obviously Chicanos are not Indians in an ethnic sense!

All persons with dark skins in the United States suffer from racial discrimination depending on how dark they are, but those who are members of non–Western nationalities suffer also from Anglo–American chauvinism, that is, from national oppression. As indigenous peoples (members of ethnic communities with territories), Native Americans are discriminated against both racially and nationally.

Statistical information is lacking for those self-identified Indians who live a Native American way-of-life, but based on what data exist, it is likely that at least half a million do so. The Bureau of Indian Affairs (June 1973) has enumerated 542,897 (about 65 percent) who live on or adjacent to federal reservations, including those living in the former reservations of Oklahoma, and all Indians and Alaska Natives of Alaska, most of whom are living in rural villages. And according to the 1970 census, 32 percent, excluding Eskimos and Aleuts, still speak an Indian mother tongue, which is the supreme indicator of nationality.

The importance of language in maintaining ethnic consciousness is well-known. The fact that one-third of all Indians still speak their own language is surprising given that the U.S. government has practiced a deliberate policy of cultural genocide for two centuries. For example, speaking an Indian language in federal Indian boarding schools, until relatively recently, was forbidden and severely punished. One-third seems a significant percentage, but when we compute the numbers of members of specific Indian nationalities rather than individuals, the percentage becomes even higher. In rough percentages, we find that 93 percent retain their mother tongue among the Navajo, 81 percent among the Iroquois, 68 percent for the Papago-Pima, 67 percent for the Apache, 42 percent for the Sioux, and from 34 to 66 percent for the various Pueblo groups (computations based on Tables 16 and 18, U.S. Dept. of Commerce, *Subject Report: American Indians* 1973). For the Eskimo the percentage, according to the linguist, Michael Kraus, is about 73 percent. Thus among the larger nationalities the majority of members have retained their own language. (This, of course, is in addition to English which the vast majority of Native Americans now speak, although literacy is another matter.) In fact, the percentages are astonishing, ranging from 34 to 93 percent and averaging over two-thirds, that is, *double the national average* for the ''all-Indian'' category reported by the Census.

It is also important to look at the Native American population in relation to other oppressed, non-white minorities, in order to gain a better perspective of their position in U.S. society. There are 48 million non-whites in the country, or about 24 percent of the total population. Blacks comprise 28 million, and for this reason alone their struggle for civil rights and social equality is paramount in U.S. society. In addition, their overwhelming numbers in the working class, particularly in basic industry, makes Black liberation a key one in the struggles of all working people. There are in addition 16 million Chicano, Puerto Rican, Mexican and Latino (including several million undocumented workers), whose fight against national oppression in many ways resembles that of Native Americans. Finally, there are four million American Indian, Eskimo, Asian, Hawaiian and ''others'' (Perlo 1975:11). Of this number, as we have previously stated, only about one million are Native Americans. But it is not the size of the population that is the most significant factor in the Indian question.

Territoriality
A key factor is that of territoriality. Sutton (1975:ix), an authority on land tenure, states: ''. . . Only the Indians represent a truly 'territorial' minority, and their constant quest for equity in . . . society stands alone in being founded on a recognized body of treaties and laws.'' In weighing the factor of territoriality, we must make a distinction between race and nationality even more strongly than we made it above.

In past centuries, in the rush for land and empire, a number of Native American peoples and nations were annihilated. Yet, despite the fact that millions died, many groups managed somehow to survive as nationalities. Today, the larger numbers and better-known peoples, some without reservations and others sometimes divided among several reservations, include the 23,000 Apache; the 9,921 Blackfoot; the 66,150 Cherokee; the 41,946 Chippewa; the 23,562 Choctaw; the 17,004 Creek; the 35,000 or so Eskimo; the 21,473 Iroquois; the 27,520 Lumbee; the 96,743 Navajo (according to the Navajo Census, 154,000); the 16,690 Papago, Pima; the 10,087 Keresan, Pueblo; the 14,248 Shoshone, Paiute; the 47,825 Sioux (Dakota); and the 7,635 Yuman (U.S. Dept. of Commerce, Bureau of the Census 1973:188–189). (These figures are conservative.) Altogether there are 115 officially-recognized peoples and nations with populations of 2,300 or greater. Actually, these groups are mini-nationalities which have been victimized because of their aboriginal, land and resource-owning status. (See map of United States.)

Native Americans are not evenly dispersed among the 50 states. Some states have large concentrations and, in this sense, can be referred to as Indian states. In terms of actual numbers, five states account for almost one-half of the Native American population of the United States: Oklahoma (97,731), Arizona (95,812), California (91,018), New Mexico (72,788), and Alaska (51,528). (Again, the numbers are conservative.)

There is a more important way of looking at the Indian states. In these states the Native American peoples constitute a significant part of the state population, even with official undercounting: more than 16 percent in Alaska, 7.29 percent in New Mexico, 5.47 percent in Arizona, 4.89 percent in South Dakota, and almost 4 percent in Oklahoma and Montana (*Akwesasne Notes* 1972:9). Moreover, if we use the concept of Indian country rather than Indian state, that is, disregard state boundaries which intersect regions of Native American concentration, we find that there are large areas of the United States and Alaska where indigenous peoples are the majority population. The Navajo Nation, to cite an obvious example, consists of 19,400 square miles and occupies parts of three states, principally Arizona, in an area as large as the combined size of Massachusetts, Vermont, and New Hampshire. As Faherty (1974:244) points out, "though Indians constitute a small minority of the total national population, they are highly concentrated in the Southwest, Oklahoma, the Dakotas and Alaska." In these regions they can be a powerful political force, and the nationalities aspect of the Native American struggle must be viewed in this light.

Alaska is the largest Native American region, with Athabascan, Haida, Tlingit, and Tsimshian Indians, Inuit and Yupik Eskimo, and Aleut groups. Furthermore, Alaska Natives are the vast majority in most regions of the state, especially in north, western and southwestern Alaska, the whites living predominately in the urban areas of Anchorage, Fairbanks and Juneau.

The Southwest, principally Arizona and New Mexico, is the second largest region. Here live many traditional Indian populations on collectively-owned lands. Many of the largest federal reservations are in the Southwest, the Navajo Nation being the largest in terms of both population and acreage. Other peoples include the Hopi and Zuni, the Rio Grande Pueblo villages, the Apaches, the Pima and Papago, the Ute, and the Yuman groups.

Oklahoma, the "Red Land," is next, having been created from Indian Territory in 1907. In the eastern portion are the Cherokee, Choctaw, Chickasaw, Creek and Seminole, all originally "removed" by the military in forced marches from southeastern United States during the 1830s. In the western portion are the Plains tribes—Southern Cheyenne, Arapaho, Comanche, Kiowa, Pawnee and others, in addition to remnants of eastern peoples who were also "removed" during the last century.

Oklahoma is followed by the Northern Plains states, chiefly South Dakota and Montana, each with a number of principal reservations, many carved out of the Great Sioux Nation. Much of the actual land use has been temporarily lost to white control through the government's forced land allotment and heirship policies. Pine Ridge, scene of the 1973 Wounded Knee demonstration, is the second largest federal reservation, but Sioux Indians also live on several other large reservations. There are also Crow, Blackfeet, Northern Cheyenne, Bannock, Shoshoni, Gros Ventre and other peoples.

There are smaller areas of Indian concentration in other regions of the country, for example, the Chippewa area of Minnesota, the Longhouse (Iroquois) communities of New York State, the Seminole in Florida, the fishing peoples of Washington state.

California's high number of Native Americans, in addition to native California Indians, reflects primarily the movement from out of the state into the urban centers in the decades following World War II. In California the movement has been mainly to the Los Angeles–Long Beach and the San Francisco–Oakland metropolitan areas. Thus, another way of looking at the population distribution is a tripartite breakdown into urban, reservation, and rural non-reservation peoples.

Urban

Some authorities see an unmistakable trend of people moving from the reservation and rural regions to the urban scene. They cite the fact that the 1950 Census found over 50 percent of all officially-designated Indians living on reservations, but the 1960 Census found only 43 percent reservation residents, and by 1970 only 39 percent lived on reservations (Sclar 1972:194–195). This assumption may be unfounded, however, due to the built-in bias in the U.S. Census, enumerating procedures for the earlier censuses which undercounted off-reservation Indians, thereby skewing the proportion between urban and rural. As mentioned earlier, according to a recent BIA survey, about 65 percent live on or adjacent to reservations, villages and the like; the remainder, presumably, are urban.

Nevertheless, for many years and increasingly since World War II, Native Americans have been forced to migrate to the major cities in increasing numbers to search for employment or to avail themselves of government training programs. In the big city, however, they face bureaucratic indifference and find themselves in the lowest ranks of the urban proletariat, more often than not, unemployed or underemployed. Median income is $4,568 for men and $2,023 for women. Most hold unskilled jobs. Among those with jobs, nearly 45 percent are blue collar workers; more than 35 percent are women.

In the big cities Native Americans suffer not only poverty, unemployment and racism, but also social isolation and a deep sense of cultural loss. Their multi-national origin and dispersal among the general population makes political organization difficult.

Those cities in rank order with the largest numbers of Native Americans (excluding Alaska) are the Los Angeles–Long Beach area of California (reportedly 60,000); Tulsa, Oklahoma; Oklahoma City; New York City; the San Francisco–Oakland area of California; Phoenix, Arizona; Minneapolis–St. Paul, Minnesota; Seattle-Everett, Washington (which also includes 3,000 Eskimos); Chicago, Illinois; Tucson, Arizona. In Alaska there has been a migration from Eskimo and Indian villages to regional centers, such as Nome and Bethel, where Alaska Native peoples predominate.

Reservation

Reservations were created first in the east, primarily as areas of refuge for dispossessed Indian peoples. By 1790 the eastern peoples and their great alliances and confederacies, like that of the Iroquois, had been defeated after a long, courageous struggle. The defeat of the eastern Indians paved the way for the Indian Removal Act, initiated in 1830 under President Andrew Jackson. The forced removal of the eastern and southeastern Indians, which violated the early treaties, caused untold misery, suffering and thousands of deaths; it was, in fact, a policy of genocide. Even so, there were those who escaped removal by fleeing into the hills, or who for other reasons were not sent westward to Indian Territory beyond the Mississippi River. Today, their descendants live on 18 small state reservations located mainly in New York, Connecticut, Maine, Pennsylvania, and Virginia. (There are also 17 federal reservations in the east, but these are located mainly in the Great lakes region.)

In an article on the contemporary legal status of Native Americans, Theodore W. Taylor (1974:255), a former Deputy Commissioner of the BIA, states:

> Indians on state reservations have some special relationships to state and local governments. In New York for the Iroquois, in Maine for the Passamaquoddy and Pennobscott, and in Virginia for the Mataponi and Pamunkey, for example, the states provide for elementary and secondary education either through the provision of schools . . . or through payments to county and local public schools for the Indians' tuition and school books. . . State reservation land is not taxed in any state, and in some instances this may be the only economic benefit of the reservation to the Indians. However, the state reservation for the Miccousukee in Florida is relatively large for the number of Indians involved and has economic potential.

The great majority of indigenous nationalities, however, are on federal reservations, federal recognition being based on treaty, statute, agreement or precedent. Taylor (1974:255) states that "except for the Lumbees of North Carolina, most larger Indian groups are federally recognized and are eligible for special services and programs." But a more accurate way of looking at the evolution of federal reservations is that those peoples and nations who could not be annihilated were confined instead to reservations, for many years under guard of the military and under the control of the Indian Agents.

Federal reservations, found mainly in the west, are much larger than state reservations. They more nearly constitute the original homelands, although considerably reduced from former territories. Their creation closely parallels the evolution of treaty-making. The greatest number, nearly 260 of the 400 treaties with Indians, were made between 1815 and 1860 during the great westward expansion of commerce, industry and settlement following the War of 1812. Most of the treaties "concerned the exchange and cession of lands or the establishment of boundaries for Indian lands" (Oswalt 1973:571).

Federal reservations, at least in the letter of the law, have a measure of self-government with a number of powers: (1) choose a form of government and operate under it; (2) define conditions of membership; (3) regulate domestic relations, prescribe rules of inheritance; (4) levy taxes, regulate property within tribal jurisdiction; (5) control the conduct of members; (6) and administer justice (Cohen 1971a:122). The 1973 Wounded Knee demonstration, however, exposed the way in which these rights have been subverted by the government. Nevertheless, federally-recognized nationalities currently have at least token autonomy, which is expressed in their incorporation under federal charter to conduct business affairs as collective entities, and to practice limited self-government. As Taylor (1974:255) correctly points out, under U.S. law Native Americans living in organized Indian communities may be citizens of four different governments—tribal or village, county or city, state, and federal government. This results in a complicated maze of contradictory relationships and overlapping legal jurisdictions which move steadily in the direction of eroding Native American civil, land, water, mineral, hunting and fishing rights. Of course, Native Americans do not accept the contemporary legal practice of overlapping jurisdictions but prefer in most cases to return to a more sovereign status, as interpreted in many early treaties and agreements, where state, county or city jurisdiction has no force and federal powers are clearly delimited.

Rural Non-reservation
Finally, there have existed for many years one hundred or more distinctly Native American communities which are unrecognized legally by either state or federal government. Taylor (1974:254) estimates that over 42 percent of U.S. Indians are not recognized by the federal government. He gives the following examples: the Yaqui of Arizona, the Miamis in Indiana, the Wyandots in Kansas, the Houmas in Louisiana, and the Metis in Montana.

The majority of these non-reservation but primarily rural groups are concentrated in four regions: the Atlantic coastal area, especially in the southeast; the Great Lakes region, especially in Michigan and Wisconsin; in Oklahoma where the reservations were terminated; and in California and Nevada (Spicer 1969:134). The groups in each area have had a different history. Those in the east, for example, are the descendants of Indians who lived in the original 13 states and include the Creeks in Alabama, the Mohegans in Connecticut, the Nanticokes in Delaware, the Wampanoags at Mashpee in Massachusetts, the Narrangansets in Rhode Island, the Chickahominys in Virginia, and the Lumbees in North Carolina.

Oklahoma presents another unique situation. By 1870 twenty nationalities had been forcibly relocated to Indian Territory. The 1887 Indian Allotment Act—a ploy by white landgrabbers and speculators to seize Indian lands—and the 1898 Curtis Act dissolved the larger peoples and nations in Indian Territory (Oklahoma) as political entities and, for all practical purposes, put an end to collectively-held lands. The Curtis

Act was aimed primarily at the "Five Civilized Tribes," because the
Creeks and Cherokees in particular were opposed to private property
through land allotment.

The Creek, Cherokee and Choctaw Republics were Indian nations of a
new type, which had been formed under the impact of European conquest. They evolved agrarian-based economies, held extensive properties (including slaves), devised their own writing systems, founded
schools and academies, and lived under their own systems of courts, law
and order. Their local and national governments were stable and probably
as well managed as most states of that day. Yet by 1906 these nations had
been "deprived of their governments, their Tribal courts abolished, and
their chief executives stripped of their power" (Washburn 1971:82).

Today, Oklahoma remains very much an Indian state, the Cherokee
population alone numbering over 25,000, most of whom are full-blooded,
Cherokee-speaking, poor people, dispossessed of land and resources.
Education rates are among the lowest in the country, just the reverse
of the former state. The Indians of Oklahoma have suffered mainly
at the hands of state interests although federal services are extended
in certain categories, such as the Employment Assistance and Relocation Program, and limited recognition is now given to the "tribes" as
quasi-political entities.

Terminated nationalities form yet another category of unrecognized
Native American peoples. After World War II, vested interests through a
change in government Indian policy launched a new attack on Indian
lands and resources. In 1953 Congress began passing a series of termination laws under which nine specified nationalities would be "freed" from
federal services and reservation status. Two timber-rich reservations were
terminated—the Klamath of Oregon and the Menominee of Wisconsin—
along with the Paiutes and Utes of Utah, smaller groups in Oregon and
Texas, and the Indians in California.

Alaska is another case in point. Very few reservations were created in
Alaska, although villages have quasi-political status. With Alaska state-
hood in 1958, and especially after the discovery of oil ten years later, the
economic motive for the expropriation of lands and resources became over-
powering. But before the state of Alaska and the corporations could
gain control over large portions of Alaska occupied by the Alaska
Native peoples, aboriginal land claims had to be settled. This led to the
Alaska Native Claims Settlement Act of 1971. As Gus Hall (1974:124)
has written:

There are 375 million acres in Alaska, but the Indians, Eskimos and Aleuts who are among the most starved, ill-clothed, and ill-housed peoples of the nation receive only 40 million acres of the poorest lands under the terms of the land claims act. . . The remaining 90% of the land goes to the federal government to give away to the monopolies. In the fabulously rich North Slope oil region Native Alaskans get only surface or hunting rights on most of the area. The underground oil treasure is left for the Gulf, Exxon and other pirates.

Not one cent of the land claims settlement, which was less than $1 billion, went directly to the people who needed it—the 55,000 impoverished Native Alaskans (sic). Instead, $462.5 million is to be paid out over an eleven-year period to shareholders of twelve Alaskan corporations, who will dispense it somewhat like the government poverty programs.

And today, almost ten years after the act was passed, Alaska Native peoples have still to receive the lands promised them. Thus, in this sense, they are being terminated, having been deprived of their aboriginal claim to most of Alaska as recently as 1971.

Sovereignty is the collective authority of a people to govern themselves.

Hank Adams,
Indian activist

2

INDIAN
SOVEREIGNTY

For the last decade there has been a trend for writers on Indian affairs to cite in an upbeat fashion former President Nixon's 1970 Message to Congress, later reaffirmed in his 1974 State of the Union address, that his administration would put an end to the repressive policies of termination, (abolishing the reservations, ending treaty rights and federal services), and that there would be a reform of the Bureau of Indian Affairs. Nixon's Indian platform impressed Alvin Josephy who, in his anthology, *Red Power* (1971), prominently featured the 1970 Message in its entirety. Wilcomb Washburn, a historian on Indian-white relations, interpreted the 1970 Message as giving "hope that at long last an equitable solution to the Indian problem may be within reach" (1971:245). And John S. Warren, writing in the *Montana Law Review* (1972:264), stated that "fortunately for the Indian and the White, the trend [the deterioration of tribal self-government] appears to have changed: the executive branch has officially abandoned the belief that Indians are incapable of governing themselves."

At first, it seemed that the Nixon administration would fulfill its promises. Then, in November of 1972, there began the Trail of Broken Treaties Caravan to Washington, D.C. (*Trail of Broken Treaties, Akwesasne Notes*, 1973). The TBT Caravan was organized one year after a smaller caravan had gone to Washington to protest the circumvention of the authority of the Indian Affairs Commissioner to institute the promised reforms within the BIA. The failure of the Nixon administration to recognize the TBT's 1972 protest and to give its spokespersons a hearing (a courtesy historically given Indian delegations visiting the nation's capital), or to consider its well-conceived program of meaningful reform, the "Twenty Points," led to a "sit-in" at the BIA offices. Any notion about the administration's "liberal" Indian policies vanished altogether when the building was surrounded by police and the demonstrators harassed and later pursued by the FBI back to their reservation homes. Subsequently, the "overly sympathetic" Indian Commissioner and virtually his entire staff were fired or forced to resign because of their alleged soft policy toward the demonstrators.

Even before the TBT sit-in at the BIA headquarters, it was evident that Nixon's program for Indian self-determination was not going to be translated into action. For one, there was the intransigence of the Indian Service bureaucrats. As D'Arcy McNickle (1973:viii) saw it: "Every effort by a team of young Indians brought into the Bureau to translate the President's Message into program activities was effectively nullified by oldline employees, some of them Indian, who evidently resented being supplanted by the young activists."

There was a more fundamental road-block which lay in the Department of Interior itself: the well-documented conflict of interest problem. How can Interior be the guardian of Native American lands and resources, safeguard the Indian interest, at the same time it is subject to the corporations and energy monopolies? Thus suspicions began to grow that Nixon's Indian reform was simply a case of political phrasemongering designed to garner bipartisan support for his administration by drawing upon widespread sympathy among many non-Indians for the "plight" of the American Indian.

At this juncture, on February 27, 1973, several score of determined Oglala Sioux and their supporters began their 71-day occupation of a South Dakota hamlet, Wounded Knee. The punitive handling of this protest by the Nixon administration, under the direction of General Alexander Haig, the ruthless condoning of armed vigilante attacks on the protestors, the military over-kill philosophy evidenced in the number of armoured personnel carriers, weaponry and troops deployed, the tactics of terror, starvation and murder used, the callous disregard by federal authorities of the solemn agreement made with the Indians, and finally, the arrest of hundreds on conspiracy and other serious charges, these developments soon exposed the sheer hypocrisy of the new policy of "Indian self-determination."

Ironically, the key issue at Wounded Knee in 1973 was self-determination, the right of the Oglala Sioux to determine for themselves the nature of their Indian government, to control it and to end the abuses to their treaty rights, including the violation of their civil rights in the unpunished murders of Indians by whites.

Any further illusions about the integrity of the Nixon administration were soon dispelled by the disclosure of the burglarizing of the Democratic Party National Committee headquarters at the Watergate complex in Washington, D.C., and the indictment of the Vice-President for tax fraud. As John Pittman (1973b:6) so succinctly put it, Watergate "unveiled a long-time and ongoing conspiracy to deprive the U.S. majority of Constitutional safeguards against authoritarian rule. . . ." The Nixon administration was beginning to treat all Americans like Indians! This was the real conspiracy in the country and not the supposed conspiracy charged by the Feds against the Oglala Sioux and the American Indian Movement leadership.

At the heart of the 1972 Trail of Broken Treaties and Pan-American Quest for Justice was the demand that the U.S. government restore to Native American nationalities their Indian sovereignty. "Sovereignty," Hank Adams has said, "is the collective authority of a people to govern themselves" (Nickeson 1973:23). Adams is an Indian long involved in the fishing rights struggle in the state of Washington. As he explains:

> Sovereignty was once affirmed for the Indians in their right to make treaties—the right of a nation. Chief Justice John Marshall ruled on that right [in 1832] when he said that nations do not have to be equal in size or strength to enter into an equitable treaty. All that was needed was the sovereignty to make the treaty and the ability to carry out its stipulations.

The issue of Indian sovereignty is clearly embodied in the manifesto of Twenty Points, the Indian position paper, which was presented to the government by the TBT Caravan. The Twenty Point program was a collective document, formulated by eight national Indian organizations and endorsed by four others, so that it represented a broad spectrum of Native American opinion and support.

McNickle (1973:ix) points out that seven of the Twenty Points are directly concerned with "the restoration of the treaty relationship disestablished in 1871 [by Congress] and with other aspects of treaty review, implementation and enforcement." Looking at the document another way, we find that fifteen of the demands "seek a redefinition of relations between the Indian peoples and government on federal, state and local levels, and propose the establishment of institutions in keeping with such relations according to a proposed timetable" (Pittman 1973b:73).

> The nub of these 15 demands is the assertion of the sovereignty of "Indian tribes and Nations," and the insistence that "all Indian people in the United States shall be considered to be in treaty relationship." The remaining five demands call for restoration of the Indians' land base to 110 million acres, including 40 million acres in Alaska; protection of the Indians' religious freedom and cultural integrity; guarantees of the right of self-government and the establishment of means to implement that right; control by the Indian communities of governmental functions for health, housing, employment, economic development and education (Pittman 1973b:73).

The Ford administration continued the "self-determination" policy as expressed by Nixon. This policy was then embodied in law in the 1975 Indian Self-determination and Education Assistance Act. The Act (U.S. Code, Congressional and Administrative News 1974:7775–7804) supposedly corrects BIA bureaucratic abuse by allowing tribal organizations to contract for their own services and to become more involved in government policy and decision-making functions. Title II of the Act amends the 1934 Johnson-O'Malley Act by "strengthening" federal support for, and Indian participation in, Indian education.

Although reformist in that it facilitates the parental and community control of Indian education, its business model, on the other hand, for contracting out services in the BIA, education and health fields may actually dismantle federal services to Indians; thus "self-determination" becomes, in practice, federal termination of services. Rather than real self-determination, the Act is viewed by Indians as merely the contracting law.

The Carter administration, on the other hand, reversed even the self-determination rhetoric of Nixon! The Nixon rhetoric of protecting Indian resources and promoting self-determination vanished entirely with the unveiling of Carter's energy program. Interior Department Solicitor Leo M. Krulitz has attacked Indian self-government and expressed the administration's frustration with the fact that, historically, Native Americans were inadvertently placed on energy-rich lands containing coal and uranium. The Coalition of Energy-Rich Tribes (CERT), the "Indian OPEC," was totally ignored by Carter in the development of his energy program. Yet the rapid exploitation of conventional fuels (coal, oil, gas and nuclear), which was the essence of Carter's program, depended largely on Indian resources.

Real Self-Determination

The United Nations Charter recognizes the right of all peoples to self-determination, and its Covenants on Economic, Social and Cultural Rights, and on Civil and Political Rights, each begins with the article (The National Lawyers Guild 1977:50): "All peoples have the right of self-determination. By virtue of that right they freely determine their political status and freely pursue their economic, social and cultural development."

> Self-determination means a people's right to choose whatever form of political organization and relationship with other states it desires. It does not necessarily mean independence, although it may very well and often does. It may result in a people choosing to be associated with or dependent on another state. They may choose confederation with other less-than-totally independent peoples. They may choose supervision by the United Nations. The key, however, is that the people themselve choose through an expression of their will free from outside influence (National Lawyers Guild 1977:53).

The National Lawyers Guild points out, however, that "not every disenchanted group of people within an existing independent state is entitled to self-determination" (1977:53). Mere cultural or religious differences, such as among ethnic and religious minorities, are not enough. International standards have been developed and, according to the study undertaken by the Guild, Native Americans in the United States meet those standards and are therefore entitled to exercise the right of self-determination.

The standards or criteria which define a state for the purposes of international law are (1) a permanent population, (2) a defined territory, (3) an effective government, and (4) the capacity to enter into relations with other states (National Lawyers Guild 1977:11). According to the Guild's study, Native Americans meet these four criteria.

A similar view of Indian sovereignty is to ask what are the powers exercised by sovereign nations, and have Native Americans exercised these powers? According to a study undertaken by the Institute for the Development of Indian Law (Berkey *et al* 1977), they include power to select a form of government, judicial powers, power to determine membership, power over domestic relations, power to tax, the ability to wage peace, war and to extradite, and the power to make treaties. The study states that "Indian governments have traditionally exercised all the powers of sovereign nations," and "the United States and other nations of the world have recognized an Indian nation's right to self-government" (Berkey *et al* 1977:11).

Most Native Americans take this view of Indian sovereignty, the right of each and every indigenous nationality to determine for itself just exactly what its relationship shall or shall not be to the United States of America. The National Congress of American Indians, for example, at its 1974 annual convention, issued an "American Indian Declaration of Sovereignty." Marxist-Leninists, however, point out that self-government flows from a people having the prerequisites of a nation, and a nation is a historical concept, not an absolute category existing forever in time. The question of sovereignty, therefore, depends on the nature of the Indian community, its social and ethnic characteristics within a given historical period, and not on the wishes of individuals. It is objective reality and objective reality alone that ultimately determines the national question.

History of the Indian Sovereignty Concept

In colonial times and during the formative years of the fledgling United States, the dominant powers recognized the sovereignty of the Native American peoples. Upon the "discovery" of North America the European powers recognized the right of Native American tribes and nations to the possession of their lands. "The law of discovery as formulated by the European powers simply established which country would have paramount right as among themselves in the exploration and conquest of the new lands" (Warren 1972:255). The European power which then asserted the "law of discovery" over a given region would have an exclusive right to trade, and, more importantly, at least for the agrarian-based English colonies, it would have the right to purchase the land from the Native Americans in question.

All the competing European powers recognized the Indians' right to occupancy, for it was in their interest to do so, to have rules in this mercantilist "game" of conquest, rules which would protect and regulate the interests of the competing trading monopolies. At stake were eight millions of square miles of land, or more than twice the size of all Europe itself.

The Indians' right to occupancy (or possession), according to European legal notions at the time, was alienable in but two ways: either by purchase or by conquest. But even under the right of conquest, the European powers were supposed to observe the Indians' right of occupancy. The conquering power was to tax and to govern only, the conquered Indian population then becoming subjects or citizens of the conqueror, but their property, that is, the land, would remain unimpaired.

Later, with the birth of the United States, the "Americans" also recognized this doctrine of tribal sovereignty in their early treaties with the Native American peoples, primarily, according to contemporary scholarship, as an expedient war measure.

> By the time of the American Revolution the Continental Congress had super-seded the French in the struggle for control of the new land and the Indian tribes had become pawns in the war between the British and the Americans. Primarily as a war measure, the Americans, following the British example, treated the Indian nations as sovereigns, hoping thereby to win the favor of the various tribes and enlist their support in the Revolution. (Iowa Law Review 1966:656).

The first treaties between the European powers and the Indian peoples were essentially treaties of peace and friendship, and were designed to define the boundaries between the competing European colonies and the existing Indian peoples, nations and confederations. This was true, also, initially, in the first treaties made by the United States after the revolution (Oswalt 1973:57). It was only later, during the 19th century, that treaty fraud became an oppressive strategy used by an expansionist United States bent on the internal conquest of the Native American land base and the consolidation of the capitalist system.

Spicer (1969:12) provides us with the clue as to why the "Americans" were at first anxious to gain the friendship of, or at least, to neutralize the Native American peoples and nations. He reminds us that the great majority of Indians at the end of the colonial period were *not* living "as politically subordinated and culturally dominated people." This explains the dignity of the language of the early treaties which tended to treat the Native American peoples as sovereign powers. In reality, until the end of the 18th century, there were in North America many nations (in the generic sense of the term), both Native American and European, which competed for political and economic dominance. These competing nations included the five rival European states: Holland, France, England, Spain and Russia. To the Indians, however, the five European powers operated more like two dozen different nations. As Spicer (1969:14) describes it, the French in the northeast behaved differently from the French in the south. There were the Puritans and other different kinds of British in New England. There were also the descendants of Dutch colonists in New York and Connecticut, the Pennsylvania Quakers, upper and lower-class Virginians, the Carolinians, the "ever aggressive Georgians," the Spaniards in Florida, and "the grow-ing nation of Cumberland settlers or 'Long Knives.'" Native Americans, on the other hand, were seen by the Europeans as fifty or sixty nations.

The concept nation (derived from "natio" in Latin) is more than 2,000 years old and originally meant the ethnic aspects of a community of people—family, language, customs and beliefs. "Originally applied to only tribal communities, the concept was later extended to the populations of territories, states, individual nationalities and, with the decay of feudalism and the birth of capitalism, also to a qualitatively new formation . . ." the modern nation (Fedoseyev 1977:18). It was in the earlier, pre-capitalist sense that European powers applied the term to Native American societies, meaning *a people,* the inhabitants of a specific territory who share common customs, origins, history and language, or related languages (see *The American Heritage Dictionary of the English Language*).

Today, however, nation is used in a more precise, scientific sense in the socialist world, by national liberation movements and working-class parties. Nation is seen as a historical community welded together by economic ties, which are its determining property. This definition emphasizes classes, which were not present in tribal, i.e., pre-class societies. Thus there is in the modern nation the *social,* i.e., economic ties of people and the intrinsic unity of classes and strata these ties create, as well as the *ethnic,* i.e., language, territory and features of the "culture, way of life, beliefs, traditions, mentality and psychology shaped by the geographical environment, common origin and centuries of historical development. . ." (Fedoseyev 1977:18).

Among the Native American "nations" of the 17th and 18th centuries were the following regional groupings:

(a) East of the Mississippi River and South of the Ohio the great part of the population spoke languages of the Muskogean family, of which there were four major group which came to be called Creeks, Choctaws, Chickasaws and Seminoles. . . (b) Widespread in the north from the Mississippi to the coast were many Algonkian speaking peoples—for instance, those of the central coast who came to be called the Delawares; those of New England, such as the Narrangansetts, Pequots, Mahicans, Abnakis, and others; the Powatans, Chickahominies, and others in tidewater Virginia; the Ottawas, Chippewas, Potawatomis, Kickapoos, Fox, and numerous others of the Great Lakes region. (c) The Iroquoian Five Nations of the New York area and the Cherokees of Tennesee spoke related languages as did some others who belonged neither to the great Muskogean or Algonkian [language] families (Spicer 1969:14).

And in the West were another fifty or so different Native American peoples of many differing language stocks, cultures, economic patterns, and social organization.

In the early years, and especially before the U.S. revolution, it was anyone's guess as to which of the rival European and Indian nations would become politically dominant. It is within this context that the European powers dealt with the indigenous peoples pretty much as their sovereign equals, despite notions of cultural superiority.

Indian Sovereignty Redefined

Spicer (1969:14) states that by about 1700, the Europeans numbered altogether no more than 200,000 people, whereas the Indians numbered 300,000. It was only as the Indians became outnumbered that the balance of political power shifted and, with it, a reinterpretation of the doctrine of Indian sovereignty by the European nations and English colonies. One can roughly correlate the deterioration of the doctrine with the growth of U.S. hegemony over the native peoples. Washburn (1971:220) explains that by the 17th century "in New England and Virginia, and progressively later in the other colonies and in the later states of the Federal Union," U.S. military success occurred usually when the white population curve going up crossed that of the Indian going down.

Washburn (1971:49) also sees the defeat of the French in the "Great War for Empire" (1756–1763) as "the beginning of the end for the *defacto* independence of the Indian nations." Spicer (1969:11–12), on the other hand, indicates a slightly later date: "By hindsight it appears clear enough that the 'Americans' as early as the 1790s were on the road to dominance." He adds that the year 1794 is a useful marker, because on that date the "Americans" were victorious in the Battle of Fallen Timbers. This signalized the opening of the Ohio Territory to white colonization and settlement, and the defeat of the Indian peoples living there. We would choose the date of 1813, for in that year Tecumseh was killed in the battle on the Thames in the "French–Indian War" (in reality, he was fighting for a new Indian confederation of many nations which could halt further U.S. aggression). Tecumseh's death signaled the last hope of forming a united Indian resistance east of the Mississippi, although Black Hawk courageously fought a rear-guard action after 1816. By the time of the resistance of the Indians in western United States in the middle of the 19th century, the "American" nation was too strong to defeat. The military resistance by western Indians, on the other hand, delayed the expansion of the U.S. frontier for yet another hundred years. It was this resistance, then, which was clearly the primary factor causing the Europeans to deal with Native Americans as sovereign entities more than any European notions of morality, or the inherent political rights of indigenous peoples.

The Northwest Ordinance of 1787, prior to the writing of the U.S. Constitution, set forth the manner in which the "unsettled areas" to the northwest of the existing colonies should be dealt with. This laid the basis for an *ideal* federal policy toward Native Americans. The Ordinance states:

> The utmost good faith shall always be observed towards the Indians; their land and property shall never be taken from them without their consent; and in their property, rights, and liberty, they shall never be invaded or disturbed, unless in just and lawful wars authorized by Congress; but laws founded in justice and humanity shall from time to time be made, for preventing wrongs being done to them, and for preserving peace and friendship with them (quoted in Washburn 1971:55).

Yet, almost immediately after the Revolutionary War, the rights of the Indian nations were violated. For one, unprovoked acts of aggression were committed against the Cherokees by the North Carolinians. These acts were so outrageous, reported Henry Knox, Secretary of War under the Confederation, "as to amount to an actual although informal war of the said white inhabitants against the said Cherokees" (Washburn 1971:54). And in the old Northwest, the fertile regions north of the Ohio River, the encroachment of white squatters soon resulted in organized Indian resistance. The defeat of General Arthur St. Clair's 200,000-man army with a loss of 600 men in 1791 was the worst defeat ever suffered by U.S. forces in its Indian wars. In 1794, however, Indian military resistance was broken and a humiliating "peace treaty" forced upon the nations of the old Northwest. The Treaty of Greenville opened the lands of Ohio to white entry "legally." It was this defeat which Tecumseh had hoped to overturn when, a few years later, he began organizing a united Indian revolt in alliance with the British against the invading U.S. frontiersmen, but which, in the end, proved unsuccessful.

An inkling of how the new "American" government was to deal in the future with the Indian nations, Wax (1971:46–47) reminds us, is the fact that Indian affairs were located in the War Department instead of the Department of State. Had Indian affairs been lodged in the State Department, Native Americans would have more likely been treated as foreign and therefore sovereign nations.

Nevertheless, despite this pragmatic or *real* policy of aggression which came eventually to dominate the American Indian frontier, an *ideal* federal Indian policy was hammered out by Henry Knox and Thomas Jefferson. This was done within the framework of the new federal union of separate states, formerly the colonies. Knox (Washburn 1971:55) averred that the different Indian nations ought to be treated as foreign nations and not as subjects of the various states, although the states should retain the right of pre-emption of all land within their boundaries. Jefferson's contribution to the evolution of this more limited doctrine of Indian sovereignty was to deny the exaggerated European claims to land title based on "discovery" or observation of the shore line of a continent, and "the indefensible, or rather, undefendable claim to total sovereignty on the part of those (the Indians) who could not maintain it. . ." (Washburn 1971:55–56). His position was a middle one, namely, the right of pre-emption. By pre-emption is meant the recognition of the legal right of the Indian nations to their lands, but at the same time recognizing the "legal right" of the federal government to purchase Indian land "when the Indian nations wished to sell it." Under this interpretation, the United States could legally declare war to prevent an Indian nation from selling to a rival European power.

Actually, Knox and Jefferson were anxious to work out the separation of powers between the economically competitive colonies, on the one hand, and the newly formed federal union on the other. The need for federation was born of the need for the rival colonies to free themselves economically as well as politically from the English monarchy, but once freed and independent, the question then arose, which would have primary jurisdiction over the lands and resources of the Native American peoples, the federal government or the individual states?

It should be noted that the Indian peoples were left out entirely in these deliberations. The Indian nations were not states and therefore never had the opportunity to decide how they should fit into the national constitutional scheme. This political "oversight" is made obvious from a casual observation of any U.S. or state maps, including those from the earliest times. In each and every instance the boundary lines of the individual states transect those of the Indian nations, later reservations. The anomalous status of Indian sovereignty with respect to the separation of federal and state powers is thus made readily apparent.

Due to this historical reality of the evolution of Indian sovereignty, from one of full sovereignty to one of limited sovereignty, we must be concerned with two systems of legal interpretation: the doctrine of Indian sovereignty as defined in federal treaties and court decisions, and sovereignty as legislated by Congress through its laws and statutes. These bodies have not always defined Indian sovereignty in the same way. Indeed, a third governmental body, the federal Executive, has from time to time intervened to instrument Indian policy in terms of its own interpretation.

The Role of the Federal Executive

Congressional acts began to contradict Indian sovereignty as early as 1790 with the enactment of the first Indian Trade and Intercourse Act. A series of acts led to a permanent act in 1834, Section 25, extending criminal jurisdiction to the United States for crimes committed by whites against Indians within Indian territory. This section was interpreted ``to mean that the only criminal jurisdiction left to the Indian governments covers crimes between Indians within Indian territory'' (Berkey *et al* 1977:56). The conflict with the federal Executive, however, first came to a head during Andrew Jackson's presidency, 1829–1837.

The election of Jackson to the Presidency signalized the victory of the southern, slave-owning states over treaty-protected Indian lands in the old Southwest, especially when gold was discovered in the Cherokee Nation. In 1832 the Indian Removal Act was passed by Congress and the forced relocation under inhuman conditions begun of dozens of the eastern peoples to Indian Territory beyond the Mississippi River. As a consequence, the doctrine of Indian sovereignty was reinterpreted with a view to justifying this genocidal dispossession. Chief Justice of the Supreme Court, John Marshall, began the capitulation when he ruled in *The Cherokee Nation v. The State of Georgia* (1831) that ``the Cherokee Nation, though a 'State' was not a 'foreign State' but a 'domestic dependent nation.' '' Then in *Worcester v. The State of Georgia* (1832), Marshall, having previously ruled the Cherokees dependent, now attempted to limit their dependence to the federal government and not to the State of Georgia. The Court ruled that Indian nations are to be ``considered as distinct, independent political communities,'' that they had not given up the right to self-government, and, furthermore, according to the Constitution, the laws of Georgia did not apply to Cherokees living within their allotted boundaries (Warren 1972:256).

In response to Marshall's decision Jackson was said to have replied: ``John Marshall has made his decision, now let him enforce it.'' Jackson then defied the Court in favor of states' rights, in this case, Georgia's, leaving Marshall to ponder just how long the Constitution and the federal government could last. The central point, however, is that under pressure from several southern states which coveted Indian lands and resources, the Supreme Court was forced to modify its earlier definition of Indian sovereignty, thereby legalizing Indian removal.

> Marshall clearly indicated that Indian nations were not foreign states in the constitutional sense of the word. Although he recognized tribal sovereignty over internal tribal matters, or least to the extent that it did not come into conflict with federal law, he thought the existence of any external sovereignty was highly questionable (*Iowa Law Review* 1966:675).

Meanwhile, administrative authority over Indian affairs, which further eroded Indian sovereignty, was being legislated: the Act of July 9, 1832 authorized the Commissioner of Indian Affairs to manage Indian matters, and that of June 30, 1834, authorized the President to draw up regulations to implement Indian legislation. The BIA thus plays a major role in determining Indian policy and programs since it is required by law to implement Congressional acts. The Snyder Act of 1921 is only half a page in length, but "the regulations implementing this act . . . put the Manhattan telephone book to shame" (Berkey *et al* 1977:34).

Administrative authority has extended its control over tribal land and property, including inheritance questions and "trust responsibility" of lands, over tribal money, membership, and tribal laws. The Secretary of Interior must approve all laws passed by an Indian government; yet there is no federal statute which specifically requires Secretarial approval. Rather, approval power was written into Indian constitutions under the 1934 Indian Reorganization Act to ensure that BIA supervision of Indian governments would continue (Berkey *et al* 1977:40–41).

The U.S. Congress

Treaties, ratified by the U.S. Senate, have historically governed U.S.–Indian relations. Thus the role of Congress has always been important. Since the treaty process traditionally has been considered a compact between independent nations, ratification tended to add to the prestige of Indian sovereignty.

Oswalt (1973:57) provides us with a summary of treaty-making.

> Treaties with Indians were negotiated by the President of the United States and were binding when approved by the Indians and two-thirds of the U.S. Senate . . . in all nearly 400 treaties were negotiated. The greatest number, nearly 260, were arranged between 1815 and 1860, during the great westward expansion of White settlers following the War of 1812. The majority of the

treaties, 230, involved Indian lands. These concerned the exchange and cession of lands or the establishment of boundaries for Indian lands. A block of 76 treaties called for Indian removal from their lands. . . . Nearly 100 treaties dealt primarily with boundaries between Indian and White lands and affirmed the friendly relations between a tribe and the United States. This was the general nature of most early treaties. Two tribes, the Potawatomi and Chippewa, each negotiated 42 separate treaties, which is a record number.

The basis of Indian rights today, and especially in the recognition of Indian peoples as separate, domestic nations, is clearly defined in most of the treaties which have been made by the government in the past. Oswalt (1973:569) tells us that "treaties were considered in the same light as other statutes of the United States Congress." In some cases the treaties even required U.S. citizens to have passports to venture onto Indian lands. There were also several gestures towards having Native American representation in Congress. In the first treaty ever made with Native Americans, the Delaware (Lenape) in 1778, there was a provision for them at a future date to consolidate with other Indian peoples and form a state with the Delaware as the leaders. "In a treaty of 1785 and another of 1830 it was proposed that Indians send a representative to Congress, but again this possibility was never realized" (Oswalt 1973:571).

These and other historical facts establish that sovereignty was recognized by the Executive Branch and Congress many times in the past. As Indian power waned, however, in the face of growing U.S. numerical, industrial and military superiority, treaties began to regulate the control of the Native American peoples and nations more than they constituted bi-lateral agreements between equal powers. Oswalt says that this shift took place in 1849 in a treaty with the Navajo. By the 1860s the United States was making treaties which could be amended in most cases, unilaterally by Congress. State interests, especially those states on the Indian frontier, began to influence a Congressional policy, which was contrary to Indian sovereign rights. This was primarily over the land question. "In 1861 a treaty with the Arapahoe and Cheyenne Indians recognized the power of the President, with the assent of Congress, 'to modify or change any of the provisions of former treaties . . . to whatever extent he may judge to be necessary and expedient for their best interests'" (Washburn 1971:72–73). Moreover, Congress began to enact laws which conflicted with the treaties they had previously made. Thus Congress has amended Indian treaties, although international law recognizes only a few instances where a treaty can be unilaterally changed without the consent of the other party (Berkey *et al* 1977:53–54). In 1902 the Supreme Court formally recognized the authority of Congress to abrogate treaties which had been negotiated with Native Americans.

In 1871 Congress put an end to treaty-making altogether. In the 1860s the Senate and the House argued over their respective powers—the House appropriated funds for Indian treaties but did not have the power to negotiate them; the Senate had the power to negotiate treaties but not to fund them (Jorgensen 1978:10). The massive power of eastern Republicans in Congress forced the Act of 1871 which allowed for speedier domination of the Indians and the expropriation of their resources. In ending treaty-making with the Indians, Congress recognized that the political relations of the federal government with Native Americans were no longer the same as those between equals. Native American peoples and nations had been reduced to a state of powerlessness and rendered dependent upon the unilaterally-dictated terms and conditions set by the dominant nation or power.

> Recognizing this, the House tacked a rider on the Indian Appropriations Act of March 3, 1871, that marked the abandonment of treaty-making with the Indian nations and recognized that tribal sovereignty was merely a straw man whose existence continued to be sustained only by judicial decisions. This rider stated: "No Indian nation or tribe within the territory of the United States shall be acknowledged or recognized as an independent nation, tribe, or power with whom the United States may contract by treaty. . ." (*Iowa Law Review* 1966:661).

The rider, on the other hand, did not invalidate any pre-existing treaty. And yet, the abrogation of treaty-making was a recognition that Congress had come to hold plenary and supreme power over "sovereign, self-governing" Indian peoples and nations. Through riders to its money bills, Congress has passed legislation harmful to Indian sovereignty and completely unrelated to its appropriation acts.

The power of Congress over formerly sovereign Native American nationalities has now become entrenched. Federal Indian policy has been embodied in several major pieces of legislation: the Indian Removal Act of 1830, the Indian Trade and Intercourse Act of 1834, the 1885 Major Crimes Act, the Indian General Allotment Act of 1887, the Indian Reorganization Act of 1934, Public Law 280 in 1953, and the Indian Civil Rights Act of 1968. These acts have severely limited the doctrine of Indian sovereignty as guaranteed originally in federal treaties. In addition, House Concurrent Resolution 108, passed in 1953 and setting forth the policy of termination, had the effect of law.

The passage of the Indian Trade and Intercourse Act provided for the eventual replacement of original treaties by statute. It marked the adoption by the government of the frontiersman's notion that the federal government "had an absolute right to all its territory and that the Indian occupant could therefore be evicted at will" (*Iowa Law Review* 1966:663). It supported the notorious Indian removal policies of the Jackson administration discussed earlier, specifically the Indian Removal Act. (The significance of the Major Crimes Act is that, although it did not take away Indian jurisdiction, it nonetheless forced United States jurisdiction on Indian people in cases of murder, manslaughter, rape, arson, etc., which is a clear violation of Indian sovereignty.)

The Indian General Allotment Act robbed Native Americans of two-thirds of their remaining land base and fostered policies of forced assimilation into white Anglo society and culture. The "plum" of citizenship was offered Indian individuals who would take up individual land allotments and foresake collective life. The provision which permitted the sale of surplus reservation land after allotment represented the interests of the frontier white communities and vested economic concerns that wanted to open up the reservations for settlement.

The Indian Reorganization Act (IRA), on the other hand, reversed the old line assimilationist policy for one of cultural pluralism. The IRA was the New Deal's answer to a century of abuse and mistreatment inflicted on Native American communities; at least, this was the way the Act was represented by its liberal adherents. It must be admitted that it took a different line from that of the Allotment Act in some important aspects.

> The IRA allowed for the consolidation of Indian land and the purchase of non-Indian land. It made legal the creation of tribal governments with constitutions and charters. The IRA made available modest loans to tribal resources (irrigation and the like). And the IRA also called for the establishment of schools on home reservations so that Indian children could stay at home (Jorgensen 1978:17).

Yet it also increased the powers of the Secretary of Interior over Indian government, and it clashed with traditional Indian political organization. It only vaguely recognized the Indians' right to their own cultures, and the proposals to give land and schools have remained mostly paper promises. The kind of sovereignty recognized, in fact, was internal tribal sovereignty, as was admitted by Senator Wheeler, one of the bill's co-sponsors. Wheeler stated that the purpose of the bill was "to stabilize the tribal organization of the Indian tribes by vesting such tribal organization with *real though limited* authority and by prescribing conditions which must be met by such tribal organizations" (*Iowa Law Review* 1966:664). Congress in the 1930s saw limited, internal sovereignty as good public policy, but it did not, in the IRA legislation, recognize what the legal scholars have termed unextinguished sovereignty.

Starting with the Indian Claims Commission Act of 1946, Congress returned to narrow individualism, reversing its policy of so-called corporate collectivism under the IRA. By 1953 this policy was fullblown. House Concurrent Resolution 108 called for the termination of reservations, the ending of the federal relationship, the "freeing" of the American Indian to take his "equal place" in society. The attack upon Indian sovereignty was 100 percent! It was not until the Kennedy administration in 1961 that a moratorium was called to the disastrous termination policy.

Part of termination was Public Law 280, which gave five states complete criminal jurisdiction over offenses by or against Indians: California, Nebraska, Oregon, Minnesota and Wisconsin. "The statute also gave other states the consent of Congress to assume civil and criminal jurisdiction over Indian territory by making appropriate changes in their state constitutions or laws. In 1968 the law was amended to require the consent of the Indian nations. . ." (Berkey *et al* 1977:63). This, of course, violated many treaties and ignored Indian sovereignty.

The Indian Civil Rights Act placed certain restrictions on Indian governments, although it gave Indian individuals the protection of the U.S. Constitution. In the past, "courts have stated that Indian governments were not subject to constitutional requirements because they existed before the establishment of the U.S. and the Constitution. . . ," but now, "Congress has restricted the freedom of an Indian nation to maintain a governmental system consistent with its own laws and customs" (Berkey *et al* 1977:64–65). Ironically, while seeking to protect the civil rights of Indian individuals, it has infringed upon the sovereignty of Native American nationalities.

The Indian Civil Rights Act was handed down to Native American peoples unilaterally by Congress and in almost total disregard for its detrimental impact on Indian sovereignty. The abuses that Indians had been complaining about, and supposedly what the Act corrected, were more often than not due to corruption in tribal government. But this is caused indirectly, if not directly, by the nature of the tribal council system, itself a product of the neo-colonial operation of the Bureau of Indian Affairs. The Act, called also the Indian Bill of Rights, was supposed to extend to Native Americans those constitutional guarantees which other citizens enjoy. Congress, however, modified some of these rights, in other areas neglected to extend them, and in certain other areas imposed restraints more extensive than those of the U.S. Constitution (Warren 1972:260). One of the rights which Congress omitted is the Constitutional right to keep and bear arms!

According to the American Civil Liberties Union, the Indian Civil Rights Act can be viewed as an entering wedge by both federal and state governments into the internal affairs of the Indian tribe. The question arises: Whose rights are paramount, the civil rights of an Indian individual, or the sovereign rights of a Native American nationality?

The Courts

The U.S. courts have supported Indian sovereignty more consistently than either the Federal Executive or Congress. Two early important rulings, *Cherokee Nation v. Georgia* and *Worcester v. Georgia,* have already been analyzed. Although the Supreme Court ruled in 1889, in *Stephens v. Cherokee Nation,* ''that the Indian tribes were in no sense sovereign states,'' the concept of internal sovereignty has been preserved. In *Talton v. Mayes* (1896) it was held ''that the powers of the Indian tribe are not derived from the Constitution, treaties, or statute, but rather are inherent powers of limited sovereignty which have never been extinguished'' (*Iowa Law Review* 1966:659).

On the other hand, in 1886 and 1903 the Supreme Court rendered decisions which conflicted with the principle of Indian sovereignty. The validity of the Major Crimes Act was upheld in *U.S. v. Kagama.* In *Lone Wolf v. Hitchcock* the Court again upheld the actions of Congress, stating that Congress has plenary power in Indian affairs.

In a well-argued paper written for the 1977 Geneva Conference, attorney Robert Coulter (1977) explains the legal limitations of U.S. courts to redress the wrongs done to Native Americans: these are the political question doctrine, the rule of ''Tee-Hit-Ton,'' and the plenary power doctrine. All have a direct bearing on the sovereignty question and illustrate the power of Congress over Indian policy.

The political question doctrine holds that the courts must not decide an issue, such as the status of Native American nationalities and their sovereignty, that has been committed for determination by the Constitution to the legislative or executive branches of government. Coulter cites the case of *Lone Wolf v. Hitchcock* (1903) as an example.

The Medicine Lodge Treaty of 1867 stipulated that no cession of reservation lands would be valid unless at least three-fourths of the adult male members of the Oklahoma tribes concerned gave their consent. In 1900, however, Congress ratified an agreement grabbing two and one-half million acres for the United States and ignored the three-fourths consent stipulation. In the suit brought by the Indian governments, *Lone Wolf v. Hitchcock*, the Supreme Court considered the issue to be a political question and would not consider the Indians' claims that the cession had been obtained by fraudulent means. As a result, the Indians were denied a remedy for the gross violation of their treaty rights. There are many cases of treaties being violated, where the courts "cop out" using the political question doctrine.

Coulter (1977:9) says "the rule in 'Tee-Hit-Ton' is a shocking and, frankly, racist rule of law." It concerns Indian property rights and states that fee title to Indian land is vested in the United States, that Indians have only a mere right of possession or occupancy, subject at any time to taking or extinction by Congress.

The plenary (absolute) power doctrine gives Congress practically unlimited power over Indian affairs when the courts consider a matter a political question beyond the scope of judicial review. Thus even a Joint Resolution of Congress can instrument a policy that terminates Indian reservations, as was the case in 1953.

The States

Federal laws and regulations now take precedence over Indian sovereignty, and for a time, until 1970, it looked as if state laws and regulations would do the same. The intrusion of states into the sovereignty of the Native American nationalities is producing a crisis in federal-state-Indian relations. This came to a head particularly after World War II. State laws are not supposed to override Indian treaty rights, such as those of hunting, fishing, taxation, but, none-the-less, many states have attempted to do so, and the question is not settled yet (Kane 1965:247).

Fishing rights in Washington, Oregon, and California have been under attack by state authorities. The state of California, for example, is presently opposing Yurok fishing rights on the Klamath River. The issue came to a head, however, primarily in Washington. Dozens of Indian fishermen and women have gone to jail and suffered their nets and fishing gear destroyed or confiscated, in order to get their treaty rights before the courts. Although state intrusion into treaty rights clearly violates the federal Constitution, laws and regulations, the federal government has been strangely silent in this matter until very recently. Beginning with the 1974 decision by Federal District Court Judge George Boldt, which allowed Indians a 50–50 split in the commercial fish harvest, favorable federal decisions are being made.

The White Mountain Apache of Arizona are attempting to exert sovereignty over wildlife management by setting their own game quotas and fees; sportsmen need only reservation permits to hunt and fish. The State of Arizona, however, has opposed Indian sovereignty in this instance and sought to maintain its own regulations over the reservation. A recent U.S. district court affirmed the Apaches' right to set their own fees, seasons, and to regulate game, but it also upheld Arizona's right to enforce state regulations on non-Indian hunters leaving the reservation (Hess 1980:279–280).

Citing Public Law 280, a number of states have attempted to tax reservation Indians, but the courts, as in *William v. Lee,* have so far ruled that states have no tax authority on reservations. A more troublesome problem has been the question of Indians policing a reservation where there are resident whites. "In the case of *Oliphant v. Schlie,* and *Belgarde v. Morton,* the court upheld tribal jurisdiction over non-Indians who committed crimes within the reservation" (Berkey *et al* 1977:85), but the states continue to challenge this right on various grounds.

There has been a vicious backlash to recent favorable federal court decisions. In Washington state, "commercial salmon fishing businessmen and sport fishing groups were incensed at Judge Bolt's decision, because they had been battling Indians over these rights for years and, for the most part, winning" (Jorgensen 1978:41). Reactionary, anti-Indian interests came together to form the Interstate Congress for Equal Rights and Responsibilities (ICERR). The Western Interstate Region of the National Association of Counties, representing officials from eleven western states, joined with ICERR in 1978 to decide how to battle against Indian interests.

In 1977, Republican Representative John Cunningham of Washington introduced a bill entitled, ironically, the Native American Equal Opportunity Act. Actually, the bill called for terminating the reservations by abrogating all treaties, closing all Indian hospitals, schools, housing projects, and ending hunting and fishing rights. Nine other proposed pieces of legislation also attacked Indian sovereign rights in the areas of hunting, fishing, water jurisdiction, land claims (in Maine and New York), and Indian criminal jurisdiction. This led to the formation of a coalition of Native Americans in opposition to the attack on Indian sovereignty. Following their traditional religious leaders, a group of 180 walked across the country from San Francisco to Washington, D.C., in what was called "The Longest Walk." They arrived in the summer of 1978 where they were joined by many others to protest at the Capital. Subsequently, the bills failed to get out of committee, and Rep. Cunningham was defeated in a bid for re-election. Yet the danger remains. The right wing has not abandoned its attempt to destroy Indian sovereignty!

Indian Sovereignty Today

Despite set-backs to their status as sovereign political entities, Native Americans are unlike other oppressed minorities in that the Courts in particular have repeatedly recognized their special status. Thus the U.S. government has made over 400 treaties and agreements, 5,000 statutes, a number of Supreme Court rulings and hundreds of federal regulations, all of which pertain to Native Americans, and which define in one way or another their special relationship to the United States. This relationship, by now, has become quite a contradictory one.

> These decisions and many others, recognize: (1) Indian tribes are "distinct, independent political communities," possessing all the rights, powers and privileges of any sovereign state; (2) their sovereignty is limited in that tribes have only internal powers (e.g., they cannot make treaties with other powers); and (3) by treaty or legislation, Congress may at any time qualify the sovereignty of the tribes (Warren 1972:257).

The *limited* sovereignty remaining to Indian nationalities nevertheless includes the powers to: (1) govern themselves administratively and judicially (but under IRA regulations), (2) tax themselves, (3) handle domestic relations, (4) apportion tribal property, (5) regulate inheritance, and (6) determine tribal membership.

Many Native Americans dispute this modification of the right to original sovereignty. They point to their treaties which, for the most part, guaranteed them many of the rights of sovereign nations. They ask when was it that they agreed to give up these rights? Congress has acted arbitrarily and unilaterally in reducing Indian sovereignty. Since Native Americans did not receive full citizenship until 1924, and in some states could not vote until much later, one might ask, on what basis were Indian political interests represented in the Congressional legislation which has curtailed sovereign rights?

Yet, in terms of a multitude of legal pronouncements, Native Americans are still being described by the Courts as "distinct, independent, political communities," possessing all the rights, powers, and privileges of any sovereign state (Warren 1972:257). The primary aim of the Indian movement is to make this legal definition a political reality, to strengthen and extend sovereign rights, powers, and privileges of North American peoples and nations, which have been so badly abused and neglected.

The next chapter will describe in historical terms the *economic motive* for destroying the Indian peoples as sovereign entities. If we are to truly understand the reason why Native American leadership sees the restoration of treaty rights as the basis for ending oppression and reducing poverty, then we must focus on the cause and not the symptoms of what has been mistakenly termed "the Indian problem."

*We did not break any laws, but in fact went
into Wounded Knee to uphold laws.*

Russell Means

3

THE MEANING OF
WOUNDED KNEE

A traditional chief of the Onondaga Nation has defined an "Indian
nation" as a group of people with a distinct language, a way-of-life, a
territory, self-government, and (reflecting on the social genocide) "which
has their children, their future generations."

It may come as a surprise to non-Indians to learn that there are Native
American peoples in the United States who still regard themselves as
distinct nationalities, but such is the case. This fact lies at the heart of the
"new Indian" movement launched in the 1960s. According to this view,
despite hundreds of years of dispossession and genocide, the essence of
the Native American struggle is that of asserting the right to exist as
viable national communities.

This is particularly the view of those known as traditionalists, like the
aforementioned Onondaga chief, but all movement activists generally
subscribe to this view. Not only militant groups like the American Indian
Movement, but the National Congress of American Indians, as well, has
endorsed the principle of Indian sovereignty. Yet the demand for political
rights without sovereignty over raw materials, let alone the right to own
and control the means of production on the Indian land base, is like a
house built on sand.

The key ingredient missing from the above definition of nationhood is
the economic component. The economic question is relegated to one of

secondary significance, if it is noted at all, in the standard works by writers on the so-called Indian problem. Native American activists themselves tend to view their oppression primarily in political rather than economic terms. The fact that Indian sovereignty has been a historically recognized principle in U.S. legal doctrine, although abused in practice, has reinforced this tendency. However, the activists' demand for an adequate land base and, more recently, for fair royalty rates and lease arrangements, that is, for a larger measure of control over the means of production on the land base—primarily in the extractive industry—may be understood as relating directly to the economic aspect of the question.

There are three strands to the Native American question, each deserving of careful analysis. First, the struggle has strong characteristics of a national movement. In reality, it is many related national movements, e.g., Navajo, Lakota, Iroquois, Hopi, and so on. This is the major theme of the present chapter on Wounded Knee.

Secondly, it is an all–Native American struggle against racism, a specific form which has been directed against *all* "tribes and nations," the original possessors of North America, by *all* Euro-Americans regardless of national background. This form of racism, although infinitely deepened by the racism against Black people which arose out of slavery, was spawned by the frontier history of dispossession and genocide. It has lasted into this century and is being fueled today by the new attack on the Native American frontier by capitalism.

Finally, it is a class struggle in the sense that national and racial oppression are manifestations of capitalist exploitation, a means of deriving superprofits at the expense of indigenous peoples. In the original conquest of aboriginal North America, the Native Americans' lands and resources provided the original or "primitive" accumulation of capital. Today, the Indian and Eskimo regions of the United States and Alaska constitute cheap sources of land, water, timber, fish and minerals—especially coal, oil, gas and uranium—which are being increasingly expropriated by the multinationals. It is hardly surprising that the struggle has taken on strong anti-monopoly overtones.

Native American reservations and communities are no longer separate economic systems, although they have special characteristics which deserve serious consideration. In most cases, they have been integrated into the capitalist political economy for the last one hundred years or more. Most Native Americans are now wage workers, and tens of thousands have been driven into the cities in search of work. Others have been forced into the rural proletariat. And both groups occupy the lowest ranks of monopoly capital's reserve army of unemployed and under-employed labor. Because of national chauvinism and racism, they occupy a caste-like status in the lower ranks of the working class. Thus a lessening of their class exploitation is linked, not only with the fight against racism, but also with the struggle for self-government in their reservations and communities, to controlling the means of production and the development of resources in these areas, and to maintaining their own languages, religions, and life-ways, if they so choose.

Today the Native American movement is making three political de-mands which, from the viewpoint of history, are the central issues around which Native American peoples and nationalities have always waged their struggle: the right to a land base, to culture, and to self-government. What remains to be strengthened ideologically is the economic edge of their struggle.

The strategy of the current movement has centered on restoring the treaty process, because most treaties, to one extent or another, recognize Indian sovereignty. The key element of Indian sovereignty is the right to self-government, for Native Americans to govern themselves as indi-vidual nationalities. The exercise of political autonomy is seen as the foundation upon which U.S. indigenous societies can be revitalized, not necessarily to their original or even early colonial forms, but to a state of life which is commensurate with human dignity and in accordance with indigenous customs and traditions. Thus the strategy does not speak specifically to the class question, but, rather, to national oppression.

The occupation protest at Wounded Knee, South Dakota, in February of 1973, and the concerns raised by the Indian activists in their confronta-tion with the U.S. government forces dramatically demonstrated the continuing struggle for self-government. It is necessary to analyze this important event, in order to comprehend the current mood of the Native American peoples, to understand why they are waging an extremely bitter and militant struggle for self-government. At the outset, how-ever, one should have an appreciation for the historical background to the protest.

The 1890 Massacre at Wounded Knee

In 1868 the United States government, after an unconditional defeat of its military forces, was required to abandon the Bozeman Trail through the Powder River country and sign the Fort Laramie Treaty. It was, in this sense, a surrender treaty, because it acknowledged the sovereignty of the Teton Sioux Nation and its allies over the disputed territory.

The treaty guaranteed the right of the Teton Sioux to the land from the Missouri River west to the Wyoming–South Dakota border, with the Sioux to retain exclusive use of the territory within these boundaries. The treaty also provided for an even larger area to remain "unceded Indian territory" upon which the various Indian peoples could hunt and from which whites were to be excluded.

It was Chief Red Cloud who is said to have observed: "They made us many promises, more than I can remember, but they never kept but one. They promised to take our land and they took it." Thus within a few years, the "Americans" broke the terms of the 1868 Ft. Laramie Treaty when gold was discovered in the Black Hills.

In 1874 General George Armstrong Custer with 1,000 cavalrymen trespassed upon the Black Hills, holy land for the Sioux and other Indians, in violation of the treaty. Custer's illegal expedition confirmed the presence of gold, and the U.S. government then sent a delegation west to buy the mountains. The Sioux, however, refused to sell their sacred lands. But by this time hundreds of miners and settlers had invaded the reservation. The government then claimed the Black Hills and the unceded Indian territory, and the Army was ordered to collect the bands of Indians for deportation. The series of battles that ensued culminated in perhaps the best known engagement of the general conflict beween whites and Indians—the Little Bighorn—where Custer and his force were wiped out by the Sioux and Northern Cheyenne. Ironically, the Indian victory was termed "Custer's Massacre" whereas a real massacre a few years later of unarmed Indians by white soldiers has come down to us as "The Battle of Wounded Knee."

An Act confiscating the Black Hills region and the unceded territory was passed by Congress in February, 1877. The Sioux bitterly complained that the United States violated the procedures set down and ratified in the 1868 Treaty, but to no avail. "The United States has always maintained in public that the deal was legal, while admitting privately that it was one of the biggest swindles in world history" (Deloria 1974a:12). Then, in 1889, under pressure from politicians and vested interests in the newly established state of South Dakota, the Great Sioux Reservation was again reduced in size. It was divided into five smaller tracts and allocated to the various Teton Sioux bands, these tracts becoming the present-day reservations (See map, page 55).

SIOUX LAND CESSIONS

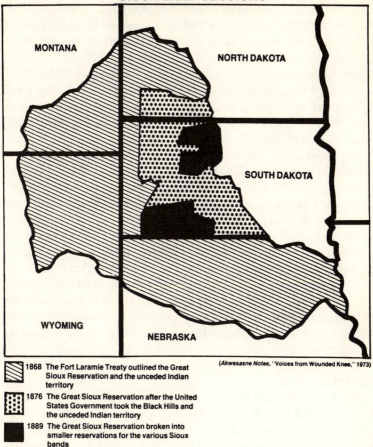

MONTANA

NORTH DAKOTA

SOUTH DAKOTA

WYOMING

NEBRASKA

(*Akwesasne Notes*, "Voices from Wounded Knee," 1973)

1868 The Fort Laramie Treaty outlined the Great Sioux Reservation and the unceded Indian territory

1876 The Great Sioux Reservation after the United States Government took the Black Hills and the unceded Indian territory

1889 The Great Sioux Reservation broken into smaller reservations for the various Sioux bands

In 1890 the government again violated Sioux sovereignty, guaranteed in the 1868 Treaty, when it sent soldiers to extinguish an imaginary uprising, the Ghost Dance religious movement. This led to one of the worst, and certainly the best known massacres of American Indians in U.S. history.

On December 29, near Porcupine Creek at Wounded Knee, the Seventh Cavalry, bent on revenge for Custer's death and the U.S. Army's defeat at Little Bighorn, brutally massacred not only unarmed men, but also women and children. The Indian death toll was nearly 300 of the original

350. The wounded survivors were taken to the Pine Ridge Agency after dark. The barracks were filled with soldiers, and no one would open their doors to the Indian wounded for shelter. Finally, the Episcopal mission was opened, the benches taken out and hay scattered over the rough flooring. Dee Brown, in *Bury My Heart at Wounded Knee* (1970:418), points out the irony of this tragedy. It was the fourth day after Christmas, and the season's greenery was still hanging from the church rafters when the first torn and bleeding bodies were carried in. "Across the chancel front above the pulpit was strung a crudely lettered banner: PEACE ON EARTH, GOOD WILL TO MEN."

The Sioux never forgot Wounded Knee. The Sioux author, Vine Deloria, Jr., describes a visit to Wounded Knee as his strongest boyhood memory (1971:238–239). He says that his father would often point out survivors of the massacre and that the reservation people always went out of their way to assist them. "For a long time there was a bill in Congress to pay indemnities to the survivors, but the War Department always insisted that it had been a 'battle' . . . This does not, however, explain bayoneted Indian women and children found miles from the scene. . . ."

By such brutal massacres, by treaty fraud and other nefarious practices, but mainly through starvation—the calculated killing of tens of millions of buffalo, the Plains Indians' food staple—the Sioux and other peoples were finally defeated and reduced to the status of captured nationalities on the reservations.

The Hungry Years

General William Sherman aptly defined a reservation as "a parcel of land, inhabited by Indians and surrounded by thieves." With the final defeat of the Indians and their forced confinement to reservations, the U.S. Congress unilaterally ended treaty-making with Indian tribes and nations, and the western frontier was declared closed.

Once on the reservations, despite treaty rights to the contrary, the Indian peoples came under the brutal colonial control of the Bureau of Indian Affairs and were at the mercy of Anglo–American economic interests. It was then that the federal authorities, missionaries and traders began their long war of attrition against aboriginal economy, society and culture. Brandon (1961:363) aptly terms the years from 1870 to the 1920s as "the Indians' darkest hour." He states that "there was no doubt much more silent suffering than will ever be related." Spiritual culture was proscribed by the authorities, children were made to feel ashamed of their "blanket Indian" parents, the reservations had a concentration camp air, and "hunger was the big reality for those confined peoples who could only secure their dinners out of promised government subsistence." Meanwhile, the U.S. public was persuaded that Indians were a "vanishing race":

> This image, which gained prominence at the beginning of the twentieth century, was captured in James E. Fraser's statute of a bent and battered Indian sitting on an equally forlorn horse, both with heads bowed. According to the title of the statue, this was "The End of the Trail." At about the same time, in 1909, Joseph K. Dixon, working with the Bureau of Indian Affairs, arranged "The Last Great Indian Council." It included 21 representative Indian chiefs, scouts, and warriors, and was intended to be a farewell to a people on the verge of extinction (Faherty 1974:242).

The United States, already a leading capitalist power by the end of the nineteenth century, had been able to develop rapidly in large part because of its ability to seize Indian lands. Not only the crops grown on these vast lands and the minerals mined, but the capital generated through speculation underwrote the Yankee state. Thus it was that U.S. capitalists, assured of their final conquest of the Native Americans as indigenous peoples, could afford philanthropic works. In 1906, for example, President Teddy Roosevelt persuaded his friend, J. Pierpont Morgan, to finance Edward S. Curtis' ambitious project of making 40,000 photographs of the "vanishing Redman." It was within this context, also, that the Bureau of American Ethnology and the American Anthropology Association were founded at the turn of the century, to "reconstruct" Indian cultures before the Indians' "inevitable disappearance before the tide of civilization."

With the confinement of Indians to reservations, the conquest of indigenous society seemed complete. What still remained, to cinch the bourgeois mission of Manifest Destiny, was the destruction of the Indians' political economy, the eradication of spiritual life and social institutions. The old collectivities were to be destroyed: tribal land and resource management, government, religion and the extended family. This was discretely referred to as "assimilation" or "acculturation" rather than genocide. "An elaborate rationale based on the 'superiority' of white economy, culture and religion made a program of destruction and exploitation of Indians seem one of philanthropy and assistance" (Council on Interracial Books 1971:264). The policy of the U.S. government then shifted from one of outright genocide to cultural and social genocide, and the slogan, "Kill the Indian, but save the man," was coined.

The four agents of the new genocide under the colonial pattern were the Indian agent, the mission church, the federal boarding school, and the white trader. Of these four it was the Indian agent or superintendent who exercised the most power.

The Indian agent "possessed and exercised the powers of a dictator. He could put Indians into prisons, determine their sentences, break up families, take children from their parents, decide where an Indian should place his residence, and prescribe his daily routine" (Wissler 1966:286). The agent had two powerful "weapons": rations of food and clothing to give out at a time when reservation Indians depended on assistance to stay alive, and the newly appointed Indian police to enforce the regulations of the government.

In 1883 the government framed a criminal code to do away with "demoralizing and barbarous customs." Many Indian traditions and practices were termed "Indian offenses" and considered as crimes. "Give-away feasts, the sun dance, the time-hallowed way of burying the dead, even the building of a sweat lodge, were now punishable by a jail sentence" (Erdoes 1972:175).

According to Burnette and Koster (1974:19–20), it was religion which bore the brunt of the general attack on Indian culture. ". . . The spiritual leaders and healers known to Whites as 'medicine men' were the focal point of the persecution, because they were the bearers of Indian religion, the transmitters of oral tradition and ritual. . . ." Thus, in the Sioux country, the U.S. Army crushed the Sun Dance.

The Sun Dance, or *wi yanyang wacipi,* is probably the most famous of the seven rituals in the Sioux religion. It is a flesh sacrifice by votaries who ask a blessing for themselves, for their people, and all living things. Its political significance is its function of maintaining tribal solidarity. And that is why it was suppressed by white authorities.

An even more repressive legal instrument than the "criminal" code was the Dawes Severalty or General (Indian) Allotments Act of 1887. The Allotment Act, as it is generally termed, destroyed Indianness in a hundred different ways. Senator Pendleton of Ohio, in arguing for its passage, declared that "they must either change their mode of life or they must die!"

By simple legislative theft, half of the Native American land base was lost through this Act. Allotment destroyed Indian economy by forcing the transfer of communal lands to private ownership. Those lands "left over" were then declared surplus by the government and sold to whites.

About 90 million acres of Indian land was thus lost, with only the Southwestern peoples escaping the full impact.

We can cite the example of the Oglala Sioux on the Pine Ridge Reservation. The Oglala are one of the Teton Sioux bands. During the 1880s, under the reservation system, they had adapted from a hunting to a ranching economy with comparative ease. This was because lands were still held in common under traditional land management custom. But later, the forced shift from communal livestock grazing to individualized allotted farmlands proved disastrous. Deloria (1974b) explains that they had developed large communal cattle herds by 1916 and were relatively prosperous. They also raised some of the finest horses in the region. They refused allotment, however, and continued to maintain their traditional form of government. But in 1917, the Oglala Indian agent sold their cattle, supposedly for war needs, and leased their lands out to white cattlemen. "The cattle market broke following the war, making it impossible for the Oglalas to re-enter the cattle business. Large corporate farm operations began to move into western South Dakota to practice the new techniques of dry-land farming which had recently been developed" (Deloria 1974b:68).

At the same time that the government forced allotment on the Oglalas, it also devised the notorious leasing system by which a number of small Indian allotments are leased as one unit for small rental payments to wealthy white ranchers. In short order, the white cattlemen and farmers gained a stanglehold over Oglala economy which they have never surrendered.

The destruction of Native American religion and economy, like that of the Oglala Sioux, more easily facilitated the attack on traditional government, because these spheres of life are closely linked in aboriginal society. A man no longer became a chief in the old way. "Those who did what the white agent wanted became chiefs and were given fine, two-story houses, so that everybody could see that it payed to do as one was told. Those who disobeyed were removed from office. The old nomadic democracy of the Plains vanished" (Erdoes 1972:174).

Under such repressive practices, Native American resistance to authoritarian rule and colonial confinement took on non-political forms. "Bureau personnel encountered sullen apathy, a sense of deep grievance, passive resistance, subtle sabotage, a high incidence of drunkenness, uncooperativeness, and mourning for the past" (Lurie 1971a:434). Religious revitalization movements occurred, only to be repressed by the authorities.

Nevertheless, pockets of resistance survived. These holdouts were contemptuously called "conservatives" by the Indian agents, as opposed to "progressives" (those who cooperated with the government), but are known today by the more accurate term, traditionalists.

Traditionalists comprise significant elements of the Haudenosaunee (Six Nations Iroquois) in New York state and Canada, the Miccousukee in Florida, and the Hopi in Arizona. In fact, most Native American nationalities have their traditional adherents who steadfastly seek to maintain their political independence and ethnicity, often at great personal sacrifice, including imprisonment.

At Pine Ridge in 1973, the poorest and most oppressed of the reservation masses, under the leadership of their traditional chiefs and assisted by the American Indian Movement, rose up in the face of the U.S. military-governmental complex and declared themselves an independent Oglala Nation, attempting thereby to reverse a century of national oppression.

The 1973 "Occupation"
On February 27, 1973, Wounded Knee was "occupied" by several hundred Oglala Sioux and their supporters, with the goal of returning at least this historic site to the control of the Oglala people. They sent three demands to the U.S. government: (1) the Senate Subcommittee on Administrative Practices and Procedures, headed by Senator Ted Kennedy, should launch an investigation of the Bureau of Indian Affairs and the Department of the Interior for their handling of the Oglala Sioux Nation; (2) the Pine Ridge Reservation tribal constitution, chartered under the 1934 Indian Reorganization Act, should be suspended and the Oglala Sioux allowed to freely choose their own form of government; and (3) Senator William Fulbright, head of the Senate Foreign Relations Committee, should investigate the 371 treaties between the federal government and Native American peoples because of the government's failure to honor its Indian treaties.

A number of critical issues sent the activists to Wounded Knee: racism, economic exploitation, government mismanagement of the reservation, and, above all, the denial of the right of the Oglala masses to run their own affairs on the Pine Ridge Reservation.

There had been a number of racially-motivated and unpunished murders, often by police, in Indian country during the year prior to Wounded Knee. These included the murders of Yellow Thunder in Nebraska, Shenandoah in Pennsylvania, Smith and Oakes in California, Celaya in

Arizona, High Pine in Montana, and Badheart Bull in South Dakota. The American Indian Movement (AIM) was in the leadership of the Indian demonstrations that protested these murders.

A high point in the intensity of these and other protests was reached in the 1972 Trail of Broken Treaties to Washington, D.C., described earlier in a previous chapter. By 1972 AIM had grown to become the nation's largest militant Indian organization. At Pine Ridge a number of AIM chapters had sprung up, principally because of AIM's popularity after the Washington, D.C., demonstration, as well as because of its leadership in combatting racism in the South Dakota area.

AIM's protest of the Yellow Thunder murder in February of 1972 is an example of its successful use of direct action. Raymond Yellow Thunder, an elderly Oglala man from Pine Ridge,

> . . . was beaten in Gordon, Nebraska by two White men, thrown naked into an American Legion dance, beaten again, and locked in an auto trunk. His bruised body was found two days later. His attackers were released without paying bail and charged with second degree manslaughter. Incidents like this had happened many times before, but this time the people decided to do something about it (*Voices From Wounded Knee* 1974:13).

When the authorities tried to cover up the circumstances of Yellow Thunder's death, relatives and friends at Pine Ridge turned to AIM. AIM then led two thousand protesters to Gordon, Nebraska, and forced an investigation into the case.

Meanwhile, sinister forces at the national as well as state and local levels began to view AIM with alarm, seeing it as a threat to the *status quo* in Indian–white relations. These forces conspired to stop AIM before its militant tactics "infected" the reservations. At Pine Ridge, homeland of the Oglala Sioux, this conspiracy bore fruit. The catalyst was Richard Wilson, the ultra-conservative, newly "elected" president of the Pine Ridge Tribe.

> While AIM was becoming popular, two members of the John Birch Society, Eugene Rooks and William Rooks, were spreading rumors among tribal councilmen and other officials that AIM was a communist organization and was trying to take over the Oglala Sioux government and establish a base on the Pine Ridge Reservation. One of the most gullible persons to fall for Eugene Rooks' propaganda was Dick Wilson. Soon Rooks was successful in convincing not only Wilson, but almost all of the tribal councilmen, as well as BIA Superintendent Stanley Lyman. Rooks, Wilson, Lyman, and other persons in government were more scared of AIM, not because they were supposedly communists, but because they felt AIM was a threat to their jobs (*Voices From Wounded Knee* 1974:15).

After the Washington, D.C., "sit in" in which a number of Sioux had participated, Wilson set out to punish AIM members who were returning to the reservation. He "fired" the tribal vice-president for supporting AIM and augmented his reservation police force with a $62,000 grant from the Bureau of Indian Affairs.

The Wilson police force soon became known as the "goon squad" after it began a campaign of arrests, beatings and harassment. AIM members, including Russell Means, an Oglala in the organization's leadership, were banned from the reservation in violation of their civil rights. Theoretically, this was to prevent futher protests, but, in reality, the tribal police "had a tendency to lean very hard on all of Wilson's political opponents" (Deloria 1974b:71). Means, for example, had threatened to run against Wilson in the next tribal election.

The Oglalas organized to oppose the regime of Wilson and Lyman, the BIA superintendent. An Inter-District Tribal Council (IDTC) was formed to fight corruption in the reservation government and in the BIA. There had been charges of misuse of funds and other irregular if not corrupt practices. In December, 1972, the IDTC demanded, but without success, the resignations of Wilson and Lyman.

In the meantime, AIM was active in the fight against racism and exploitation in the nearby towns contiguous to the reservation. In mid-January it held a Chicano–Indio unity conference in Scottsbluff, Nebraska, and in February, it led two hundred people in a demonstration at Custer, South Dakota (the county seat) to press for a first-degree murder indictment of the killer of Wesley Badheart Bull.

By February, things were coming to a head. AIM was in Rapid City, organizing civil rights hearings and meeting with the mayor. Wilson, who had ignored the murder of Badheart Bull, began issuing press releases calling upon the local officials in Rapid City and other nearby towns to kill all AIM members. And he challenged AIM to come to Pine Ridge and face his "goon squad."

It was at this time that the Oglala Sioux Civil Rights Organization was formed at Pine Ridge, to combat the tribal president's increasing harassment of reservation citizens. A series of impeachment attempts were made, but Wilson, with the behind-the-scenes support of the BIA, refused to call the council into session.

Early in February, three Oglala Sioux councilmen filed impeachment proceedings against Wilson for the fourth time in his ten-month old adminstration. It was then that the tribal president declared a state of emergency, citing the AIM "danger," called in the federal marshals and, at the same time, postponed his own impeachment hearing. "The federal government, whose various agencies had been keeping close surveillance on AIM since the occupation of the BIA building in Washington in November, was more than willing to step in and support the tribal president . . ." (*Voices From Wounded Knee* 1974:22).

Thus the government's military build-up on Pine Ridge was begun *before* the Wounded Knee protest. Federal marshals were sent in on the pretense that, in neutral fashion, they would be simply helping out local authorities, but this was not the truth of the matter. As a documented study (*Voices From Wounded Knee* 1974:23–24) of the protest reports:

> While the marshals may have come to Pine Ridge partly to protect Wilson and the BIA building, it is clear they were sent by the government to coordinate some kind of attack on the American Indian Movement, which was effectively leading Indian people in revolt against the whole BIA system. High-level officials of the U.S. Marshal Service, the U.S. Attorney's office, the FBI, and the BIA were on the scene in Pine Ridge days before Wilson's impeachment hearing. The director of the Marshal Service flew in from Washington on a plane provided by the Pentagon. . . .

Later, after Wilson successfully manipulated his own impeachment trial, hundreds of protesting Oglalas moved to the reservation community of Calico to consider what to do next. There they voted to call in AIM for assistance. The Oglala chiefs advised the people to "take your brothers from the American Indian Movement and go to Wounded Knee and make your stand there . . ." (*Voices From Wounded Knee* 1974:31). At Wounded Knee the leaders said that the only options open to the United States government were to either wipe out the old people, women, children and men by shooting them, or to negotiate the protestors' demands.

The hamlet was no sooner "occupied" by the demonstrators than it was blockaded by federal marshals, the FBI, the Bureau of Indian Affairs police, the federal border patrol, and elements of the U.S. Army. In short, a federal army had come to South Dakota and another 1890 massacre was in the making.

The military presence at Wounded Knee was in violation of federal law (18 USC 1385), which stipulates that the use of U.S. military personnel and equipment to quell "a civilian disturbance is unconstitutional in the absence of a presidential proclamation or Congressional authorization." Yet the 82nd Airborne was there in civilian disguise, and the U.S. Army furnished 16 armoured personnel carriers, 400,000 rounds of ammunition, 100 protective vests, a Phantom jet, three helicopters, 120 sniper rifles, 20 grenade launchers, and a host of other equipment. The 200 Indians, on the other hand, had fewer than 50 rifles, half of which could not be fired because of their poor condition. A Vietnam veteran inside Wounded Knee later testified: "We took more bullets in 71 days than I took in two years in Vietnam. It was horrible. The Army fired at everything that moved" (Garbus 1974:454–455).

After the blockade had been in effect for two weeks, the government issued an ultimatum: everyone must leave the village by the evening of March 8th or the military would come in shooting. Russell Means, Oglala AIM spokesperson, expressed the sentiments of those inside when he said: "We came here and bet our lives that there would be a historic change for our Nation. The government can massacre us, or it can meet our basic human demands. Either way, there will be historic change" (*Voices from Wounded Knee* 1974:51). It was at this point that hundreds of other Oglalas came to their assistance. According to Deloria (1974b: 76–77), "the roads to Wounded Knee were jammed by cars filled with Indians . . . determined to stop the federal marshals from killing their relatives." The line of cars was nearly seven miles long.

Sections of the non-Indian public were by this time also voicing their support and sending material aid. Angela Davis, for example, led a Communist Party, USA delegation to Wounded Knee in a demonstration of solidarity. And the National Council of Churches representatives vowed to stand between the Indian activists and the military, if need be, to prevent the government from killing the protesters.

With the outpouring of public support, the government's March 8th ultimatum was thwarted and the blockade temporarily lifted. The government then hoped that the demonstrators would disband, but, instead, more supporters poured in. These included many of the "revered medicine men and several well known holy men" (Deloria 1974b:75). On March 11th these leaders met in an all-day council at Wounded Knee. At the end of their deliberations they solemnly announced their declaration of an independent Oglala Sioux Nation, based on the terms of the 1868 Treaty. "They . . . voted to send delegates to the United Nations, and to address the White House in Washington, D.C., on the fact they were going to be independent. . . They asked the American Indian Movement to effect that change" (*Voices From Wounded Knee* 1974:64). It was this act, and the support it received from the majority of democratic-minded Americans, which eventually brought the U.S. government to the negotiating table.

The extent to which non-Indians were sympathetic to the Oglala declaration of independence was revealed in a nation-wide public opinion poll. *The New York Times* (as quoted in *Akwesasne Notes* 1973:6) declared editorially:

> Perhaps for the first time since the British people's revolutionary war of 1776, the American people gave their support to an armed insurrection against the government of the land. The Lou Harris Poll showed 51% of those questioned supported the Independent Oglala Nation at Wounded Knee.
>
> 21% of those asked opposed the native people. The balance of 28% said they weren't sure of where they stood. Harris reports that back of this public reaction is the 76% conviction that American Indian people have not been treated well—in fact, 60% said treatment was downright "poor."
>
> 50% of those asked felt that the treaties had been broken, and that native people had not been given a chance to determine their own future through self-government. 93% of those asked answered that they had followed the Wounded Knee incident through the media.
>
> Most sympathetic to the cause are persons in the East, those who live in the suburbs, young people under 30, the college-educated, Blacks, people with incomes over $15,000, union members, independent voters, and Catholics. That means that support cuts through a wide swath of the American people, Harris says.

In spite of growing public opinion in favor of the Oglala protest, federal forces after the March 8th crisis closed in for a second round of armed confrontation. But in the meantime, four hundred supporters had rallied at Wounded Knee. Furthermore, "six of the eight district chairmen withdrew their support from the tribal council and threw in with the occupiers, which meant that the Oglala militants had three times more support from the tribe's own elected officials than Wilson did" (Burnette and Koster 1974:238).

A peace agreement favorable to the demonstrators was signed on April 6th. It included the promise of a federal investigation into the situation at Pine Ridge and a presidential treaty commission to re-examine the 1868 Treaty. The government, however, balked on honoring the terms of its implementation, and it was not until the 7th of May that the protest actually ended. Later, the government treacherously reneged on its promise for a treaty commission, and over 400 federal indictments were handed down against the Wounded Knee activists.

Despite these later developments, a moral victory was won by the Oglalas at Wounded Knee. Above all, they succeeded in bringing to the court of national and international opinion the vitally important question of Native American self-government. Self-government was seen by the protesters as the key to the other issues. The documentary account, *Voices From Wounded Knee* (1974:2), makes this point clear: ". . . For 71 days no federal law enforcement personnel or Bureau of Indian Affairs officials had any authority in Wounded Knee. For 71 days, through countless battles and negotiating sessions, and despite the government's blockade of food, fuel, and medical supplies, *a self-governing community was built*" [my emphasis, S. T.].

The significance of Wounded Knee, 1973, therefore, lay in the fact that an independent Oglala Sioux Nation was declared. On March 11th, 14 of the 18 chiefs, "traditional and still-respected leaders of their people, as well as eight of 20 members of the Bureau of Indian Affairs corporate tribal council . . . met with the American Indian Movement leaders and declared their independence from U.S. government control and domination" (AIM 1973:9).

The original Oglala government had ceased to be recognized by the United States after the 1890 Massacre. For almost one hundred years the situation had been as the journalist, John Pittman (March 9, 1973, *Daily World*) describes it:

> The Constitution of the United States (Article I, Section 8, paragraph 3) dele-
> gates to Congress the power of regulating commerce with foreign nations . . .
> "and with the Indian tribes," thereby recognizing the Indians as autonomous
> nationalities. But throughout the history of the United States, the Congress, as
> well as the Executive and Judiciary, has treated Indians not as autonomous
> nationalities but—in the words of jurist Hugh Brackenridge—as "the animals
> vulgarly called Indians."

An alien political system, the government-controlled tribal council system, was imposed on the reservation in 1935 under the terms of the Indian Reorganization Act. Thus at Wounded Knee, for the first time since 1890, representatives of the United States were forced to negotiate with the "traditional and still-respected leaders" and their grassroots supporters, who had proclaimed their independence as an Indian nationality. It represented also the first time in over one hundred years that the United States had dealt with any Indian people whatsoever which had proclaimed its sovereignty.

The Reservation Political Economy
Wounded Knee points up the

> conspiracy between government and private interests that has dispossessed the Indian peoples of 97 percent of their land (1.9 billion acres), reduced them to chronic hunger and abysmal destitution, and today is continuing the theft of the remaining 3 percent (55 million acres) and attempting to drive them into monopoly capital's reserve army of unemployed and underemployed labor (Pittman 1973:66)

The loss of the Oglala Sioux land base and the destruction of a viable economy reflects the situation found generally on reservations.

The 11,000-member Oglala Sioux Tribe on the Pine Ridge Reservation occupies 2,500 square miles. The reservation is the second largest of the 267 federally-recognized land areas still remaining in the possession of Native Americans. The reservation originally encompassed approximately four million acres, but, today, less than one-half remains in possession of the Oglalas; 1 million acres are now owned by whites, and 1.5 million are leased to white ranchers. As recently as World War II, the government took 200,000 acres for a gunnery range. In 1975 this area, one-eighth of the reservation, after finally being returned, was signed over by the Wilson regime to the U.S. Park Service for long-term use.

Beginning in 1904, under the terms of the Indian Allotment Act, the reservation was divided into 8,275 individual allotments. Only 146,633 acreas were allowed to remain in tribal ownership, most of it wasteland. "By 1930, 655,000 acres had been fee-patented and sold by individuals. In that same year, 904,000 acres had passed into heirship status, and most of that acreage was leased out to non-Indians" (*Wassaja* 1974:14). The fragmentation of the allotted lands through heirship has meant that up to as many as 100 people now own one parcel of land. The BIA arranges for the Indian heirs to lease their parcels to whites, often without permission and at low prices. Those at Pine Ridge realize on the average $300 per year. "The land is leased primarily to white ranchers who make the real money. The landowners live on welfare. They are the have-nots, traditionalist in values, suspicious of government" (*San Francisco Sunday Examiner & Chronicle*, March 18, 1973).

Today, reservations like Pine Ridge are being exploited increasingly by big business, by large food processing chains, by mining and electric power conglomerates. The economic stranglehold over reservations by business interests is often also the deciding factor in Indian political life.

Deloria (1974b:69), in speaking of Pine Ridge, relates that "more than one election was decided by large and anonymous contributions by groups of ranchers. And more than one tribal administration was suspected of being obligated to the white ranchers, who sometimes controlled nearly 80 percent of the reservation lands through the leasing-unit device."

In 1928 the Brookings Institution issued its landmark Meriam Report. It found, among other things, that in the 25 years since the Allotment Act the Indians' economic status on the reservation had become one of extreme poverty. Little has changed since then, despite the 1934 New Deal reform, the Indian Reorganization Act.

Census figures for South Dakota testify to the general economic oppression of Native Americans in that state. The 1970 Census reported 32,365 Indians in South Dakota, 4.9 percent of the state's total population. Per capital income is about $1,100, which is 44 percent of white income. Among Indians and "others" (mostly Asians), 50.5 percent live officially in poverty, as compared to 16.3 percent in the white population. The economist, Victor Perlo, (*Daily World,* March 6, 1973) found:

> Unemployment of Indian males reached 25.3 percent, as compared with 2.8 percent for white Anglos. However, the Census only counted 53.4 percent of the adult Indian males as in the labor force, as compared with 75.8 percent of the white Anglo males.

> Obviously, many of the Indian males not included in the labor force are really unemployed. Excluding those who are in school or in institutions, or over 65, or disabled, one arrives at an unemployment percentage for Indian males (in the labor force but unemployed) of 39.8 percent.

Unemployment for Indian women is 12.5 percent, as compared with 4 percent for white Anglo women, but there is no statistical method for estimating the uncounted unemployed, Perlo informs us. State welfare statistics show that "while only 7.1 percent of those under 18 in South Dakota are Indian, Native people receive nearly half the state's aid to dependent children" (*Voices From Wounded Knee* 1974:12).

In summary, we see that unemployment and poverty among South Dakota's Native Americans vastly exceed that of whites, in a state where much of the land base, at least technically speaking, is owned by the Indians.

The figures given above include those who live in urban areas and who are more likely to be employed, although underpaid and discriminated against. Even so, the Indian unemployment rate for Rapid City, South Dakota, is 22.3 percent compared with 5.4 percent for whites. Burnette and Koster (1974:271) call South Dakota "the Mississippi of the North" and Rapid City "the capital of anti-Indian racism." The Indians are racially segregated four miles outside of town in the "Sioux Addition."

When we turn to Pine Ridge Reservation itself, we find that "nearly 70 percent of the Oglala Sioux are unemployed or underemployed, and per capita income is an incredibly low $800 a year" (*San Francisco Sunday Examiner & Chronicle,* March 18, 1973). One-half of those who work are employed in the tribal government–BIA bureaucracy. There is almost no industry on the reservation, except for the tourists who visit the Wounded Knee massacre site, and they leave little money. "Most businesses, like the 'trading post' general store-gas stations in the outlying reservation districts, and the Sioux Nation supermarket in Pine Ridge village, are owned by whites and charge prices significantly higher than stores off the reservation" (*Voices From Wounded Knee* 1974:121).

The Bureau of Indian Affairs has done little to encourage economic development. "The government spends some $10 million annually for various programs—such as one to help get drop-outs back in school—the system is designed primarily for subsistence. Thus, there is $880,000 a year for welfare, but only $17,000 for planning and industrial development" (*San Francisco Sunday Examiner & Chronicle,* March 18, 1973).

These conditions led Edgar Cahn (1969:2) to point out that "$8,040 a year is spent per family to help the Oglala Sioux Indians out of poverty. Yet, median income . . . is $1,910 per family. At last count there was nearly one bureaucrat for each and every family on the reservation."

Clearly, government bureaucrats are among the primary beneficiaries of "Indian money." In addition, however, on most reservatons there is a class of assimilated Indians with petty entrepreneural aspirations or quisling tendencies, who cooperate with the government bureaucrats in their neo-colonial management of Indian lands and resources. At Pine Ridge these persons are commonly designated "mixed bloods."

> The mixed-bloods tend to live in and around [the town of] Pine Ridge, where the BIA and tribal government offer as many as 600 job positions. Patronage is the order of the day and the tribal president dispenses the jobs—to his friends and family. "Jobs are so scarce," said one politician "that a janitorial job becomes a political appointment" (*San Francisco Sunday Examiner & Chronicle,* March 18, 1973).

It is this strata which dominates the tribal council system on most reservations. Thus, the much discussed problem of "Indian factionalism"—

full-blood vs. mixed-blood, conservative vs. progressive, pagan vs. Christian—is, at heart, a result of colonialism and oppression.

"Self-government" at Pine Ridge

The tribal council system of government was conferred on the Indian peoples in 1934 by a progressive Democratic administration and a liberal Indian commissioner, John Collier. Its great positive feature was the ending of allotment policy, thus temporarily halting the loss of lands. Liberals hold the opinion that the IRA's self-government provision has been of equal benefit, but Native Americans leading the current protest movement hold a different opinion. Wounded Knee, 1973, has exposed to public view the kind of "self-government" that has in fact been imposed, not conferred, on Native American nationalities at the expense of traditional forms of government, which in most cases were more democratic. Although Collier, known as a reformer and frequently attacked for his "socialistic" views, was a proponent of cultural pluralism, he nonetheless saw Indian affairs as colonial administration (Philip 1977: 118). His objective was to get the government to follow indirect rather than direct rule.

At Pine Ridge, as on all the federally-recognized reservations, Indian "self-government" is patterned along neocolonialist lines. The Secretary of the Interior may veto any measure passed by the 20-member Oglala tribal council, and the BIA superintendent really runs the reservation. As a result, at Pine Ridge "many of the eligible voters boycott the elections of the tribal council, held every two years, considering it alien to their traditional method of choosing leaders" (Pittman 1973:68). Many Oglalas consider the council corrupt as well. At best, the council is an advisory body to the superintendent and his line staff, and a relatively powerless one at that.

This kind of "self-government" has been a thorn in the side of the Sioux Nation for over 40 years. It has enabled white economic interests, in collusion with federal authorities, to manipulate the reservation economy while, at the same time, giving the illusion of Indian democracy. As a matter of record, the "Sioux full-bloods" opposed the IRA from the beginning, on the basis "that any governments organized under the Act could be dominated by mixed-bloods who had already sold their lands and simply hung around the agencies looking for a handout" (Deloria 1974b:198).

D'Arcy McNickle (1973:x) has described the aboriginal Sioux political system before it was suppressed and then replaced by the IRA form of government.

> Like other Plains tribes, the Sioux had no centralized government, but each of the major divisions of Sioux-speaking people was made up of local bands or camps organized around one or more leaders. Decisions were arrived at within the local group without outside interference. An elected council, such as the 1935 constitution established, displaced the camp structure and made no provisions for traditional leadership. . . The effect was to place control of tribal affairs in the hands of members who were in part assimilated into the white political system, were often of mixed-blood, and were not at home in the Sioux language.

Robert Thomas studied Pine Ridge government in 1964. His findings were presented in a paper entitled "Powerless Politics" and subsequently quoted in Ernest Schusky's monograph, *The Right to Be Indian* (1969). Thomas found that nearly all the former institutions on the local level have disappeared except the traditional religious groups, "which have carried over from aboriginal times" (Schusky 1969:471). That is, virtually the only major Oglala institution which has survived the Euro-American conquest and the reservation system "are the old native religious groups," the very groups *not* represented in Pine Ridge government under the IRA constitution.

In this respect we should note the leadership taken by the religious chiefs during the negotiations at Wounded Knee in 1973. The chiefs continually emphasized the disgust of the Oglala people with the BIA's puppet tribal council and their desire to return to a government of Indian origin. On March 19, 1974, 1400 Oglalas petitioned BIA Superintendent Stanley Lyman for a referendum to this effect. The petition appeared to be legally binding under the government's own IRA regulations, but, as an investigation by South Dakota's Senator Abourezk later brought out, "the BIA field officials falsified voter eligibility figures" in order to ignore it (Burnette and Koster 1974:242).

Thomas (Schusky 1969:471) found that the "country Sioux" tend to look at the tribal council "the same way that many urban working-class people look at the police force and city government. They see it as a foreign coercive feature in their daily lives."

> The country Sioux certainly do not see the tribal council as representing them nor as making decisions for them. . . The criterion for selection of tribal councilmen by those few Sioux who do vote in an election is not that the tribal councilman can represent them or their opinion, but because they feel that a

particular person knows how to handle Whites. . . A tribal councilman thus may be tremendously competent or incompetent, socially responsible or irresponsible. Invariably they are very marginal to the community and sometimes even personally disliked.

Given this situation, it is hardly surprising that the Oglala strategy has been to reassert the doctrine of Indian sovereignty as specified in the 1868 Ft. Laramie Treaty. Indian self-government is seen as the means by which the dispossession can be halted and a beginning made toward restoring economic viability to the reservation, the means also by which racism and impoverishment can be dealt with more effectively, and the disintegration of Oglala life—the social and cultural genocide—reversed.

In June, 1974, the first Indian International Treaty Conference was held on the Standing Rock Sioux Reservation. It was attended by 3,600 people from 97 Native American nationalities. This number represents a record turn-out for Indian country, considering the militant and grass-roots nature of the meeting, which is without historical precedent. Significantly, a newspaper headline of the event read, "Indian movement united around sovereignty issue."

Ever since the smashing of Indian military resistance toward the end of the last century, the erosion of treaty rights has quickened. The public has some appreciation for this historical fact, but few fail to realize that it has been federal legislation enacted by Congress under the guise of "for the Indians' own good" that has seriously weakened the doctrine of Indian sovereignty.

The IRA

The 1934 Indian Reorganization Act in many ways strengthened the government's control over Indian peoples. Cohen, for example, explains the serious limitations of its self-government provisions.

Felix Cohen, now deceased, was the foremost authority on Indian law (see his *Handbook of Federal Indian Law*, 1971a). From 1933 to 1948 he was assistant solicitor in the Department of the Interior. His observations, therefore, on the New Deal period in Indian administration are extremely relevant.

On the origin of the concept of self-government, Cohen reminds us that self-government is not a new or radical idea, but, rather, one of the oldest ingredients of American democracy. Indians practiced self-government before the European immigrants came. "It took the white colonists north of the Rio Grande about 170 years to rid themselves of the traditional

European pattern of the divine right of kings or, what we call today, the long arm of bureaucracy, and to substitute the less efficient but more satisfying Indian pattern of self-government'' (Cohen 1971b:18).

This fact leads Cohen to the following contradiction: the discrepancy between the U.S. government's continual recognition of the Indians' right to self-government, its lip service to this ideal, on the one hand, and on the other, its continual taking away of this historic right.

Cohen attempts to answer this question by recalling some of his experiences when he worked inside the Department of Interior to implement the IRA, and in particular, the chartering of the Indian tribal councils. He found that ''while every official was in favor of self-government generally, by the same token he was opposed to self-government in the particular field over which he had any jurisdiction'' (Cohen 1971b:23). In short, Cohen pin-pointed the perennial problem of trying to institute needed reforms in government only to have them blocked by bureaucratic intransigence.

There was also deliberate sabotage of the reforms at the Indian Agency level of the BIA. Cohen states that the superintendents almost immediately violated many of the rights granted under the federal charters to the newly formed tribal councils. He tells of instances ''. . . where decisions and ordinances that were not supposed to be subject to review by superintendents or by the Commissioner of Indian Affairs have been rescinded or vetoed by those officials. Tribes without independent legal guidance frequently acquiesce in such infringements upon their constitutional and corporate powers'' (Cohen 1971b:24). This is an important point, because, in fact, the BIA continues to violate tribal constitutions in its dealings with Indian nationalities. A recent example is the 1966 Hopi Tribal Council ''lease'' of Black Mesa, held jointly with the Navajo Nation, to Peabody Coal to strip mine.

According to the Hopi constitution, the council has the responsibility to ''prevent the sale, disposition, lease or encumbrance of tribal lands or other tribal property.'' Hopi lands can be leased only if there is a constitutional amendment voted on by all the members of the Hopi Tribe. Because the Hopi are sharply divided politically (the traditional villages are not represented by the tribal council, having refused IRA, etc.—see Clemmer 1976), the government knew it could not possibly obtain such a constitutional amendment. It therefore used another section of the constitution to interpret matters favorable to the exploitation of the reservation by big business. This section authorizes the council to ''exercise such futher powers as may in the future be delegated to it by the members of the tribe *or the Secretary of the Interior* [my emphasis, S. T.]. In 1961 the Secretary of the Interior, in response to a "Hopi tribal council resolution," used this section to delegate the power to the "council" to lease Black Mesa.

The interference of the BIA in tribal elections has been going on for a long time, IRA regulations not withstanding. Cohen, for example, documents BIA interference with the Blackfeet and Choctaw, and San Ildefonso Pueblo in the early 1950s (1973:531–533). He writes: "In a democracy any interference with the right to vote is, of course, subversive of all other rights. . . Quite the contrary, however, is the recent record in the Indian country. During the period 1950–1952 interference with the right to vote increased, chiefly along two lines: the use of federal funds to influence local elections, and direct interference with local election arrangements."

There have been other negative consequences of the IRA as well. Cohen, for example, deplores the fact that various bills which were introduced into Congress to achieve the objectives of IRA, specifically to turn over the Indian Bureau's functions to the Indians, "generally end up by giving new powers and new millions of dollars not to the Indian tribal councils, but to the Indian Bureau" (1971b:26). Furthermore, how the BIA went about its business of implementing IRA is illustrated in the "model constitution" which it drew up and pressed upon the Indian peoples. And "it was the BIA, of course, that approved or disapproved the constitutions drawn up by the tribes and nations" (Council on Interracial Books 1971:266).

Thus, many of the intended liberal reforms of the Act, the legislation which authorized the tribal council system of government, were subsequently subverted by the BIA.

What Cohen failed to see in 1949 was that the Indian New Deal Reforms, embodied in the IRA, were nonetheless based on the premise that the solution to the Indian question is assimilation. Passage of the IRA, therefore, continued the line taken by Congress earlier when it passed the 1924 Snyder Act conferring citizenship. The Snyder Act was passed without a murmur of dissent in Congress largely because it continued the long-standing Indian policy of *forced assimilation into bourgeois society*.

An important motive behind IRA was similar in intent: IRA was to correct some of the bureaucratic abuses which had held back the supposed inevitable assimilation towards "full citizenship." The Act was to move the Indian from wardship to citizenship. But what kind of citizenship? Citizenship for Indians and their integration into U.S. class-stratified, color-conscious society, with its historical frontier mentality toward Native Americans, is hardly equal to that enjoyed by members of Congress. American "citizenship," i.e., political assimilation, has deprived U.S. Indians of governing themselves under their own forms of political organization protected by their own sovereignty.

What is the end product of bourgeois assimilation, embodied in a multitude of legislation and policies ranging from the 1887 Allotment Act to the BIA's relocation and employment assistance program of the 1950s? For the many Indians now living in cities, supposedly integrated or assimilated, we find that their change in residence and political status from reservation to urban has been ". . . from one area of poverty to another. In the conditions of growing automation and cybernation, of racist discrimination by both employers and trade unions, the untrained, unskilled Indian newcomers land on the bottom of the job ladder, receiving the lowest wages for the dirtiest, most onerous work, and living in the worst conditions of urban blight and official neglect" (Pittman 1973:71–72). In the city Indian people face a multiple bureaucratic system: the BIA, welfare, employment office, health department, police system, city government, a county structure, local school system, etc., in all of which they have no effective voice.

It is true that Congress vested in the "Indian tribes" the power in 1934 to organize at the local level and to write a constitution. But the constitution was modeled after the U.S. form of parliamentary democracy. Real decision-making was limited by the veto power of the Secretary of the Interior and the bureaucratic intransigence of the BIA. Congress viewed this kind of limited authority as good public policy in the 1930s, a shift from colonial to neocolonial policy, at a time when sweeping changes were occurring in the country. It was anybody's guess whether the capitalist system would survive the Great Depression. Millions were without work, hundreds of thousands demonstrated in the streets, and there was even talk of revolution. Within this context there were those in Congress who were anxious to tinker the system together again, and concessions were made to ordinary working folk, to the poor and the minorities. In the case of the Indians, the liberal concession was one of "self-government," but self-government under the IRA did not mean that Congress was "recognizing inherent rights or unextinguished sovereignty" (Iowa Law Review 1966:664).

The Indian Resistance

If history teaches anything it is that the oppressed should have no illusions about those in power who represent interests vastly different from their own. Yet when former President Nixon announced a new Indian policy of "self-determination," many "friends of the Indian" believed that at long last the federal government would undertake a much overdue reform. Then came the awakening:

> Not only did the Nixon Administration fail to press Congress for adoption of enabling legislation to implement the promises, but other Nixon measures—revenue-sharing with the states, increasing military expenditures, policies fostering racial animosity among the white majority against the non-white minorities—in effect nullified the gesture of a new policy for the Indians and exposed its demagogic intent (Pittman 1973:79).

Not only the political demagogy of the Nixon Administration on the Indian question, but also the true condition of Native Americans under capitalism was exposed at Wounded Knee in 1973. And this exposure was the result of a new unity that had been forged between traditional Indians and the "new Indian movement" militants, between those on the reservations and those now living in urban areas. Evidence for this unity is the fact that on the opening day of the trial of AIM leaders on conspiracy charges arising out of the occupation, 65 traditional leaders of the Oglala Sioux people appeared in court. Many were in a white man's court for the first time, some never before off the reservation. Most were women, one 91 years old, and some were survivors of the 1890 Massacre. Their spokesperson was Frank Foolscrow, a traditional chief:

> We are all Oglala people. . . We come . . . to tell everybody who will listen that we stand with our brothers Russell Means and Dennis Banks [AIM leaders]. Together we stand with our traditions, our land, our medicine and our treaty rights.

> We represent not only ourselves but the Oglala band, the Sioux Nation and concerned Indian people everywhere. We called our brothers and AIM to help us because we were being oppressed and terrorized. They answered our call. We now call upon all people to honor our people and to honor our treaty rights.

> If Dennis Banks and Russell Means go to jail for supporting the dignity of the Sioux Nation and the promises made to us, you must be ready to send us all to jail. If we cannot live with our brothers in freedom according to our ways and traditions, we are ready to join them in a white man's prison (January 23, 1974, *People's World*).

Thus, the meaning of the Indian struggle at Wounded Knee in 1973 is found in the democratic principle of self-government on which the United States was purportedly founded. Felix Cohen's warning (1971b:28–29) in 1949 is even more true today than it was then:

> The issue is not only an issue of Indian rights; it is the much larger one of whether American liberty can be preserved . . . when those of us who never were Indians and never expected to be Indians fight for the cause of Indian self-government, we are fighting for something that is not limited by the accidents of race and creed and birth: we are fighting for what Las Casas and Victoria and Pope Paul III called the integrity or salvation of our own souls. We are fighting for what Jefferson called the basic rights of man. . . .

Civilization or death to all American Savages!

A Fourth of July toast
drunk by officers in
Sullivan's expedition
against the Iroquois
in 1779

4

THE INDIAN FRONTIER
IN HISTORY

U.S. History is a history of capitalist expansion and it cannot be understood apart from Indian affairs. Two works, published in the early 1970s, bring this point home and tell what really happened on the Indian frontier. These are Vogel's *This Country Was Ours* (1972) and Jacobs' *Dispossessing the American Indian* (1972). In reviewing the two books for the *New York Times,* Michael Rogin (1972:4), a political scientist, observed that "Indian policy has not been an isolated series of crimes, but rather an integrated part of America's expansionist development." This aspect of U.S. historical development is the major theme of this and the following chapter.

Virtually all initial contracts between Native Americans and Europeans in North America were peaceful. The indigenous peoples provided the colonists with food and knowledge of how to survive in what to Europeans was an alien environment. It was only later, after white encroachment on Indian fields and villages, in a word, a grab for land, that hostilities developed. This fact shows that peoples of differing cultures can live peacefully together if exploitative economic relations can be eliminated. It was primarily the commercial interests of the European colonists that made Indian-white conflict inevitable.

The European lust for land and the commercial greed for empire was foreign to the egalitarian societies of native North America. As Wehunsonacock said to John Smith, "Why will you take by force what you may have quietly by love? Why will you destroy us who supply you with food? What can you get by war?" (LaFrance n.d.:1). This is not to say that there was no inter-tribal strife before European entry, but this has been made overmuch of by apologists for the conquest. The nature of inter-tribal "warfare" was far different from that practiced by the rival European powers and the genocidal slaughter later waged against the indigenous peoples.

To the Native American land was one thing, to the European it was another. To the Native American land was (and continues to be for many) a way of life; to the European it was a source of profit.

At the base of ideological differences over land were two diametrically opposed economic systems. The European's notion of land as private property was a reflection of the prevailing system of economic relations found in Europe at the time of American colonization. The Native North American, on the other hand, had a system of economic relations based upon the natural mode of production, in which the land was held in common. It was characterized by production for use, not profit, and it was confined to the local kin or co-residence group. Lewis Henry Morgan, the early North American ethnologist, showed that "the law of hospitality," communism in living, and the common ownership of lands marked Indian societies. He said that "hunger and destitution could not exist at one end of an Indian village or in one section of an encampment while plenty prevailed elsewhere in the same village or encampment" (1965:45). When there was a surplus, it was redistributed among the people according to traditional usage and ceremonial practice. Trade or barter was not for the accumulation of wealth; money served no purpose in Native American society. *Land never became a commodity,* to be bought and sold.

> When the white man arrived, there was not one acre from the Atlantic to the Pacific that belonged to a private person, that could be alienated from the community or assigned to anyone outside the tribe. The very idea that ancestral lands from which they drew their sustenance could by taken from the people, become an article of commerce, and be bought and sold was inconceivable, fantastic and abhorrent to the Indian. Even when Indians were given money or goods for title to their lands, they could not believe that this transaction involved the right to deprive them of their use forever (Novack 1970:10).

The notion of private property was not always a feature of European societies either. Engels, in his classic study, *The Origin of the Family, Private Property and the State* (1942), convincingly demonstrates this fact. Rather, the idea of private property took shape among Europeans as technology increased, new forms of wealth were discovered, and class formation developed. The ancient clans among the Athenians, for example, held property in common, and it was not until the later years of the Athenian state that grain, wine and oil began to be produced and traded for profit. With increasing production of these surpluses there developed a system of commodity production for wealth. Only then did land become private property. A similar evolution took place among the Celts and Germans.

Even in Christ's time, people owned just their flocks of animals and not the land itself. The Welsh, as late as the 11th century, still tilled their fields in common as village-owned lands. Clans and communal land rights did not begin to decay in Scotland until 1745, after England had established her conquest over the "wild tribes" of that land.

The European conquest of North America, and, later, U.S. westward expansion across Indian lands, had its origin in that brutal process Marx (1954:784) termed the "so-called primitive accumulation of capital": the seizure of another people's land base in the interest of the colonial powers' ruling elites and for the purpose of generating capital, by transforming that land base into large-scale private property.

A similar process had occurred at the expense of the English peasantry with the Enclosure Acts. These laws ended peasant rights in common lands—pastures, woodlots, and so on—with the result that many were forced into tenancy, or else off the land entirely and into the developing manufacturing centers to become an urban proletariat. Much the same process took place among the Celtic-speaking tribes of Ireland and the Scottish Highlands and Islands. (MacLeod [1928:152–171] documents this last in an interesting chapter on "Celt and Indian.")

In the introductory statement to this chapter it was said that the growth and development of the United States was due to capitalist expansion. Initially, this expansion was part of the world-wide system of colonialism. Vast territories in Africa, Asia, Australia and the Americas were seized by the mercantile capitalist powers of Europe for the purposes of constructing military outposts and trading centers, seizing slaves, looting for gold and silver, and acquiring land for settlement. "By political, military, economic and ideological fetters, the European powers established their absolute power in the colonies" (Woddis 1967:14). Later, after the American (U.S.) Revolution, colonial expansion moved from east to west across the North American continent as the new government added to its territory piece by piece. In both instances, however, colonial expansion was at the direct expense of the aboriginal peoples. It was they who were dispossessed of their land and either annihilated or else reduced to the status of conquered peoples under colonial rule.

The conquest and subsequent colonization of the Americas brought tremendous wealth to the colonizing powers. This was the primary motive for the conquest.

> The discovery of gold and silver in America, the extirpation, enslavement and entombment in mines of the aboriginal populations, the beginning of the conquest and looting of the East Indies, the turning of Africa into a warren for the commercial hunting of black-skins, signalised the rose dawn of the era of capitalist production (Marx 1954:823).

After the initial looting, killing and slave-taking, the economy of the colonized became the familiar one-crop kind, the fur trade in northern North America, tobacco and cotton in the southern United States, sugar and bananas in Jamaica, and so forth. At its zenith in 1910, 1,200 million people, or 70 percent of the world's total population, lived under the colonial system in one form or another (Woddis 1967:28). By 1900, a little over 90 percent of Africa, 99 percent of Polynesia, and almost 57 percent of Asia were under the colonial system.

The colonial powers made triple profits based on cheap land, cheap labor, and cheap resources. They invested in mines and plantations and made fanstastically high profits by using slave, peonage, or poorly paid wage labor. Monopoly trading firms bought up cheaply raw materials (e.g., furs in North America), often produced by or obtained from the indigenous populations. Foreign manufacturers (e.g., English merchants) made substantial profits by selling their goods in the colonies where their control of the territories created closed markets and where the goods of other colonial powers could not easily penetrate.

The looting of the New World and African slave labor financed the bourgeois revolution and the development of trade, or mercantile capitalism, in Europe. As Sir Walter Raleigh expressed it: "Who rules the trade of the world rules the wealth of the world and consequently the world itself." It paid the tab for the birth of the English factory system and the industrial revolution. The importance of the looting of the Americas is shown by the fact that, by 1800, Latin American mines were pouring $40 million a year into Europe in gold and silver, or ten times the wealth possessed by the rest of the world put together. Humbolt, for example, states that during the first three centuries of Spanish rule, at least $6 billion in gold and silver were obtained from the colonies in the Americas (Foster 1951:56).

The original or primary accumulation of capital in the United States was at the expense of both the Afro-American and Native American peoples. The enslavement of millions of Africans provided a vast source of labor for superexploitation, while the genocidal dispossession of the Indians provided the soil on which Afro-Americans were forced to toil. Thus the fate of these oppressed peoples is linked in history, although in different ways, to the accumulation of the great wealth of U.S. capitalism.

At the beginning of the American conquest, the countries of Spain, Portugal, France, Sweden and Russia all sought to uphold feudalism. But Holland, and later, England, soon became more capitalist-oriented than feudal, and thus England and then the United States emerged as major industrial nations. Through the "American" Revolution, the United States became the first country won and controlled by the capitalist class alone, although it was not until after the Civil War that its power was consolidated. This was directly at the expense of the Native American land base, as shall now be documented.

The Colonizing Joint Stock Company

The colonizing of North America was considerably different from that which occurred in Latin America under the Spanish and the Portuguese. The Spanish Crown itself took the initiative in colonizing the Americas, but the English and Dutch delegated most of their colonizing operations to private business organizations. The reason for this was that feudalism was on the wane in northern Europe by the time of the conquest of North America. The sovereigns were growing poorer while the merchant class was getting richer. Out of this context arose the forerunner of the modern business enterprise, the colonizing joint-stock company. MacLeod (1928: 129–130), upon whom we rely for the discussion which follows, asserts:

> The sovereigns of England, Holland, France, and, later, Russia, were to delegate the initiation and development of overseas empire chiefly to business organizations of this new type. The result was of profound importance in making the story of the frontier different in North America from that of Latin America—so important in results, in fact, that it is necessary that we know something of the nature and development of the business corporation on the frontier in order later to consider its peculiar effects on the course of frontier history and on the fate of the North American Indian.

The origin and development of this form of organization is traced from ancient Babylon to Rome and medieval Italy, and from there to northern Europe. Today's U.S. "Company" (Co.), England's "limited company" (Ltd.), and the "corporation" (Inc.) is virtually nothing more than a joint-stock company which has been made into a legal entity, a fictitious "person," as it were. MacLeod continues:

> In these joint-stock companies there were in the sixteenth century as today, a common or jointly held fund of assets (the "joint stock") owned by the company. In this the members ("Freemen" or "associates") of the company evidence their proportionate shares of beneficial interest (or ownership) by shares of stock they hold. . . . These stock certificates are transferable at the will of the owner and with the certificate goes not only the interest in the assets of the company, but membership in the company.

In the colonization of North America the private trading companies of North Europe became *colonizing companies;* that is, they secured charters from their respective governments which gave them privileges formerly reserved for feudal lords. No colony was initiated by the Crown itself.

> The Crown stepped in to assume direct control of one colony after another only after the foundations and much of the superstructure had been built. *Every colony was established and put on its feet, and its frontier policies, including its Indian policy, determined once and for all, by private agents to whom the Crown had delegated virtually all the powers of Government* [my emphasis, S. T.] And the first and most significant historically, in the development of Indian affairs, of these several agencies were the colonizing business corporations or joint-stock companies (MacLeod 1928:142–43).

The Dutch East India Company of 1602 climaxed the transition from the development of the simple trading company into a colonizing one. Not only did it have a monopoly on trade with the Far East, but it also was allowed the right to maintain an army and navy, wage war, secure peace, make treaties with foreign nations, conquer and rule new territories, and mint its own money. England, France, Sweden, and later, Imperial Russia soon followed the Dutch example.

In 1606 the region south of the Delaware and west to the Pacific Ocean was given by James I of England to the Virginia Company. The Company was made up of the merchants of London. The region north of the Delaware, or New England, went to the merchants of Plymouth, and hence, the name, the Plymouth Company. The Virginia Company was the first British agency to open trade relations with Native Americans. It was modelled after the East India Company.

More than one hundred of its shareholders were also shareholders in the English East Indian Company, and the same prominent businessmen were active in both. Thomas Smyth, a prominent businessman of the period, for example, had been a member of the company which took over Raleigh's American rights. After 1606 he was at the same time governor (i.e., in modern parlance, president) of the Russia or Muscovy Company, governor of the East Indian Company, treasurer of the London Company, governor of the Bermuda Company . . . and a director of the Levant or Turkey Company. Interlocking directorates so early! (MacLeod 1928:135).

In 1602 the Pilgrims organized into an unchartered joint-stock company in association with some English businessmen. Their agreement stipulated that "at the end of seven years each colonist should come into possession of a house and garden; and during the seven years each colonist was to devote four days' labour each week for the company, and two for himself" (MacLeod 1928:135). The Pilgrims rested on the Sabbath but the mathematics are clear: Four-sevenths of the week was devoted to the business corporation and a lesser amount to the religious Pilgrims and the Almighty!

Massachusetts was governed under a joint-stock company chartered until 1684, after which the charter was revoked and Massachusetts made a Crown colony. As a Crown colony it became a private corporation chartered by the government for the purpose of commerce, fishing, and real estate. Citizenship could be obtained only by becoming a member in the company, and many residents were therefore disfranchised.

> . . . Instead of Massachusetts and the New England towns being a survival of ancient free Anglo-Saxon institutions on the American frontier, they were merely "founded as a result of a simple business arrangement to meet the exigencies of the colonists amid the new environment" without any uniform plan (MacLeod 1928:137).

Colonizing joint-stock companies like those mentioned above, as well as the Dutch West India Company, the Swedish South Company, the New France Company, the Sholikoff Company, and many others were the colonial entities, even more than European governments *per se,* which shaped early Indian policy in North America.

Feudalism did not completely die out during this period. In fact, it was revived for a time in North America. Feudal manors were established in Canada under the regime of the trading companies (seignories), along the Hudson River by the Dutch (patroons) while the West Indian Company was in power, and in English North America (the proprietory grant—

thirteen colonies under companies). These were a curious compound of feudalism and commercialism. For example:

> In 1664, the Duke of York, brother of the reigning King, was made proprietor of what is now New York, New Jersey, and Pennsylvania, but proceeded immediately to sell New Jersey. In the same year Carolina was granted not to one feudal lord but to six, jointly. They promptly constituted themselves a joint-stock company (MacLeod 1928:141).

The rights to New Jersey passed from York to two nobles. One of these sold out to two Quakers, one of whom was a merchant. The merchant Quaker, becoming financially insolvent, turned his rights over to three trustees who were to settle with his creditors. These trustees were William Penn and two other Quakers. They held all the rights of a feudal lord—"the right to make all laws, to admit or expel inhabitants, to imprison, execute, make war, tax, etc., and held title in fee from the Crown to all land" (MacLeod 1928:142).

An Economic Interpretation of the Revolution

In reality, business relations were at the core of European settlement in North America. In terms of wealth and privilege this resulted in colonial society resembling a many-layered cake. The British merchant capitalists were the "upper crust," the Crown being feudal decoration. Companies organized by merchants and nobles, armed with land grants and monopoly privileges, brought masses of the British poor to North America, many as indentured servants.

> These became the small farmers and artisans who formed the base of the New England economy, the objects of exploitation by merchant capitalists and wealthy planters.
>
> In the South, a different economy developed: largely cotton, tobacco and sugar cane plantations operated with Black slave labor. . . .
>
> In the seaport cities and towns, particularly with the development of the fishing and shipbuilding industries, a class of wage laborers emerged and the beginning of factory production appeared (Lumer 1975:25).

And then there were the Indians. The American Indian frontier provided the raw material—land and resources—for colonial wealth.

Conflict between England and the colonies was inevitable. As Thomas Paine, spokesman for the common man and author of *Common Sense* observed, it was rather absurd for a continent to be governed by an island.

More important was the fact that British mercantilism exploited the colonies by restricting their trade and development, by compelling them to buy British manufactured goods, and by imposing onerous taxes. The greatest hardships were borne by the lower strata, but the "American" merchants and planters, too, wanted freedom from the British monarchy to make their own profits in the colonies. The common enemy brought the several classes together and the American Revolution (1775–1783) was the result.

The American Revolution was the first successful colonial revolution in modern history. The Revolution affirmed in action as well as theory the right to national self-determination, because the United States was the first independent state in the New World to emerge after European colonization, which had destroyed the earlier aboriginal governments.

The basic pre-requisite for self-determination, for nationhood, is economic self-sufficiency. By 1750 the English colonies had developed a self-sufficient and interdependent economy. They produced all kinds of manufactured goods and carried on trade with Europe, Africa, and the West Indies. In fact, they produced more pig and bar iron than England and Wales combined (Williams 1961:103). Given these circumstances, it is hardly surprising that the colonists began to think of themselves as "Americans" rather than as British.

Not the least of the Revolution's interesting features, after the war had begun, was the adoption by the revolutionists of the Indian method of fighting—from concealment and relying on individual initiative—which they had learned on the frontier. As Aptheker (1975:41) observes, ". . . the nobility of England referred to the Americans as 'tricky' and 'unmanly' for they did not fight in the regulation way that the drafted and mercenary armies employed by European royalty had developed."

A key factor behind the Revolution was the conflict between the land speculators among the wealthier colonists and the British fur trade interests. "Resentment over British efforts to regulate the fur trade, and to restrict settlement and land speculation west of the Appalachians, contributed significantly . . . to the American Revolution" (Rogin 1971:1). Land speculation in Indian territory by the merchant class became a principal source of wealth.

Land use in the two instances was diametrically opposed as were the concomitant Indian policies. Land speculation for plantations and farms meant Indian removal, but in the second instance the Indian fur trapper or hunter was a commodity producer who became an integral part of the colonial system. The French, except for the Quebec inhabitants, had a more harmonious relationship with the Indians in great part because of their difference from the English colonists in economic aims and activities.

> This contrast was emphasized by Duquesne when he tried to win the Iroquois from their friendship with Britain. The Frenchman told them: "Are you ignorant of the difference between the king of England and the king of France? Go see the forts our king has established and you will see that you can still hunt under their very walls. They have been placed for your advantage in places you frequent. The English, on the contrary, are no sooner in possession of a place than the game is driven away. The forest falls before them as they advance and the soil is laid bare, so that you can scarce find the wherewithal to erect shelter for the night" (Novack 1970:14).

The British Crown also had its fur trade interests, which soon came in conflict with the interests of the land-hungry colonists. After the defeat of the French in the French–Indian war, and as a result of Pontiac's Rebellion (an uprising by eighteen Algonkian peoples in confederation against colonial intrusion), England issued the crown Proclamation of 1763. (See map, page 89.) This proclamation forbade White settlements on Indian land west of the Alleghenies. "It created a virtual Indian reservation of the land claimed by England between the southern boundary of Quebec, the watershed of the Appalachian Mountains, the northern boundary of the two Floridas, and the Mississippi" (Ewers 1939:14). The British motive was not to protect either the Indians or the colonists so much as it was to avert another uprising like Pontiac's, because the British sought to keep the agricultural-minded colonists out of an area still peopled by Indian nations which "produced" furs for a lucrative European market. More importantly, the British used the Indian situation as a pretext to confine the colonists to a small area of land which would keep them weak economically and dependent on British manufactured goods. The Crown was out to protect British pocketbooks.

Land speculators had been investing in Indian territory west of the Appalachians, gambling on a westward expansion of settlers much like investors who "play" the stock market today. The Crown Proclamation was a blow to these speculators' dealings in that it stated that settlers must leave Indian land at once. This was one of the principal causes of the colonial revolt against Britain, i.e., a dispute over conflicting economic interests in Indian lands.

Patrick Henry, George Washington, and Benjamin Franklin all had extensive investments in Indian lands (Council on Interracial Books 1971:42–48). They were incensed by the Crown Proclamation, for they considered it an infringement on their right to make profits.

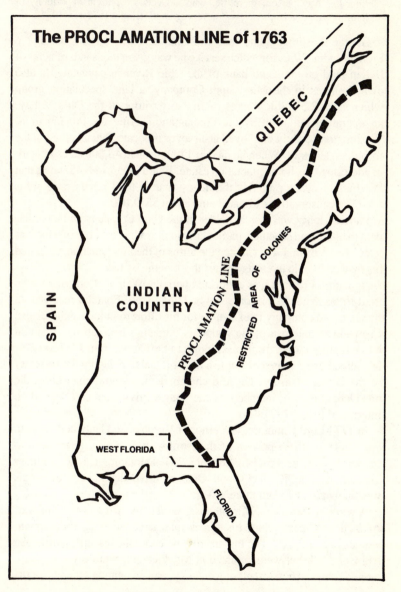

The PROCLAMATION LINE of 1763

"Between ourselves," Washington explained in a letter . . . , British restrictions hould be viewed "as a temporary expedient to quiet the minds of the Indians." Urging his friend to enter land claims for him, Washington continued, "Any person, therefore, who neglects the present opportunity of hunting out good lands . . . will never regain it" (Rogin 1972:1).

George Washington had been an Indian fighter in Virginia during the French–Indian War, for which service he was given thousands of acres of Indian land on the south bank of the Ohio River in payment. He also owned shares in the Mississippi Company, a land speculation group which held 2.5 million acres of Indian territory in the Ohio Valley, an operation outlawed by the Proclamation. After the Proclamation, Washington secretly employed a surveyor to locate valuable land in the forbidden territory. When he died in 1799, he held 40,000 acres of land, in addition to his home plantation estate. Beard (1956:144–45) notes that Washington "was probably the richest man in the United States in his time," a conservative estimate being about $530,000.

Patrick Henry was a shareholder in the Ohio Company and a participant in other land schemes, particularly in the Indian territory of what was later West Virginia. He violated the terms of the Proclamation and pitted his own economic interests against those of the British.

Benjamin Franklin was connected with the Walpole Company which tried to take over 2 million acres of Indian land. Franklin received 72 shares in the company in exchange for his effort to influence the British Crown in the interests of the Walpole Company's land scheme. Franklin was a representative from the colonies to the Crown from 1767 to 1775. He helped bribe scores of English high officials, including the secretary of the British treasury, the lord chamberlain, the lord chancellor, the president and other members of the King's Privy Council (Council on Interracial Books 1971:44).

In 1774 Lord Dunmore, Governor of Virginia, suddenly laid claim to the whole southern portion of the Northwest Territory, guaranteed to Indians under the Proclamation of 1763. Dunmore sent two military expeditions into Kentucky and Ohio to drive the Indians out. This was known as Lord Dunmore's War.

A white settler, Daniel Greathouse, started his own action in this war. At Yellow Creek, Ohio, his forces massacred unarmed Indian men, women and children. The Indians rose up under the leadership of Logan and Cornstalk but were defeated at Mt. Pleasant, Ohio, by Lord Dunmore's forces. They lost all of Kentucky, valued hunting grounds for the many tribes in that area, and the area south of the Ohio River. Washington, the "Father of our country," was probably one of the plantation farmers who provided Dunmore with the political and economic support for his action against the Indians and indirectly against the British Crown.

Dunmore's War helped pave the way for the Revolutionary War, the final separation from England and an end to the constraint against westward expansion placed upon the colonists, but the year 1776 proved too late to reverse the two hundred years of injustice to Native Americans. "With all the firey rhetoric from the great 'American' Revolutionaires, nowhere was there a voice questioning the right of the colonists to be in lands not legitimately theirs. Nowhere even was there a voice demanding a new deal for the American Indians" (Council of Interracial Books 1971:48–49). The army of "ragged continentals" which defeated the world's greatest colonial power was comprised of common people—small farmers, artisans and workingmen, including many Blacks—but the leaders were merchants, lawyers and wealthy landowners. (Not a single signer of the Declaration of Independence was a workingman, a Black, a woman or an Indian.) From the point of view of the merchants and planters, the Revolution was for freedom, property and empire. It was the wealthier strata among the colonists who determined the main course of events after the war, and it is hardly surprising, therefore, that westward expansion was the name of the game.

The Revolutionary War, like most important events in history, contained profound contradictions. On the positive side, its great liberating contribution was the overthrow of British rule and the establishment of an independent republican form of government, based on the idea of a popular sovereignty, where the people are citizens rather than subjects.

> It eliminated the last vestiges of feudalism, as primogeniture, quitrent, entail. It contributed to the termination of imprisonment for debt and indentured servitude. It provided for the separation of church and state; it helped promote some aspects of the rights of women; it led to the manumission of several thousand slaves and to the elimination of chattel slavery in the North and to some forward movement in the outlawing of the international slave trade (Aptheker 1975:41).

The Declaration of Independence postulated the equality of all men, truly a revolutionary idea for the eighteenth century. Of course, its authors meant men and not women; they meant men of property and not indentured men, enslaved men, Black men, nor the 300,000 Indians then living in the colonies. ". . . But for its time even the limited meaning of its usage was a significant advance over conditions then prevailing in the world'' (Aptheker 1975:40).

On the negative side, the original demand for the complete abolition of slavery, put forward in an early draft of the Declaration of Independence, was dropped as a concession to conservative southern planters. It remained for the Civil War, almost one hundred years later, to complete what the first revolution had begun. (And even then, the newly-freed slaves were soon forced into a system of peonage through sharecropping, the poll tax, and Ku Klux Klan terror.)

Of all the diverse segments in colonial society, the Indians stood the least to gain from the Revolutionary War. This was because of the land question. In Helen Hunt Jackson's *Century of Dishonor* (1965:16) we learn that North Carolina and Virginia, to a great extent, paid their officers and soldiers in the war by grants of Indian lands in the forbidden territory. "It was one of the great resources which sustained the war, not only by those states but by other states." It is not surprising, therefore, to learn that there was hardly a single Indian nationality of consequence which joined the colonists in the Revolution of 1776. "Had the founding fathers really believed what they professed—liberty and equality for all— they would have used their powers to bring to a halt the land grabbing of the western settlers and an end to the gross profiteering schemes of the Ohio Company and other land speculators. . ." (Council on Interracial Books 1971:49).

As a revolutionary general, George Washington ordered 40 Seneca villages burned to the ground and all food supplies destroyed in retaliation for the Indians' support of the British. (Search and destroy missions so early!) And as the first President of the United States, he presided over a "just war" to open the Northwest Territory to settlement. By then, however, he had come to favor a more "orderly" process of expansion, the mercantilist method of treaty-making.

The peace settlement of 1783 at the end of the Revolutionary War completely abolished the Appalachian demarcation line, the old frontier. Later, "the huge territory between the Appalachian Mountains and the Mississippi River, stolen from the Indians in the period between the Revolutionary War and the Civil War, was cut up into a dozen states" (Foster 1951:217). *This more than doubled the territory of the original thirteen colonies.* Almost two-thirds of the new territory was unoccupied by white people. The economic processes set into motion by the Revolutionary War continued into the next one hundred years of U.S. capitalist expansion across the continent.

Westward Expansion and the Dispossession

The 19th century saw the appearance of the doctrine of "Manifest Destiny," which claimed that God had destined the United States to take the leading role in the world. By 1819 Secretary of State John Quincy Adams was describing it as unnatural for the European sovereigns, located hundreds of miles beyond the sea, to maintain colonial possessions on the borders of the United States; and, in 1820, Congressman Henry Clay was calling openly for expanding the "American system" to South America.

The fuel which fed the fire of expansionist sentiment was the rapid growth of industrial development. It began during the war and continued at a pace into the post-war era.

> By 1800 the factory system was fairly well advanced. In the ensuing decades capitalist development flourished and capitalist wealth grew, but at the cost of the most brutal exploitation of the growing mass of wage workers and the rise of bitter, bloody class struggles. *They did so also at the expense of the Indian peoples, who were robbed of their lands and possessions and subjected to genocidal slaughter.* [My emphasis, S. T.] It was during these years that the foundations were laid for the mounting fortunes of the merchants, bankers, land speculators and other capitalist elements (Lumer 1975:25).

The Louisiana Territory in 1803 was the next piece of land taken. Napoleon, stung by the successful revolt of Black slaves in Haiti, and preoccupied by France's increasing involvement in the European war, was forced to sell the rich territory of Louisiana to the "Americans." He sold in reality what he could not defend from the land-hungry settlers; he sold what he claimed for France but did not own, for the greater part of the territory comprised the heartland of many Indian peoples.

The purchase of Louisiana was to prove an event of momentous importance to the Indians on the frontier east of the Mississippi River, for expansion across the continent onto Indian lands became the central fact of life in the United States of America during the next 100 years. As Rogin (1972:2) notes:

> Jefferson continued Washington's policy of expansion with the victim's consent. He purchased Louisiana, and hoped to remove the eastern Indians to the northern portion of the Territory. Opposing forced removal, he urged an increase in trading posts in Indian country. The tribes would incur debts, "lop off" their excess lands to pay them, and eventually move west.

In 1811 and 1812, the eastern Indians, under the leadership of the Algonquin chief Tecumseh, revolted and almost halted expansionist plans. Starting in 1805 Tecumseh and his brother, the Prophet, carried on agitation among the tribes and nations along the frontier for a defensive alliance (Foster 1951:215). Tecumseh proposed nothing less than the formation of an all-Indian republic, the union of every Indian group from Canada to Florida on a democratic basis. The plan might have succeeded were it not for the fact that the tribes were provoked into premature military action by Harrison's forces at Tippecanoe, Indiana, in 1811, before the alliance had been consolidated.

> The frontier Indians generally sided with the British [in the War of 1812], and their tribes, remnants of the Algonquins and Iroquois, together with the Creeks and Seminoles—all the way from Canada to Georgia—went into action. They suffered ultimate defeat, along with the British, and, as usual, their interests were abandoned by the British at the peace table (Foster 1951:216).

The War of 1812 was fought by the United States for markets as well as control of the Indian lands. The Yankees fought Great Britain to a draw and a negotiated peace, but the Indians, as noted above, were sold out in the negotiations. And so ended the last real hope of the eastern Indians in halting their dispossession.

During this war against Britain (lasting until 1814), a number of U.S. leaders nurtured plans for expanding the "borders of freedom" to include Canada to the north and East Florida to the south (Maruskin 1975:16). A bill was prepared for Congress which, if it had not been tabled in the Senate, would have given the president the authority to occupy and hold these lands by direct force.

A few years later, in 1819, the thirst for empire was slaked a bit when Spain gave up Florida to the expansion-minded "Americans." Spain's authority was weak and she was unable to control the situation within her borders. "Florida had become a haven for runaway slaves from Georgia. Seminole raiding parties crossed into the United States and then fled to safety back into Florida" (Ewers 1939:74). Secretary of War Calhoun sent Andrew Jackson in 1817 and 1818 on punitive expeditions. Finally, King Ferdinand of Spain agreed to sell Florida to the United States. Foster (1951:207) describes this as "another shotgun purchase; a method which the aggressive young United States, headed by merchants, industrialists, and planters, practiced with rival, land-holding powers as well as with the Indians." The native peoples of Florida, the Seminoles, along with their runaway Black "slaves" and allies, courageously fought the "Americans" during Jackson's raids. Seminole is the Creek word for "runaway," and the Florida alliance is a signal example of Black/Indian cooperation on the old frontier (Katz 1977).

A new stage in American expansionism was announced in 1823 by President James Monroe. The "Monroe Doctrine" denounced European interference in the Western hemispheric revolutions that were beginning to take place and seemed to defend the right of the colonies to national liberation. In advancing this doctrine the United States seemed to be protecting the other American states. However, by blocking the road to European intervention, the United States paved the way for its own intervention (Marushkin 1975:20–21).

Oregon Territory, that large expanse of country now comprising the states of Oregon, Washington, Idaho, and parts of Montana and Wyoming, was the next major acquisition. The Lewis and Clark expedition of 1806 had established the U.S. claim. Originally claimed by Spain, Russia, England, and the United States, it came to be held jointly by the last two powers.

The frontier at the time of Lewis and Clark's explorations was considerably east of the Mississippi, as far south as St. Louis. Even in 1840 it was still indisputable Indian country; its white population, almost all of whom were engaged in the fur trade, was quite small. But the economic panic of 1837 brought hard times, and conditions were ripe for migration to Oregon Territory. "Missionaries, travelers had written in glowing terms of the fertile valleys of Oregon . . . Each year the number of migrants increased. . ." (Ewers 1939:111–12). Not only were the missionaries, pioneer farmers, planters interested in the Territory, but businessmen looked to such colonization as a source of profitable trade, investment, and speculative ventures (Williams 1961:271).

The cry of the "Americans," "Fifty-four-Forty or Fight," bluffed out England. The Yankees did not get 54°40', nor did they have to fight, but the Oregon compromise did win them considerable new territory from England, establishing the line of the present United States–Canadian western border from the Pacific to the Great Lakes. An area five-sixths the size of the original thirteen colonies fell to U.S. expansion and was finally sealed by the Oregon Treaty with Great Britain in 1846.

Behind the westward-moving frontier, mop-up operations of clearing Native Americans from their remaining lands had begun. This occurred first of all in the Old Northwest (the area north of the Ohio River), and then in the Old Southwest (Georgia, Tennessee, Alabama, Mississippi).

At the beginning of 1826, the mid-point of that great period of expansion, Native Americans still claimed some 61 million acres east of the Mississippi River (Ewers 1939:80). West of the Mississippi they claimed a piece of Louisiana, almost three million in Missouri, and virtually all of the remainder of the territory in the Louisiana Purchase. Other parts not included in the Purchase were still unceded Indian country. (See map, page 97).

> Thus, though the United States was a thriving country with a population in the vicinity of 11 millions in 1826, over half its territory was still "unsettled" Indian country.

> Up until January 1, 1826, the average amount paid by the Government to the Indians for the land they ceded was 3-147/1000 cents per acre. Sold to white settlers at some two dollars per acre, Indian lands thus proved a valuable source of revenue to the United States [emphasis is ours] (Ewers 1939:80).

By 1825 the policy of relocating all the Indians of the United States along a strip to the west of the organized states and territories was announced. This included those tribes from Missouri, Iowa, Arkansas, and Louisiana as well as the eastern tribes. The dispossession of the Indians from the trans-Mississippi states became linked with removing the remaining eastern tribes. The same solution was used for both groups. The tribes west of the Mississippi River, however, were termed "wild" while those in the east (especially in the Old Southwest) were called "civilized." This was during Andrew Jackson's presidential administration.

Rogin (1972:2), a specialist on the Jacksonian period in US history, says that the destruction of the Indians was always Jackson's major aim.

> Like Washington, he early speculated in Indian lands, and made his first national reputation in Indian wars. He burned and destroyed Indian villages, and used the pretext of Indian violence to justify expansion into Canada, Florida and Texas. As general, treaty-maker and President, Jackson was the single man most reponsible for the dispossession of the eastern Indians. Like Washington, President Jackson condemned land speculators and assumed a stance of paternal benevolence toward the tribes. This paternalism, combined with coerced and fraudulent treaties, brought about the forced population transfer of 100,000 Indians to Jefferson's northern Louisiana Territory . . . one-quarter to one-third of the natives died in the process.

The dispossession of the Five Civilized Tribes (Cherokee, Creek, etc.) and other Indians of their lands in the South is directly attributed to the slave system. The slaveowners held political sway in eleven Southern states. All this territory as far west as Texas was bound into a system of

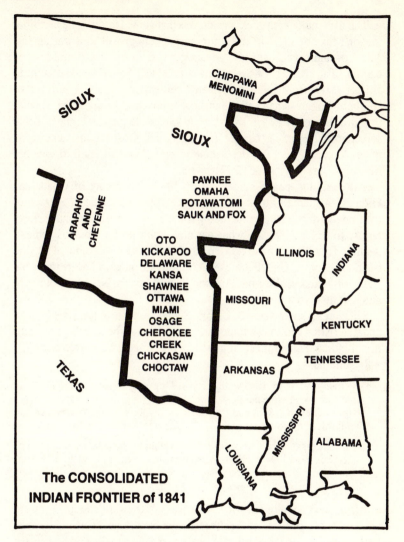

The CONSOLIDATED
INDIAN FRONTIER of 1841

big plantations. In many instances the slavemasters were absentee land-
lords who had gotten their land holdings away from the federal government through sharp practices. Their dream was to ultimately extend the
slave system into Mexico, and then to Central and South America. "In
Texas by 1858, 68 million acres had been stolen from the government,
mostly by absentee slaveowners" (Foster 1951:166).

The fifth major area of expansion was that gained through the partitioning of Mexico. In 1846 the southern planters provoked a war against Mexico, and a year later the advancing U.S. forces took the Mexican capital. The pretext for the war was President Santa Ana's attempt to collect taxes from the "American" settlers in Texas. A number of southern Congressmen called, unsuccessfully, for the complete annexation of Mexico. *The New York Herald* waxed eloquent over the possible seizure of the Mexican lands: "It is a gorgeous prospect, this annexation of all Mexico . . . Like the Sabine virgins, she will learn to love her ravishers" (Williams 1961:277).

The resulting peace agreement of 1848, the Treaty of Guadalupe Hidalgo, a shameful treaty, stripped the young Republic of Mexico of over one-half its territory, including some of the richest crop and pasturelands, to say nothing of what we now know to be fabulous mineral wealth. Together with the Gadsden Purchase of 1853, this brought into the boundaries of the United States 944,825 square miles, what are today the states of Texas, California, Arizona, New Mexico, Nevada, Colorado, and part of Wyoming.

This area, southwestern United States, retains today its Mexican characteristics and, more importantly, constitutes the heartland of traditional Indian nationalities, among them the largest, the Navajo Nation.

In summary:

> The four years 1845–1848 were epoch making ones for national expansion. In rapid succession came the annexation of Texas (1845) the establishment of our claim to Oregon (1846) and the Mexican Cession (1848). An area equal to two-thirds of the total area of the country prior to 1845 was added.

> By these cessions the number of Indians within the boundaries of the United States was more than doubled. When these new areas were acquired Indians made up the bulk of the population and held the greater part of the land (Ewers 1939:104).

Alaska was acquired in 1867. This was no "Seward's folly" (Seward was Secretary of State at the time), as the history books would have us believe, but a calculated scheme by northern industrialists, who coveted Canada as well, to acquire a base for empire. The aim of these interests was to outflank the British in North America and to give the United States a strategic bridge to Asian markets across the top of the Pacific basin (Williams 1961:319).

The purchase of Alaska from Czarist Russia brought thousands of Eskimo, Aleut and Indian peoples into the "American" orbit. It brought also a half-million square miles of territory—an area equal to nineteen of our eastern-most states—and enormous natural and mineral wealth. The full economic value of Alaska (e.g., the $200 billion oil discovery) is only now being appreciated, one hundred years after its original purchase.

By mid-century the shape of the Indian frontier had changed: the Indians were entirely surrounded. (See map, below.) The frontier had increased in length since 1808 from less than 1,000 miles to more than 3,000 miles. A series of forts ringed Indian country in the Plains. With the rapid settlement of the West in the 1840s, the whole region west of the Rockies was organized into States and Territories.

In response to expansionist pressure an intensive period of treaty making began in 1853. "Between 1853 and 1856 no less than 52 treaties were negotiated, more than in any other similar period in the nation's history" (Ewers 1939:105). The Indians lost about 174 million acres through this means.

The old frontier was a constantly shifting line with "Indian territory"

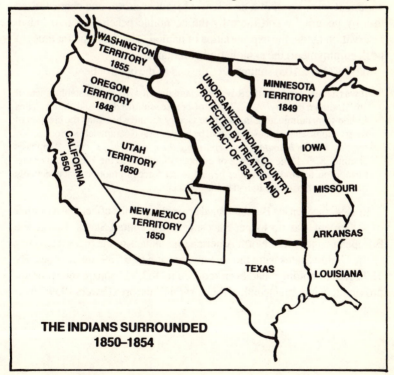

THE INDIANS SURROUNDED
1850–1854

always on the other side. The pushing aside of the rival European powers and the dispossession of Native Americas of their lands increased the territory of the United States to ten times its original area. During the expansion along the American Indian frontier, Euro-Americans met fierce resistance. With the close of the Civil War, however, the Indians' central role in retarding the rate of territorial expansion was coming to an end. The last military struggle was the Great Plains War, in reality 25 years of skirmishes and fighting between the still unconquered western Indians and the U.S. Army. The year 1866 was the first in which the full military power of the U.S. could be concentrated on the "Indian problem" in the West. This led in 1890 to what is undoubtedly one of the most notorious military actions in United States history, the massacre by white troops of unarmed Indians at Wounded Knee. This date has come to symbolize the end to Indian existence as independent tribes and nations. Thereafter, President Grant's "peace policy" drove the Native Peoples at the point of a gun onto reservations. Those who resisted faced extermination. It was then that a new kind of frontier arose, one characterized less by geography and more by the economic penetration into Indian reservation lands, the expropriation of natural resources, and (at times of peak employment) the exploitation of Indian labor.

Jacobs (1972:103) summarizes the end of the old frontier.

> It was a long step from the Royal Proclamation of 1763 to the establishment of an "Indian Territory" . . . Then, of course, followed the sad, bitter Plains Indian wars culminating in complete victory for the whites and the creation of reservations where tribesmen could be herded in and completely surrounded *by another kind of boundary line separating them from white society*. [Emphasis is mine, S. T.] The sequence of events dating back to the 1760's shows that turmoil on the Indian frontier helped to set forces in motion that eventually decided the fate of the Indian in the next century.

In 1890 the Census Bureau issued a statement to the effect that a frontier of settlement was no longer traceable in the United States. Before the European conquest of North America, the Indians of the present territory of the United States were the sole owners of 3,026,789 square miles. By 1890 Indian holdings had been reduced to 162,993 square miles, or approximately one-nineteenth of their original land area (Ewers 1939:176).

5

AGENTS OF
THE DISPOSSESSION

As to the role of the frontier settler in all this, one must ask, was he the cause of the dispossession or merely the fated instrument of economic forces already set in motion? The settler was the foot soldier in the "war" against Native Americans; he was not among the officer class, so to speak. He was not among the economic royalists who speculated in Indian lands; nor was he one of the "generals" who drew up the "battle plans" for expanding the frontier. But neither can we hold him blameless for the destruction and killing—in short, the genocide—that occurred in large part *by his hand* in the name of Manifest Destiny.

The frontier settler was more often than not an immigrant. A number were "criminals" from the poorer strata brought over from Europe. Others had fled European tyranny, including those who had been victims of the same or similar forces which later were to dispossess the Native American.

Ironically, when the English government smashed the Scotch Highland revolt in 1745 (thereby suppressing the tribal system and forbidding the use of native dress and the Gaelic language), "the disheartened tribesmen, sometimes headed by their chiefs and retaining the clan organization even in foreign parts for a time, then began a large-scale emigration to the Carolinas, Canada and other parts" (MacLeod 1928: 169). Lechmere stated in 1718 (Ewers 1939:17) that the immigrants "are generally . . . come over hither for no other reason but upon encouragement sent from hence upon notice given that they should have so many acres of land given them gratis to settle our frontiers as a barrier against the Indians."

Early in the eighteenth century the colonists realized the value of building a frontier barrier of white settlements between them and the Indians. "Accordingly they welcomed the dissatisfied and persecuted peoples of Europe who would be satisfied with land in the colonies beyond the settlements" (Ewers 1939:17). These frontiersmen or "borderers," as they liked to be called, developed a way-of-life and a philosophy quite distinct and often opposed to those who settled the coastal areas.

There were three general kinds of labor servitude in colonial North America: for the Indians, in Spanish America, there was peonage; for Blacks, chattel slavery; and for the whites, wage slavery. This last was not confined merely to whites. Many Blacks and also Indians became wage workers. Neither was chattel slavery confined just to Blacks, as evidenced by the item cited below from the *American Weekly Mercury* (Foster 1951:88). In 1729 a George Martin contracted with a ship master to transport himself, his wife and five children to the Colonies for 54 pounds.

> He paid down 16 pounds, but died on the passage. On the arrival of the vessel in port, the captain foreclosed on the contract, sold the widow for 22 pounds, the three oldest sons at 30 pounds each, and the two youngest, who were under five years of age, he sold for 10 pounds, realizing 122 pounds on a debt under 51 pounds.

Foster (1951:87) tells us that ". . . the lines of demarcation between the three basic forms of labor servitude were vague and indistinct, and they overlapped and merged." Petty thieves were shipped off regularly to the colonies as slaves. The worst example of white slavery, however, was found in the English colonies of North America. This was the practice of indentured servants. This form of white slavery was practiced by the Penns, those pious Quakers, in the colony of Pennsylvania. Their large estates were cultivated mainly by white indentured servants.

In the early days most of the indentured servants came from Ireland and Scotland with a number also from Germany. They were treated much like

Black and Indian slaves. They were bought and sold at auction, whipped and overworked at the pleasure of their masters. They were forced into slavery for seven years or more, usually to pay for their passage over. Often, members of the European lower classes were "hoodwinked" into going to America by unscrupulous labor recruiters. Thus, numbers of the European peasantry exchanged one kind of oppression for another. The price of passage charged was often exhorbitant and many sharp practices resulted. James Truslow Adams (Foster 1951:88–89) has reported on the high death rate for the eighteenth century immigrant sea traffic: "On one immigrant ship 350 passengers died out of 400, and these figures can almost be duplicated in other instances." Indentured servants constituted one-half of the 100,000 people who came to Virginia before 1700. As late as 1670 the number of whites indentured in Virginia was three times that of Blacks.

The early frontiersmen were oppressed, land-hungry immigrants. They saw the acquisition of a piece of land as the means to their economic, if not social salvation within the European class system, for the property concept was as ingrained in their thinking as it was foreign to the Indians'. There was land available along the eastern coastal areas, already "cleared" of Indians, but speculation on property values by the wealthy had driven the price beyond the reach of the poorer strata. These poorer elements were thereby forced by economic necessity, especially during periods of unemployment, to get land free by squatting on Indian lands along the ever-expanding frontier. *It is within this context, of pitting the frontiersman against the Native American peoples, that a most virulent racism arose.*

The government was duty-bound, according to the terms of most early treaties, to remove the squatters or else allow the Indians themselves to deal with them. However, more often than not the following pattern would prevail (MacLeod 1928:370):

> Trouble between Indian and the squatter would break out. The government would hasten to the rescue. Invariably it was unequal to the problem of controlling the frontier. Sometimes it drove the squatters off. More often it brought pressure upon the Indians to sell the land. In either case diasastrous irritations were set up between the frontiersmen and the native.

(Chart, page 104, portrays this cycle of Indian-white relations on the frontier.)

Many of the settlers on the frontier after the French–Indian War were demobilized soldiers. A similar situation occurred after the Civil War.

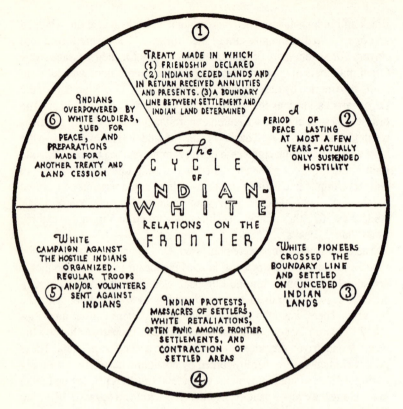

U.S. society has always accommodated its unemployed proletariat by directing them to the Indian frontier. The frontier has acted as a safety valve for the capitalist political economy which is noted for its boom-or-bust fluctuations and chronic unemployment. Some of these same processes are at work in Alaska, the last frontier, today.

The Indians in the Old Northwest Territory correctly assessed the economic position of the settlers on their frontier. In 1812 the United States proposed to the allied tribes northwest of the Ohio River that they sell to the government large areas of land where frontier squatters had entrenched themselves. The Indians, in turn, showed a not unsympathetic understanding of the settlers' situation, and an interesting alternative was suggested.

> Brothers: Money to us is of no value, and to most of us it is unknown. And as no consideration whatever can induce us to sell our lands on which we get

sustenance for our women and children, we hope we may be allowed to point out a mode by which your settlers may be easily removed and peace thereby obtained. We know that these settlers are poor, or they would never have ventured to live in a country which had been in continual trouble ever since they have crossed the Ohio. Divide therefore this large sum of money which you have offered to us, among these poor people. Give to each, also, a proportion of what you say you would give us annually over and above this large sum of money. . . . If you add also the great sums which you shall have to expend in raising and paying armies in order to drive us out of our country, you will certainly have more than sufficient for the purpose of repaying these settlers for all their labour and their improvements . . . (MacLeod 1928:372).

Needless to say, the Indians' plan was ignored.

It must be borne in mind that the invasion of frontiersmen into the Old Northwest, across the Ohio River, was occasioned as much by the profit-minded squeeze put on them by the big land speculators as by anything else. This was especially the case for the poorer settlers. Daniel Boone worked for one such land company, the Transylvania Company of North Carolina, as a land prospector, spending six years in the Kentucky country. He bought it for the company in 1775, it is said, from the Cherokees, although it is difficult to understand how they came to have title to the area. The prices later charged by that same company ranged from $2.50 to $40 the hundred acres, "a substantial piece of change in 1775, in backwoods country where a man received 33 cents for a day's work" (Brandon 1961:200).

Today, the frontiersmen have their counterparts in the white "rednecks," as they are called, countryfolk who inhabit the old Indian territories and who are the descendants of the original pioneers. For the most part, they exhibit racist attitudes towards Native Americans. Historically, members of this strata have been the petty entrepreneurs on the American Indian frontier, but they are not themselves the main bulwark of the system of dispossession which has victimized the Indians. They are, rather, the instruments of the governmental-monopoly complex which continues to this day to pit white against red. *Thus we must analyze the antagonistic relationship between the two in socio-economic rather than solely in racial terms.*

The Railroads, Primary Agent of the Dispossession
Native Americans originally controlled two billion acres of the United States at the time of the European conquest. By 1871 this had been

reduced to about 140 million acres. How did this reduction come about? It was by no means due solely to the land-hungry frontiersman. The drastic reduction of the Indian land base was effected by the U.S. government making enormous grants of land, timber, and mineral resources to corporate interests. This was the underlying force which set white against Indian on the ever expanding frontier.

Economic development in the United States increased greatly with the Civil War.

> The Civil War created a fresh demand for every kind of production including the worthless rifles, shoddy blankets, and inferior foods, that capitalists sold to the army with fatal results for thousands of soldiers. From 1860 to 1870 the value of manufactured goods advanced from $1,885,862,000 to $3,385,860,000, and the number of industrial workers increased from 1,311,000 to 2,733,000 (Foster 1951:266).

The Civil War has been called the second American Revolution, because, in losing the war, the slaveholders lost control of the government and the economy which they had dominated for a quarter of a century. Both economic systems, slave and free, had been contesting for the vast territories of the West. The outcome of the war unleashed northern capital for western expansion.

> In this process of expansion the existence of vast unsettled areas in the West had an important impact. The vast areas of unsettled land went not primarily to working people but with the connivance of the state, to capitalists for the building of railroads and exploitation of the natural wealth of these territories. In the process the Indian population was either decimated or confined to reservations on the poorest sections of the land.

> The unsettled areas in the West drained off numbers of workers seeking a better existence, leading to problems of labor shortage, to a constant flow of immigration, and to somewhat higher wage levels than those of European workers. All this gave a strong stimulus to mechanisation and the search for new labor-saving devices, and contributed greatly to the exceptional rate of technological advance of U.S. industry (Lumer 1975:25).

It was during the graft-ridden Grant administration, after the Civil War, that the ties between expanding business and the government became greatly strengthened. This led to a series of legislative acts which were detrimental to the western Indians. The most far-reaching of these, politically-speaking, was the congressional decision to end treaty-making with Indian tribes and nations. Jorgensen (1978:10–11) explains that "the massive power accumulated by the Republicans in Congress and in the eastern United States forced the Congressional Act of 1871 whereby American Indians could no longer make treaties with the government,'' and that ''this allowed for speedier domination of Indians and expropriation of Indian resources.''

Other legislation which alienated Indian lands and which forced Native American peoples into confinement on reservations include the Homestead Act (1862), the Timber Culture Act (1873), the Desert Land Act (1877), and the Timber and Stone Act (1878). It might appear that these acts were primarily for the benefit of the small petty entrepreneur, the homesteader, for example, but Jorgensen (1978:11) informs us otherwise:

> The major land legislation . . . aided the largest businesses rather than petty entrepreneurs. . . The Desert Land Act, for instance, was exploited greatly by the largest ranchers, who consolidated many 640 acre tracts into forage areas. The Timber and Stone Act allowed people to occupy 160 acre tracts of timber or stone land. The land available through mineral claims, the Homestead, Timber, Desert, and Timber and Stone Acts could be consolidated by owners in many places in the arid west, with its varied topography, but whether consolidated or not, the combined effects of these acts literally denied all off-reservation territory to Indians. The mountains, plains, prairies, plateaus, and deserts were claimed either by large businesses or by petty entrepreneurs.

The Homestead Act is the prime example of this land legislation which adversely affected the Indian lands, supposedly for the small settler but actually benefiting the wealthy. Its terms allowed for every person over 21 years of age the possibility of acquiring 160 acres of ''public land.'' If cultivated for five years, the land became the property of the settler. In practice, however, many of the alleged settlers turned out to be dummy applicants for the corporations.

A number of commercial agents were responsible for the dispossession of Indian western lands—cattle barons, mining interests, lumber concerns, land speculators, and railroads. These ''robber barons'' seized tens of millions of acres on the frontier. The land steal by the railroads was no doubt the most notorious of these.

In the name of opening the western frontier for commerce and settlement, Congress, during the 1850s and 1860s, began giving away Indian lands to the railroads. The give-away constituted 158 million acres of valuable farming, grazing, timber, and mineral lands, ''an area almost as large as New England, New York, and Pennsylvania combined, while the states turned over 167,000,000 acres, a domain nearly the size of Texas'' (Boyer and Morais 1970:22).

In 1869 the first transcontinental railroad, the Union Pacific, was completed. Other cross-country railroads soon followed. To finance the construction of the railroads, the government lavishly subsidized them with both money and lands. This amounted to about $335 million worth of land plus $707 million in subsidies—a billion dollar grab. The Northern Pacific alone got 47 million acres, an area equal to half the size of France. It was the biggest land steal in U.S. history, that is, until a few years ago when the U.S. Indian Claims Commission and the Alaska Native Claims Settlement Act arbitrarily extinguished hundreds of millions of acres still held by right of aboriginal title.

The Railroad Enabling Act of 1866 sliced some choice cuts off a number of reservations. There were sometimes 40 to 50 mile areas appropriated for railroad use on each side of a projected right-of-way. Indian communities were ejected from railroad property since, for the purposes of the Act, reservations were considered public lands (Brandon 1961:364).

Native Americans were the ones most directly affected by the railroad development, but they were not the only ones exploited. Some 10,000 Chinese laborers and 3,000 Irishmen were hired at low wages and under inhuman conditions to "throw track" on the first transcontinental railroad. There were as many casualties on this railroad line as there were combat deaths in the Civil War. And during the nationwide railway strike of 1877, "American troops fired on American workingmen as regiments under General Phil Sheridan were recalled from fighting the Sioux and thrown against the workers of Chicago (Boyer and Morais 1970:59).

A major feature of the railroad legislation during these years was the land grants provisions. These were given in a checkerboard pattern of alternate sections on either side of a proposed railroad line. The railroad would get one section and the government would retain the other alternate section. In theory the railroads were to sell their surplus land to "actual settlers" at prices no more than $2.50 per acre and, in some cases, at $1.25 per acre. The income realized would then enable them to continue construction. It is out of this context that a political alliance of "sod-busters" or settlers, land companies, and the railroads was formed, all vehemently anti-Indian. This is made clear by Clark (1947:333) in his study of the railroads in Indian Territory.

> The *bona fide* settler who wished land upon which to settle, the land speculator to whom an Indian reservation was always a Godsend, and the railroads with conditional land grants united in an effort to destroy the Indian nations and open their lands; the westerners and their representatives in Congress furnish-

ing the agitation, the railroads much of the money, the influence, and the propaganda to carry it on. Their interests were united for it required settlement to make railroads profitable and to break down the system of Indian land tenure so the grants would be validated. . . .

The negative impact of the land grant features is exemplified by what transpired in Indian Territory (later, Oklahoma) just after the Civil War. Several bills were passed which authorized federal aid to two railroad companies to build lines through the Territory, one, east-west, and the other, north-south. "These bills provided for conditional land grants . . . of alternate sections of 20 miles on each side of the railroads, as soon as Indian title . . . could be extinguished. It was unclear . . . whether it was up to the government or the rairoads to quiet the title" (Trout 1973:2). New treaties were therefore forced upon the Five Civilized Tribes—the Cherokee, Choctaw, Chickasaw, Creek and Seminole. The new treaty provisions permitted the construction of the Missouri, Kansas and Texas line, or "Katy," and the Atlantic Pacific.

> The stage was set for a powerful coalition of railroads pressing for validations of the grants, westerners (especially Kansans, Missourians, and Texans) pressing for the extinguishment of Indian title, and the establishment of a territory, and bondholders, including powerful European interests, pressing for the validation of the grants in order to protect the value of their bonds which were secured by the conditional grant lands which the railroads did not have title to (Trout 1973:7).

In addition, the railroads needed coal and railway ties for their lines. The cheapest means to fulfill these needs was to use local Indian mineral and timber resources. The Osage Coal and Mining Company, for example, supplied much of the coal for the "Katy" by expropriating Indian natural resources. This company had an interlocking directorate with that railroad line. It was commonplace for the railroads to contract with an individual Indian for timber and coal, disregarding the fact that these resources were tribal property, and therefore communally owned. Today, much the same practice continues on the part of the big conglomerates which are despoiling Indian resources, but Indian tribal councils are thus manipulated instead of Indian individuals.

The land grant provisions served to unite the Indian of the Territory against the railroads. A number of Indian leaders foresaw the outcome. They could agree with Senator Oliver P. Morton who told Congress in 1870:

> We all know how this will end. We know it will end by driving the Indians out again. . . . They went there [to Indian Territory] as a permanent home; and

now we begin the work of driving them out; first project a railroad there that must take a line of population along, must establish villages necessarily, granting land subject to the Indians' consenting to give it up, and binding ourselves to extinguish the Indian title; and whenever the Government sets about doing that it can always do it. It can always find Indian chiefs, and adventurers, and half-breeds, and Indian agents who will be able to bring about a treaty. It has never failed to do that when it has gone deliberately about the business. I therefore protest against this (Clark 1947:169).

There were also white officials like Vincent Colyer, Special Indian Commissioner, who warned in 1869 that the hidden purpose behind the construction of the railroads was to destroy Indian governments and to seize the reservation lands for speculative purposes. He spoke of two classes of interests which had combined to destroy the Indians (Clark 1947:263–64).

First, railroad companies, who, entertaining the hope that the government may despoil these people of their property—or, what is the same thing, take it for a nominal price—expect by the proposal to build a road through their country, to make vast profits out of lands or properties thus seized, on pretext of developing the country. It is well known that there is, at present, more speculation in the West in building roads than in running them. By claiming to develop the country, these corporations are clamorous for the speedy destruction of these Indian governments that stand in the way of their schemes. The other class, a very large one, comprises those who wish to occupy their lands. In the West an immense business has sprung up by which squatters make a living, not by cultivating the soil, but by dealing in inchoate titles. To this class of frontiersmen, an Indian reservation is a God-send. . . . It is then seized by some company at a nominal price—say a few cents to a dollar an acre, and the profits used to build a railroad—or, on the plea of justice to squatters, those who have intruded on it in violation of law and the rights of the Indian are permitted to keep it, sometimes as homesteads, for nothing, or for $1.25 per acre, they realizing by their illegal acts from $5 to $10 per acre, selling out to some industrious settler who comes after them, and again pouncing on some coveted reservation, and clamoring to the government for a fresh violation of public faith. . . .

Congress eventually turned against land grants for railroad companies. The populists, for one, saw them as an excessive corporation privilege which, indeed, they were. In 1886 Congress passed a law which forfeited all conditional land grants to railroads in Indian Territory, a total of almost 24 million acres. The Indians had won a limited victory. This victory was short-lived, however, for the following year the Dawes or Allotment Act was passed.

The Dawes Act destroyed Indian government in Oklahoma and accomplished what the railroads had tried for so long to do. It opened Indian Territory to white settlement, with its accompanying commercial speculation in Indian lands, just as Vincent Colyer had predicted.

> The first assault came in the western part of Indian Territory. . . . This district was opened to white settlement in 1884, and in 1890 it became the Territory of Oklahoma. A year earlier some Cherokee lands and two million acres of Creek lands were opened to white settlement. In 1891 the lands of the Sauk, Fox, and Potawatomi tribes were made available. Next, in 1892, the Cheyenne–Arapaho lands were occupied, and in 1892 the "Cherokee Outlet" succumbed to the Sooners. Other tracts were opened from year to year (Vogel 1972:189)

The remaining Indian lands were allotted and in 1906, the tribal governments declared dissolved. The two territories of Oklahoma and Indian Territory were than merged and admitted to the Union as the forty-sixth state. This was in 1907.

> Swarms of scheming white men, reminiscent of post-Civil War carpetbaggers, descended upon the Indian allottees with the aim of getting possession of their allotments by fraud and sharp dealing. Of thirty million acres allotted to these Indians, only five percent remains in Indian ownership today. Although well over a hundred thousand Indians live in the state, most of them are landless, and there are no Indian reservations remaining. Thus ended the homeland which was solemnly promised to them forever, with only its name (Oklahoma: "red people"—Choctaw) to remind us that it was once theirs (Vogel 1972:189).

Grabbing the Land

The Indian land base, constantly eroded over the years, now stands at 52 million acres. This acreage includes parts of 26 states and is the home for members of 315 different Indian nationalities. To non-Indian "Americans," this may seem like a lot of acreage, but between 1887 and 1966 Native Americans lost 60 percent of their lands. This was mainly through allotment.

Almost 90 million acres were taken "legally" under the terms of the 1887 General Allotment Act (also known as the Dawes Act), which split up reservation holdings into individual parcels. The rationale behind allotment was that individualization of collectively-owned lands would instill the concept of private property and prepare Native American people for "civilized, Christian life." The Indians would thus become integrated into Anglo–American society and the "Indian problem" would disappear. More than 100 reservations were allotted, principally on the plains, along the Pacific coast, and in the Great Lakes states. Of the approximately 150 million acres owned by the Indian before 1887, most of it guaranteed by treaties made less than 30 to 40 years before, an area more than twice the size of Oklahoma was lost. "The process lost steam after some of the big plains reservations, the principal targets, were carved up and sold, but it went along in a desultory way for many years" (Brandon 1961:366).

Allotted parcels consisted of 160 acres for family heads, 80 acres for other adults, and 40 acres for minors. Most of the remaining lands after allotment were declared "surplus" and opened by the government to white homesteading. Only 30 million acres were retained as tribally-owned land, most of which was located in the Southwest. It was the Southwestern Indians, about one-third of all those in the country at the time, who generally escaped allotment. Most of the land lost to whites was taken in the space of thirteen years (Spicer 1969:112).

Included in the Act was a twenty-five year trust period during which the allottee was forbidden to sell or mortgage the land. During this period the individual was supposed to learn the necessary technical and management skills to make a go of farming. Nothing was done, however, to aid him in acquiring these skills. When the twenty-five year period had expired, the allotment was usually either leased to non-Indians, lost through land sales (many of them fraudulent), or taken as a result of non-payment of land taxes.

Even when the Indian allottees desired to become independent farmers on their own parcels—and a number made the attempt—economic conditions present at the time discouraged it. As Lurie (1971b:35–36) notes:

> Apart from the bad design of allotment, the whole concept involved built-in obsolescence. Even if Indians had applied themselves to farming with utmost diligence, and the whites had been prevented from bilking them out of their land, the rosy future envisioned for Indians by proponents of allotment would not have come to pass. The diversified, largely subsistence family farm and the cash crop farm of a few hundred acres, provided for in allotments, had become increasingly impractical endeavors by the late 1880s, even for dedicated, experienced white farmers. This was particularly true of the Plains area, where so many reservations were located. Farmers with capital or access to credit, bought out or leased the land of those less fortunate to engage in large scale single crop or stock raising operations depending upon increasing mechaniza tion that cut down on the rural labor force.

> The same technological developments of the period also provided the expand-ing network of railroads to ship produce in quantity to the urban markets of a rapidly industrializing society. Even without mortgages or taxes to protect their land for a period from the bank and the county, if the majority of Indian

people had cut their federal ties as they were expected to do, they, like the majority of other Americans after the turn of the century, would have been pushed into the marginal economy of small independent farming or tenancy or the grinding labor of the city sweatshops and assembly lines.

One of the lone voices of dissent against the General Allotment Act was that of Senator Henry Teller of Colorado. He clearly saw the economic motive behind the policy. In 1881 he raised his objections and told Congress that allotment ''is in the interest of speculators; it is in the interest of men who are clutching up this land, but not in the interest of the Indians at all. . .'' (Spicer 1969:233).

Allotment was in direct violation of Indian treaty rights, and it struck at the heart of communal ownership. ''Indian property was communal property. The land was owned and used through the tribal entity. The very essence of Indian society was based on tribalism, and an individual's identity was important within the concept of a group'' (La France n.d.:4). Native American peoples were pre-class societies. There was social stratification based upon inherited rank and achieved status, but not socio-economic classes based upon the private ownership of property.

The allotment policy, instead of phasing out the need for the Bureau of Indian Affairs, one of the Act's intended purposes, actually increased its presence by requiring more personnel to keep up with the mounting volume of paperwork. Part of this consisted in keeping track of those who were allotted but placed in a restricted status, that is, those judged as ''incompetent'' by government bureaucrats and whose allotments were subsequently held in trust by the BIA. Spicer (1969:115) estimates that more than 100,000 people, owning about 17 million acres altogether, were put into this restricted status.

An integral part of allotment policy was an all-out attack by the Bureau of Indian Affairs, not only on communally held lands, but on all manifestations of Indian culture. Senator Henry Dawes of Massachusetts justified his bill in terms of ''civilizing the Indian.'' Christianity and the English language were forced upon Native American nationalities. In reality, however, economic greed was the underlying motive for allotment, for the result was extremely profitable for those who, by 1934, had managed to grab 90 million acres of former Indian reservation lands.

Negating another important traditional institution, that of tribal heirship customs, descent of the trust lands was to be defined by local state laws. This alien heirship system has resulted in the disastrous splintering of the alloted part of the remaining Indian land base. Additionally, further usurpation of the land took place through the right-of-way guarantees to railroads, for telegraph lines, and other "public uses" under allotment stipulations.

Neither did the Indian peoples have control over the monies, held in trust by the government, gained through the sale of their so-called surplus lands. These trust funds, under Section Five of the Act, were declared to be "at all times subject to appropriation by Congress for the education and civilization of such tribes . . . or the members thereof." This provision also enabled Christian mission churches to gain their own allotments, through the Secretary of the Interior, "for religious and educational work among the Indians."

Allotment policy was not halted until Franklin Roosevelt's New Deal administration when, in 1934, Indian peoples were given the status of federal corporations under the terms of the Indian Reorganization (Wheeler–Howard) Act. By 1934, Spicer (1969:115) estimates that about one-third of all Native Americans remained as before, under the federal trust system of tribal (or collectively-owned) land management, "although corresponding tribal [traditional] governmental systems had been eliminated." Another third "were in a new relationship of social dependency" on the government through their restricted status; and the remaining third had become independent landowners, "but their condition was not that of self-sufficient and prosperous farmers."

The fate of the Indian allottee is best summed up by Brandon (1961:366):

> . . . By one means or another, allottees frequently lost their ragtag and bobtail patches of ground to white ownership, or leased the land for messes of pottage to larger operators. Some were thus utterly dispossessed, and congregated in junkyard squatter communities here and there, or piled in by wagonloads to "visit" with any relations who still had the wherewithal for a square meal of tough beef and fried bread. Hundreds of families collapsed into permanent pauperdom.

John Collier, Roosevelt's Indian Commissioner, was an opponent of allotment policy. Some years prior to coming into the Roosevelt administration, in 1923, he had organized the Indian Defense Association and became its executive secretary (Hertzberg 1971:202). Collier sought a bill that would recognize most Indian societies as administrative and economic entities, stop allotment, consolidate the allotted lands, and place them back into tribal ownership. His bill, which became the Indian Reorganization Act, was drastically revised by Congress (Deloria 1974, chapter nine). The final bill did successfully stop further allotment, but it failed to consolidate the allotted holdings. This failure has perpetuated Indian land fractionalization through the heirship system, resulting in the ineffective utilization of the remaining land base, especially for those Native American groups which were heavily allotted. Furthermore, in that the actions of the newly created, governing tribal councils, established under the IRA legislation, were subject to the approval of the Secretary of the Interior, and their day-to-day operations were under the management of the Bureau of Indian Affairs, the political independence to redress the problems of allotment has been pretty much stultified.

The 1934 reform slowed down the great reservation land robbery which had been underway for 50 years, but, in another sense, it ushered in an era of Indian resource acquisition by indirect rather than direct means. It marked the end of the colonial epoch for Native American tribes and nations, and signalled the beginning of neocolonialism.

*But the Wasichus came, and they have
made little islands for us and other little
islands for the four-leggeds, and always
these islands are becoming smaller, for
around them surges the gnawing flood of the
Wasichu; and it is dirty with lies and greed.*

Black Elk

[*Wasichu*—Sioux for fat-taker or greedy
person.]

6

THE INDIAN FRONTIER
TODAY

Towards the end of the last century, the Indian frontier disappeared as a
line formally demarcating westward expansion. The former territories of
the indigenous nationalities had been drastically altered, the peoples
shifted about the country in many cases and, finally, forcibly confined
to reservations. Then, through the 1887 Allotment Act, even these
last refuges, the reservations, were further reduced in size. Thereafter,
the means by which Native American lands were "ripped off" became
more subtle, but the results were equally as devastating to the Native
American peoples.

The United States emerged from World War II as the foremost capitalist
power in the world. Other capitalist nations had either been defeated or
almost destroyed economically by the war. U.S. foreign policy makers
opened a new "Pax Americana" and the "cold war" was launched by
industrialists attempting to seize foreign markets vacated by a devastated
Europe. At home, Big Business moved into the government with greater
influence than ever before. This was due in large part to the war effort.
President Franklin Roosevelt had been forced to load his wartime ad-

ministration with representatives of Wall Street in order to get their support against Nazi Germany.

> Edward Stettinus, chairman of the board of United States Steel and vice president of General Motors, became Secretary of State while Bernard Baruch, Nelson Rockefeller, Dean Acheson, Marriner S. Eccles and Lewis W. Douglas, as well as scores of oil executives, dozens of vice presidents of steel and auto, and hundreds of other businessmen and their lawyers took over positions of control in the awarding of war contracts and the deciding of policies (Boyer and Morais 1970:332).

Thus there arose what President Eisenhower termed the "military-industrial complex." Eisenhower knew what he was talking about, because it was during his administration that public power and the great wealth in tidelands oil were given away to the corporations. A major part of the new "give-away" to capitalism was the government's post-war attack on Indian lands and resources, and the forging of a reactionary Indian policy dubbed "termination."

Termination, a New Kind of Dispossession

The less oppressive "liberal" Indian policies associated with John Collier, commissioner of Indian Affairs in the Roosevelt administration, were hampered first by the Depression and then by World War II. After the war there was a swing back toward the 1887 policy of direct, forced assimiliation, a stepped-up attempt to deprive Native Americans of their remaining reservation land base. As Oswalt (1973:584) observes, "the Federal Government began to divest itself of diverse obligations to Indians much more systematically than ever before." Jorgensen (1978:22) agrees, saying that "corporate collectivism gave way to termination of federal relations and a renewed push to get Indians to sever their reservation ties and move to the cities."

This renewed, forced assimilationist policy started as early as 1949 when Congress established an Indian Claims Commission to settle for all time the Indian land claims against the United States. Under the chairmanship of ex-President Hoover, the commission recommended the termination of the special federal administrative relationship. By 1953 this view had become dominant in Congress (Spicer 1969:140).

The Relocation Program was launched in 1950. Under Relocation, "surplus" reservation populations were "encouraged" to seek employment in the larger cities: Dallas, Chicago, Denver, Cleveland, Los Angeles, San Francisco and others.

House Concurrent Resolution 108, better known as the termination resolution, was passed in 1953. It stated that Indians should become subject to the same laws as other citizens of the United States as rapidly as possible. "It also declared that nine specifically designated groups of Indians . . . should be 'freed' at the earliest possible time from federal supervision and control and called on the Secretary of Interior to submit recommendations for bringing this about" (Spicer 1969:140).

In the same year Public Law 280 transferred civil and criminal jurisdiction over Indian reservations to several states and authorized other states to assume such jurisdication if they so desired. Another law repealed federal prohibition against selling alcohol to Native Americans.

In 1955 BIA health services were transferred out of the Interior Department and into Health, Education and Welfare, under the Public Health Service, Indian Division.

In 1956 programs for off-reservation education in BIA schools were "beefed up," as were some vocational training programs for adults. The focus in these programs was on the service industry (e.g., cooks and bakers), clerical skills (e.g., typists), and on the trades (e.g., carpenters, welders); significantly, it was not on management skills, investments, or the professions (Jorgensen 1978:26).

The policy of termination ended officially in 1961, but not in reality. An omnibus bill, later called the Indian Resources Development Act of 1967, was part of this trend. Fortunately, it was defeated in Congress, in great measure due to united Indian opposition. Intended by the administration as the ultimate solution to the "Indian problem," if passed, it would have vested all final authority over Native American land transactions in the hands of the Secretary of Interior. "The proposed legislation, like the General Allotment Act and the termination legislation before it, would have dissolved Indian tribes and sent potential wage earners to the city" (Jorgensen 1978:28).

The Alaska Native Claims Settlement Act was passed in 1971, in which Native Americans gave up their claims to most of Alaska by virtue of aboriginal title and accepted, instead, a money-land settlement. "With the termination of the Indian Claims Commission in 1973 and the partial implementation of the Alaska Native Claims Settlement Act the same year, the Federal Government will have discharged its last major responsibilities involving land" (Oswalt 1973:385). To put it another way, Native Americans have self-terminated their ownership to hundreds of millions of acres of land. Much of the land claimed, especially by Indian peoples in the lower forty-eight states, was no longer occupied by them due to white encroachment, but, in the eyes of the courts, was still theirs by virtue of aboriginal title.

House Concurrent Resolution 108 was clearly the most direct statement of the post-war termination policy. House Concurrent Resolution 108, in reality not a bill but having the force of law when carried out as policy by the agencies of government, called for the termination of all reservations and the elimination of federal recognition of Indian nationalities. In the name of making Native Americans "just the same as everybody else," two of the largest reservations were terminated from federal status, along with several smaller groups. The two large peoples, the Klamath of Oregon and the Menominee of Wisconsin, were deprived of their lands and vast timber reserves for a cash settlement.

As already mentioned, the Eisenhower administration of the 1950s was marked by its give-away of natural resources to corporate interests. The termination of timber-rich Indian reservations was another hallmark of these years. The post-war boom in wood products, especially for new housing, had made Indian timber extremely valuable. It would appear that behind the supposed termination objective of "integrating" Indians into "mainstream America," there was a hidden economic motive: to get at Indian timber reserves.

The influence of timber interests on U.S. Indian policy is illustrated by that now famous exchange between Paul Bernal, a Taos Pueblo Indian, and Senator Clinton P. Anderson of New Mexico, who was chairperson of the Interior Committee for two years until 1963. At issue was the Taos Pueblo claim to their sacred Blue Lake area in New Mexico. Bernal was speaking to Senator Anderson (Cahn 1969:66–67):

> My people will not sell our Blue Lake that is our church, for $10 million, and accept three thousand acres, when we know that 50,000 acres is ours. We cannot sell what is sacred. It is not ours to sell." I said to Senator Anderson: "Only God can take it away from us. Washington is not God. The U.S. Senate is not God!"
>
> I said to Senator Anderson: "Why do you want to steal our sacred land?"
>
> Senator Anderson said: "Paul, I like you. But there is timber on that land, millions of dollars of timber."

Klamath Termination

The events leading up to the Klamath termination are complicated. At Klamath, as on many reservations, social disorganization, the deterioration of Indian culture, and the formation of economic stratification led to bitter factionalism. On most reservations, especially where there are allotted lands, there is an Indian element favoring an end to collective ownership. For those families who are comparatively better off, termination has meant *per capita* payments, which could be used for repairs to homes, for the purchase of vehicles and appliances, or even investment in small businesses. For the poorer people it has meant simply a much needed monetary windfall.

In the Klamath case, the 2,000 enrolled members of the tribe were all English-speaking; acculturation had made considerable inroads. The Klamath had instituted a tribal council system long before the IRA, passed in 1934, and since 1913 they had been developing their reservation timber resources. "In the 1950s, private companies were cutting the timber on a sustained yield basis and the Klamaths were receiving about $2 million annually, which was distributed on a per capita basis, resulting in yearly income of from $3,000–$4,000 per family" (Spicer 1969:141).

In the face of rising unemployment after World War II and decreased farm earnings, the Klamath were forced to rely increasingly on their *per capita* payments. The payments became, in a sense, a dole, but one which was drawn from the earnings of their timber resource. In that the payments were still inadequate for large Indian families (even for the cost of living in the early 1950s), it is hardly surprising that by 1958 more than 70 percent chose to terminate their trust status under the federal government and to divide up the money realized from the sale of their timber lands. And yet, twenty percent were "so confused or uninterested that they did not vote," while five percent voted against termination (Spicer 1969:142).

The management of Indian timber resources by the Bureau of Indian Affairs has continually been a subject of criticism by the Indians. Although we have no information for the Klamath on this score, we can suppose that the situation reported by the Chinook Tribe in the state of Washington, in December of 1955, might very well apply also to the Klamath situation.

Claude Wayne, representing the Chinook tribe, told the joint Senate–House committee investigating government timber sales policies that methods of the Bureau of Indian Affairs constituted robbery and dishonesty toward his people.

Wayne and two CIO International woodworkers witnesses joined in calling for sale of the timber in smaller tracts to permit maximum competitive bidding and to halt monopoly timber grabs by such giant corporations as Rayonier, Inc. (*People's World*, December 5, 1955).

The testimony further brought out that eighteen independent logging firms had gone out of business in the past six years because they could not compete with Rayonier in bidding to get timber.

Indian timber commands much lower prices than timber sold on the open market. One union witness said that Indian hemlock brought $4.47 per thousand board feet and Douglas Fir, $10.85. "The same class of timber was then bringing $18 and $37 on the open market, Bishop said. He said also that 'the Indian not only gets skinned on his price, but gets shorted on his scale as well.' He cited a truckload of Indian timber that 'shrank' from 9,000 to 6,000 feet between the landing scale and the check scale" (*People's World*, December 5, 1955).

These practices have favored the growth of monopoly in the timber industry. The low price Rayonier was paying for Indian timber, let alone questionable practices by the BIA, enabled them to bid competitively on Forest Service timber adjacent to their holdings. "'In this way,' Irving explained, 'Rayonier has blocked small companies from getting timber, yet held its average price paid for all its stumpage far below the prices being paid by its smaller competitors'" (*People's World*, December 5, 1955).

A deep division had developed among the Klamath over the years and much of it centered around the management of their timber industry. Spicer (1969:141) refers to "a history of fruitless efforts to reach agreement concerning tribal management of the rich timber resources, and uncertainty and distrust of the federal government." All administrative expenses of the BIA agency for the tribe were paid out of the tribal timber money; yet, there was little real participation by the Klamath themselves in the policy decisions or management of their industry.

A tribal corporation had been proposed and rejected in 1929, a tribal cooperative plan was rejected in 1933. A proposal for liquidation of the tribal holdings was opposed in 1947. The Klamath Termination Bill of 1954 proposed final closure of the tribal roll in six months, the adoption of a management plan for the timber resources at the end of 18 months, and complete termination of federal trusteeship within three years. The two authorized delegates of the tribe who appeared at the hearing on the bill opposed the termination, and the tribal chairman held to the position that the tribe was not ready for federal withdrawal. It was clear, however, that there was strong sentiment among tribal members opposing this position. Various studies revealed that confusion and a lack of understanding were rampant (Spicer 1969:141).

When the author was on the reservation in 1949 as a young archaeology student, it was common knowledge that Weyerhauser Timber Company was after Klamath timber. President Eisenhower had appointed an Oregon business man, Douglas McKay, to the position of Secretary of the Interior, and McKay was in charge of carrying out the administration's "give-away" of the public's resources, including Indian timber. Given these facts, it seems likely that, aside from the internal complexity of Klamath political organization, there was a strong outside economic motivation for Klamath termination on the part of timber interests which worked hand-in-glove with the government. These were among the background factors leading to Klamath termination.

Menominee Termination

In the early fifties the Menominee won an $8.5 million lawsuit against the federal government for the BIA's mismanagement of their timber industry. The Menominee were one of the few, relatively better off Indian tribes in the country at the time—they owned their own forest and sawmill—although poor in comparison to their non-Indian neighbors in Wisconsin. The money from the judgment was placed in trust by the government. When the Menominee voted for a per capita distribution of the money, the distribution was made conditional on the agreement to terminate their reservation status. Under this kind of political pressure, and without foreseeing all the negative implications of their action, the Menominee, in a questionable voting procedure, agreed to termination. Even then, the vote of 169 "for" and five "against" represented less than ten percent of the eligible voters; yet, the government let the vote stand, for it was in accord with their policy of terminating Indian tribes (Lurie 1971b:39).

The several thousand Menominee were partially self-supporting before termination. Afterward, they became almost completely pauperized. Much of their land, which was not taxable when held in trust by the government, was sold at forced auctions to make up defaulted state property taxes. White speculators began selling Menominee land and lakes as vacation home sites; the National Park Service sought to acquire a 24-mile section of the scenic Wolf River lands, the heart of the Menominee Nation; and tribal funds were used up through per capita payments to unemployed tribesmen. The reservation became the 72nd county of Wisconsin, the tribal council became a corporation, the tribal rolls were closed, and the Bureau of Indian Affairs withdrew. Ten years after termination, Menominee County was one of the ten most depressed counties in the United States (Meyer 1971:46).

Among other things, termination meant converting the communally owned Menominee land to private title, held by a corporation, Menominee Enterprises, Inc.

Many Indian families had to rebuy their own homesites. The government's hospital and school were closed . . . by the state.

The newly–established county government had to contract with neighboring counties for basic services such as jails and judges. Menominee children, no longer with legal status as Indians, went to school with children from an adjoining county and . . . the drop out rate climbed. The county has no health facilities now.

Faced with property taxes for the first time, some low income families lost their newly-purchased land through delinquency. Others on state welfare had to sign over to the state bonds issued them by the tribal corporation, thus losing their annual dividends from the forest products, a subsistence income for many. The mill and forest, the bedrock of the tribe's chances, ran into economic setbacks unforseen by the federal planners.

During the 1960s, millions of dollars in special federal aid were directed to the county by the War-On-Poverty and other programs, but even this belated assistance did not alter the tribe's basic social and economic problems (*Akwesasne Notes* 3(8):16–17).

Later, an active political resistance emerged. This was the organization known as DRUMS—Determination of Rights and Unity for Menominee Shareholders—the drum having religious significance in Menominee culture. DRUMS' leadership charged that the tribal corporation, under pressure to stay afloat financially, had been converting Menominee lands into a tourist playground for affluent Milwaukee and Chicago non-Indians.

DRUMS was able to win seats on the 11-member Voting Trust which managed the land sales, but they did not have enough votes to control the Trust. The main stumbling block, besides a conservative Indian clique, was the First Wisconsin Trust Company of Milwaukee. The First Wisconsin Trust had been empowered to vote a block of 48,000 shares for minor and "incompetent" Indian stockholders, and it consistently voted with the management of Menominee Enterprises, Inc. Thus it became a target for picketing by DRUMS (*Akwesasne Notes* 3(8):16–17).

A coalition of Menominee forces, together with their non-Indian supporters, began lobbying for federal legislation that would restore Menominee land and resources (what was left) to reservation status, and to reconstitute the Menominee Tribe as a legal entity. These efforts were partially successful.

In 1974, thirteen years after the original termination, Congress passed the Menominee Restoration Act. The Act restored federal services and gave self-government (a Menominee Restoration Committee was set up), but the tribal role must be re-opened and updated, the land and other assets returned to federal trust status, before the Menominee tribe can be fully reconstituted under federal charter. These are very difficult procedures, and subsequent events, beyond the scope of our discussion here (for example, internal questions and disagreements on how to respond to the 34-day occupation by the Menominee Warrior Society of the Alexian Brothers Abbey, the Brothers' double-cross, the tremendous backlash by racist forces, and the operations of the transition government) have seriously split the Menominee people on strategy and weakened the initial coalition.

The Politics of Termination

Termination began under Commissioner of Indian Affairs Dillion Meyer of the last Truman administration. Ironically, Meyer was the former director of the War Relocation Authority, the Japanese-American detention camps, which was a shameful blot on US democracy. It is significant, therefore, that the BIA's Relocation Program for Native Americans was launched during Meyer's tenure. But the foremost proponent of termination was Senator Arthur V. Watkins of Utah.

Watkins called termination "freedom" legislation, the same term given the General Allotment Act of 1887. The political motivation behind termination by politicians like Watkins was to settle old grievances with the Indian peoples, particularly over the tax-free status of their reservation lands. This situation rankled some Congressmen from the Western states who reflected the views of their business-minded constituencies. Their aim was to "integrate" Indians into the capitalist "free enterprise" system without any further economic assistance, and turn the remaining Indian lands over to the corporations, land companies, ranchers and small businessmen.

Utah, Watkin's state, denied the political franchise to Native Americans until 1956 on the grounds that Indians were not paying taxes on their trust land (Jorgensen 1978:25). Interestingly, Watkins was later appointed chairperson of the Indian Claims Commission by Eisenhower. This act in itself should indicate a hidden purpose behind the handling of Indian land claims, going beyond the supposed administration of justice in the matter of Native American land rights

Termination as official federal Indian policy was low-keyed, but not really abandoned, during the Kennedy and Johnson administrations of the 1960s. The Nixon administration, in spite of talk of Indian "self-determination," stepped up the drive to exploit Indian resources, to the detriment of the nationalities concerned, but under the guise of tribal economic development. Indian peoples are now being pressured to divest themselves of their sovereign right over raw materials in their reservation and village areas, not to mention treaty lands. Under the Carter administration, it was not only the timber-rich reservations which were under attack, but all energy-rich Native American nationalities were endangered because of their water, coal, oil and uranium reserves. And the Reagan administration pursues the same line.

This new economic war zone also includes millions of acres of non-reservation lands, those which are under Indian claim by reason of an aboriginal title, illegal seizure, and broken or fraudulent treaties.

Land Claims as Termination

The settlement of Native American land claims is another kind of termination which has been a major characteristic of the contemporary "frontier." In 1949 the U.S. Indian Commission was set up to adjudicate the claims of all Native American tribes. Since then, about two billion dollars has been claimed by Indians for broken treaties, land thefts, and the destruction of necessary resources. By the end of 1975, the Indian Claims Commission had awarded $561 million concerning 370 separate claims.

> All of the judgement funds have not gone to the claimants. Attorney's fees have been set at 10 percent of the final award, while the federal government has exacted funds for off-setting costs—costs incurred from services rendered to the claimants . . . during the reservation period. Indians have been mightily embittered by the Indian Claims Commission Act and the large sums guaranteed to attorneys (Jorgensen 1978:23).

A land claims commission dealing fairly with Native Americans would be one which would reverse the 200-year policy of taking away the land. Instead, the settlement of the hundreds of claims has been to force claimants to accept money rather than receiving a portion of the lands claimed, even when those lands lay in the public domain and could easily be returned. Clemmer (1973:25) states:

> Rather than being a simple gesture of good will, the Commission was established as a practical action aimed at systematizing and speeding the quieting

of Indian title, which was, and is, very real. For instance, Felix Cohen undertook a study of federal Indian law for the Solicitor's Office in the 1920s [*Handbook of Federal Indian law*, 1941] which indicated that the U.S. Government acquired sovereignty but not actual ownership of Indian lands upon establishing hegemony over those lands as a result of a treaty with European power. Rather, ownership passed to the U.S. Government only when the lands in question were either purchased or ceded by the Indians in question.

According to the Kennedy Report on Indian Education (US Senate, 1969), Native Americans now hold only two percent of the land whereas formerly they had 100 percent. Furthermore, that two percent is often poor agricultural land, thousands of acres of eroded, partly eroded or otherwise worthless land.

Aubrey Grossman (1970), attorney for the Pit River Indian land claim in California, has argued that this reduction came about by robbery, wars begun by the government for the sole purpose of getting Indian land, treaties coerced by the U.S. military, violations of treaty rights, fraud, gross-underpayment, and treaties not agreed to by the Indian peoples involved. In various governmental actions and statements, continues Grossman, the U.S. government, while not admitting any illegalities as to the 98 percent of the land taken, has nevertheless admitted that a substantial amount of the land was taken illegally. This admission is made in the Kennedy Report and also in the Indian Claims Act. Having admitted that a great deal of land was taken from Native Americans illegally, the government nevertheless maintains the position that no matter how clearly it is proved that certain specific lands were taken illegally, these specific lands cannot be recovered.

This is in marked contrast to the law for the white man, points out Grossman. If a non-Indian illegally, or with force, takes another's land, the latter is entitled to go to court and get an order that the land be returned. This fact leads Grossman to the conclusion that where the illegality of the taking is admitted and the particular land that was taken cannot be returned to the Native American people in question, then it would seem highly practical that land presently owned by the government, and not being put to use, should be returned, at least as a first step.

Grossman's reasoning in the Pit River brief is significant because an economic base is the *sine qua non* for a sovereign society, and land is the cornerstone of that base.

We are the rightful and legal owners of the land. Therefore, we reclaim all of the resourceful land that has traditionally been ours with that exception of land

now owned by private individuals. On this land we will set up our own economic and social structure retaining all of the values which are commensurate
with Indian life . . . (*The Dispossessed* 1970:9).

So reads a proclamation by the Pit River people during one of its land
occupations in California!

Of special significance to Native Americans in these land claims are
the large, non-treaty areas in the west and Alaska, which are claimed
under original title. It is estimated that these lands include most of
Nevada, one-third of California, parts of the Northwestern states and
almost all of Alaska. Now, of course, with the bourgeois settlement of
claims in Alaska and California, most of these rights have been officially
liquidated, although not to the satisfaction of Native Americans.

The significance of land struggles like Alcatraz and Pit River lay
in the fact that Native Americans reoccupied a symbolic portion of
these lands and dramatically brought their just claims to the public's attention. Heretofore, the long, legally complex and unfairly administered
procedure of taking the matter through the land claims court was the only
means available, and then, the public scarcely ever heard about the claims.
The Indian people who are associated with these militant protests want their
HOMELANDS, or a significant portion of them, returned to tribal status.
They are no longer willing to settle for a token monetary compensation.

Take the case of the so-called public domain of Nevada—who actually
owns it? Historian Jack Forbes (1965) points out that the state seized the
lands which constitute Nevada from the Native Peoples without benefit of
treaty, cession, or compensation, thus violating the Fifth Amendment to
the Constitution: "No person shall . . . be deprived of life, liberty or
property, without due process of law; nor shall private property be taken
for public use without just compensation."

The seizure of land in Nevada since 1868 also violates the Fourteenth
Amendment which guarantees property rights and due process of law to
"all persons born or naturalized in the United States." Of course, Native
Americans were not formally granted citizenship until 1924, the Supreme
Court having ruled that they were domestic aliens—a patently racist
decision, adds Forbes..

California Land Claims

Few people realize that of all the states in the Union, at least until the
recent land steal in Alaska, "progressive" California has one of the worst
records of dispossessing Native Americans.

The first act of California when it became a state in 1849 was to deprive its aboriginal citizens of both land and citizenship, which some Native Peoples held under Mexico. California's action was in violation of the Treaty of Guadalupe Hidalgo, and therefore, should have been declared unconstitutional. Yet, the federal government did not intervene.

As early as 1787, and from that time on, the federal government

> . . . took Indian land—as much and whenever—farmers, railroads, mining companies and lumber companies wanted. However, the official policy—stated by Presidents, Congress and the Supreme Court—was that no land would be taken without the consent of, and payment to, to particular Indian tribes. The way of securing this consent was through treaties. . . .
>
> In California, unlike the rest of the country, the treaty procedure broke down. The reason? Gold. [Over $15 billion altogether.] (Bailin and Grossman 1971).

In 1851–52, a federal commission negotiated eighteen treaties with California tribes. Under the terms of these treaties, the California Indians ceded 5 million acres in exchange for reservations totalling 8.5 million acres. Even so, they were forcibly deprived of these 8.5 million acres— some were excellent lands—when California's gold miners, through the state legislature, pressured the U.S. Senate not to ratify the treaties. The treaties were then conveniently "lost" in the Senate archives and forgotten, except by California's Indians.

Within the next few decades, the Native American population of California declined to 16–18,000 from their original estimated number of 150–200,000. Vigilante raids killed entire village populations, including ranch hands and servants. Such was the racism on the California frontier! The state undertook an all-out, undeclared war on the Indians. "Men hunted Indians for the profit their scalps would bring as well as the conviction that Indians impeded the swift takeover of land and gold . . . 4,000 died from massacre between 1847 and 1852 alone" (Bailin and Grossman 1971:4).

After growing Indian agitation and expressions of concern from some white groups, the government, which cannot be sued without its permission, allowed Indian claims to the 8.5 million acres through the California Indian Jurisdictional Act of Congress in 1928. But it was not until 1944 that the United States finally reimbursed California's Indian citizens for the 8.5 million acres not received. Even so, a ceiling of $1.25 per acre was placed on the value of the Indian land. There seemed to be no possibility of getting back any portion of the stolen lands, for in most cases the government had already sold these lands to white interests.

In the 1944 settlement, however, the federal government devised an ingenious legal maneuver to further defraud the Indians of a just award. The amount awarded was almost $18 million. But against this award the Act stipulated that "off-sets" should be charged, service and articles presumably delivered following the execution of the treaties but, in reality, most of which were never received. The tribes and rancherias were charged also for coercive expenses and open instances of government corruption, for example, official thievery and speculation in treaty goods not delivered but which were resold.

California Indians have paid through these deductions for all government operations up until the 1930s. Furthermore, the government made a nice profit on its Indian lands transactions since it awarded California Indians only the equivalent of $1.75 per acre for lands which had been sold originally to whites for as much as $2.00 to $4.00 per acre. "Off-sets" totaled over $12 million and were deducted from the total award, leaving only a little over $5 million for the claimants. This was divided up into *per capita* payments without the consent of the Indian people and whether or not one's tribe was actually a party to the 1852 treaty negotiations. *California Indians realized about $150 per capita as a result of this settlement!*

When the U.S. Indian Claims Commission was set up in 1949 for all the Indian claims in the U.S., California Indians were forced to settle the remainder of their claims. Litigation dragged on for 18 years until, in a compromise settlement forced on them, they were given 47 cents an acre for the additional 75,000,000 acres of land illegally seized by the United States.

Once again, the settlement was on the government's terms: administrative costs to run the Indian bureaucracy, which Native Americans loathe but cannot do without under the present system of Indian administration, were again deducted from the final settlement. They were even charged for some of the same facilities for which the earlier claims award had deducted as "off-sets," and for lands they had never been allowed to occupy. They have been allowed only 47 cents an acre for California's rich lands, based on the "fair market value" in 1851, and with no accumulated interest for all the years the lands had been withheld from them.

The final award was settled in 1964. After much procrastination and the compilation of a new role of California Indians, checks were issued in 1972 just a few days before Christmas. The timing made it difficult for those wishing to refuse their checks as a form of protest to do so.

Nevertheless, a number of people did so. A news story in *Wassaja* (January, 1973:22) summed up the Indian viewpoint: "Today, checks are being mailed to California Indians in payment for 95 percent of the State of California, at the price of 47 cents an acre, with no payment for loss of water rights, mineral rights, billions of dollars in gold taken from Indian land, or for the thousands of lives lost in the genocidal onslaught against the Native Peoples. . . ." Thus there are many cases where checks have been rejected or, at least in one known instance, remain uncashed, framed and hung on the living-room wall in silent mockery of the "justice" dispensed by the U.S. government.

Who Owns Shasta County?

The main holdout against the 47 cents an acre settlement were the several hundred members of the Pit River Tribe in northern California. In an election the tribe voted to reject the claims award, but the government arbitrarily nullified the election results and convened a second "election." This time voters of remote or doubtful Pit River ancestry were found and, in the expectation of a monetary windfall, outvoted the traditional/ethnic Indians. Undaunted, the real Indians continued their fight to regain at least a portion of their ancestral lands.

Among California's many Indian peoples, the Pit Rivers are held in high esteem. The reason may be found in the Pit Rivers' tragic history, their will to survive, and their great fighting spirit.

Historically, one of the most numerous of California's Indian nationalities, the Pit Rivers were almost totally decimated by the onslaught of the Gold Rush. They were forced underground in order to survive, their eleven bands dispersed, "each family striving desperately to survive against such odds as extreme poverty, actual starvation, sickness, hunted down like wild game" (*Wassaja*, January, 1973:8).

> Early in the 20th century, the bands began to reorganize, and gradually, by the time of the California claim hearings in 1964, they had completely revitalized their tribal structure.

> More than any other tribe in California, the Pit Rivers have retained their language, and a great deal of their cultural heritage (*Wassaja*, January 1973:8).

The Pit Rivers originally held approximately 3,386,000 acres of land, today comprising three counties in northern California. (See map, page 132). On July 2, 1959, the U.S. Claims Commission ruled in favor of the Pit claim, "That in 1853 they were the exclusive owners of this land and

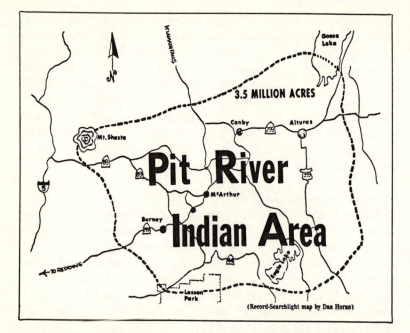

(Record-Searchlight map by Dan Horan)

that this title was taken away from them illegally without compensation
. . . by the passage of a federal statute'' (*The Dispossessed* 1970:13).

The United States Supreme Court has held also that, when the United
States has taken land away from an Indian people without compensation,
it thereby violates the Fifth Amendment to the United States Constitution. The legality of the Claims Commission's decision was further
strengthened by *25 US Code 4* which provides that "in all trials about
the right of property in which an Indian may be a party on one side,
and a white person on the other, the burden of proof shall rest upon
the white person, whenever the Indian shall make out a presumption
of title in himself from the fact of previous possession or ownership"
(*The Dispossessed* 1970:12).

Despite this decision reached by the Commission, the Pit River Indians
were not permitted to reoccupy their claimed lands. Instead, they, along
with other California Indian peoples, were forced to accept a monetary
compensation for the lands lost. Therefore, starting in 1970, the 529-
member nationality decided to step up its efforts to get back the land.

Inspired perhaps by the occupation of Alcatraz Island in 1969, in
which many California Indians had participated, the Pit Rivers adopted

the tactic of publicly occupying a portion of their claimed 3,368,000 acres, "owned" by big business. Pacific Gas and Electric, along with Pacific Telephone, Kimberly Clark Lumber Co., Southern Pacific Railroad and several others were, in effect, squatting on Pit River land—the so-called public domain—without benefit of any law, treaty, or deed of sale. Ninety percent of the Pit River claim was held by U.S. public land agencies, like the Forest Service, or by the aforementioned large corporations.

Their first action took place on June 5, 1970:

> One hundred fifty members of their tribe tried to occupy a site in Lassen National Park, which they claimed still belonged to them, and were ejected by federal police. The following day another 150 Indians who had moved onto land held by the Pacific Gas and Electric Company were dispersed, and 34 Indians arrested. Later that week 17 more were jailed for trespassing (Josephy 1971:232).

In October, 1970, 60 Pit River Indians and their supporters were brutally beaten and arrested at Four Corners in another occupation of their ancestral lands. The landless Pit River tribe had attempted to establish a quonset hut school-cultural center on their claimed land. "We expected arrests," wrote the Pit River writer, Darryl Wilson. "We received brutality, beatings and threats of machinegun fire. We also received manacles that peeled the skin from wrists. And we were chained together. Our situation was unfit even for war criminals" (Council on Interracial Books 1971:322).

What the Pit River Indians want is contained most succinctly in their proclamation made in the summer of 1970 (Josephy 1971:232–234).

> TO THE PRESIDENT AND THE PEOPLE OF THE UNITED STATES
> In defiance of the treaties signed with Indian tribes in California and across the nation, the federal government is in the process of relinquishing its duties to the American Indian.
>
> This process, called termination, has had a particularly devastating effect on the Indians of California. To add to the injury, the state of California has not assumed its responsibilities promised to its Indian citizens, the original owners of the land.
>
> Therefore it is up to the Indian people themselves to run their own affairs.
>
> Therefore let it be known by all concerned that the Pit River Tribe makes the following demands:
> 1. That the U.S. Government and the large corporations, including PG&E, PT&T, Southern Pacific Railroad, Kimberly Clark, Hearst Publications, and the Los Angeles Times-Mirror Corp., among others, return all our land to us

immediately. No amount of money can buy the Mother Earth; therefore, the California Land Claims Case has no meaning. The Earth is our Mother, and we cannot sell her.

2. That the U.S. Government and the large corporations pay back to us the profits they have made from the land since 1853, and that they make an accounting to us immediately. The land was taken illegally, against the principles of the Constitution.

3. That reparations be made to all California Indians for the deaths, suffering, and poverty forced on Indians for over 100 years.

4. That the federal government and the large corporations undo the damage they have done to the land, and that they make reparations to us for the damage done. Where the forest has been cut away, it must be restored. Where the rivers have been dammed, they must be allowed to run freely.

5. That all Indians be allowed religious and cultural freedom, and be allowed to teach their children the Indian way of life and be proud of that life. Further, that Indian studies be instituted in schools around the country, so that all citizens will know the true story of the Indian. The stereotype of the Indian that exists must be erased.

These demands are inseparable, inter-related, and must all be carried out in full force together.

The Pit River claim of nearly 3.5 million acres covers property in Lassen, Modoc and Shasta Counties. Shasta County was selected by the Indians as representative of how their lands are being exploited by large corporations and the U.S. government. The information which follows is from a discussion manual to a documentary film on the Pit River land struggle, *The Dispossessed* (1970). In the film the narrator makes the main point:

> "The rulers of Shasta County are an intricate part of the vast yet tightly controlled military and industrial complex which runs the country and much of the world. The key interest of this complex is control: control of products, control of markets, control of people and control of countries" (*The Dispossessed* 1970:8).

Table 2. lists the eight largest businesses in Shasta County, and therefore in Pit River country.

PG&E is by far the largest business in Shasta County. It owns 52,525 acres with an assessed valuation of over $320 million. Its wealth is concentrated along the Pit River in a series of dams and powerhouses. PG&E is the largest privately owned utility in the world and has close ties with giant banking and oil interests. In 1969 PG&E made a total profit of $175 million. Fifty-four percent was from public power sales. It gets

TABLE 2.

THE LARGEST BUSINESS IN SHASTA COUNTY

	Assessed Valuation	Acreage Owned*
Pacific Gas & Electric	$ 320,000,000	52,525
Pacific Telephone	27,000,000	6
Fruit Growers Corp. (affiliated with Sunkist)	23,000,000	82,217
Southern Pacific Railroad	15,000,000	165,617
Hearst Publications (San Francisco Examiner)	7,000,000	38,823
Publishers Forest Products (Los Angeles Times)	2,000,000	25,515
Kimberly Clark (paper products)	8,500,000	82,806
U.S. government	—	50% of total

SOURCE: *A Discussion Manual for "The Dispossessed," etc.*, 1970.

* Total acreage claimed is 3,368,000 acres.

cheap federal power from the Bonneville Power Authority, and yet it lets the public build its dams and power-houses. It monopolizes the free use of many of California's rivers, and it then generates its cheap power for sale to the public at exorbitant rates. PG&E has already captured the public power generation of five of California's irrigation districts, two county water agencies, a municipal utilities district, and the California Water Project (*The Dispossessed* 1970:6, 40).

In 1923 the Federal Government granted PG&E a license to erect power plants along the Pit River. Congress had buckled under severe pressure from utility lobbyists, overturned the Raker Act and passed, instead, the Federal Water Power Act, thereby deserting its public power principles. Over the years PG&E has captured every power-generating and water district in northern California except two. Public power accounts for 25 percent of the company's annual profits from electricity sales. It is now also getting into the water business—the California Water Project. There are still eleven small municipal power cities in northern California. PG&E is trying to put them out of business and consolidate its historic theft of the public domain, the major part of which are Indian lands.

At Pit River, despite PG&E inferences to the contrary, the company owns nothing. All it has are licenses. The Federal Water Power Act vested ownership of water power sites in the people; it created the Federal

Power Commission with authority to grant fifty-year licenses to public and private utilities for power development of the rivers. Now, fifty years later, many of these licenses are due to expire. "This means that 18 percent of PG&E's hydroelectric capacity is subject to recapture by the public by 1975, and all of it by 2013 (Petrakis 1970:28).

The Pit River occupation must have greatly embarrassed PG&E officials, lest the public be reminded that the company is in reality a squatter on the public domain. It therefore moved behind the scenes against the Indian demonstrators, but, of course, it left the dirty work to local law enforcement agencies.

> The arrest of these Indians, coupled with the refusal to arrest Pacific Gas & Electric Company, demonstrates, conclusively, an unconstitutional functioning of the legal and judicial system in Shasta County. . . . We refer to the control by PG&E of the legal machinery and public officials; and the lack of any control or influence, and the lack of rights, possessed by the Indians (Grossman 1970:11).

Petrakis (1970:33), writing in the *San Francisco Bay Guardian*, characterized PG&E as:

> . . . a huge public parasite that dominates the political life of the state, compels the public to create vast public works in its behalf, usurps the public's lands, rivers and technology, buys off and intimidates the press and even picks the men who "regulate" it on the state Utilities Commission and the Federal Power Commission.

Anger at the U.S. government for its subsidizing U.S. timber interests at the expense of Indian resources appears entirely justified, to judge by the experience of the Pit River Indians. About 40 percent of Shasta County is owned by the federal government; yet, most of the economic benefits go to big business, and not to the public, nor to the Indians. The lumber and paper products industry is one of the largest of these.

> . . . Companies like Kimberly Clark, L.A. Times, Sunkist, and U.S. Plywood contract with the federal government to buy the timber. They cut the trees for paper and lumber products which they sell at a profit. They make money off the public land without accepting any of the direct responsibility of land ownership such as paying property tax (*The Dispossessed* 1970:8).

Kimberly Clark owns 82,806 acres in Shasta County with an assessed valuation of $8.5 million. It is one of the largest distributors of paper products in the world with plants in Japan, South Africa, Holland, Mexico, England, Puerto Rico, Australia, Singapore, Germany, Colombia, Italy, France, El Salvador, Canada, Thailand and the Philippines.

Between 1968 and 1969, its sales in Japan increased by 50 percent; Mexico, 30 percent; Philippines, 30 percent; and England, 20 percent.

These are but two examples of the large corporations which squat illegally on lands which by all rights should be returned to Native Americans.

The Railroads Today

The huge land grants given to the railroads in the third quarter of the nineteenth century continue to plague non-Indians as well as Indians. In 1972 the National Coalition for Land Reform joined with the California Coalition of Migrant and Seasonal Farmworkers in filing a complaint before the Interior Department. Thirteen members of Congress took up the complaint and their testimony is reported in the *Congressional Record* (September 19 and November 8, 1972).

The basis of the complaint is that a number of western railroads have in effect violated the conditions imposed upon them by the terms of statutes granting land to them by the federal government. The original grants provided that they could obtain title to land extending twenty miles on either side of their proposed tracks. They were to later sell or mortgage the excess land to finance further construction once twenty miles of tracks were completed.

A number of railroads "failed" to observe these terms and, as a consequence, today own millions of acres in fertile farm and forest land as well as land on which mineral rights are being exploited commercially. The petitioners against the railroads point to the negative effects that such large, corporate land-holding patterns have on both the farm worker and small farmer in rural areas.

> Time and again they have observed the lessons of Walter Goldschmidt's 1946 study, *Small Business and the Community,* known as the Arvin-Dinuba study. The report showed that rural areas dominated by large corporations have large welfare rolls, poor schools, and all manner of social and economic problems while rural areas characterized by small farmer operations have strong civic organizations, have better schools, are better maintained, and have less unemployment (*Congressional Record,* September 19, 1972: S 15244).

A case in point is the Southern Pacific Railroad. A lawyer for the California Coalition, Sheldon Greene, cites a number of Southern Pacific's land-grant uses (*Congressional Record,* November 8, 1972:E 9227).

> The company . . . controls 200,000 acres of prime agricultural land in the San Joaquin Valley, and thus is unjustly a major beneficiary of the state's costly water projects . . . the company is illegally tapping mineral deposits, including

oil and gas leases grossing more than $3 million, and . . . it still controls land
in the Sierras, which allegedly was to have been disposed of within three years
after the road was completed in 1869.

Southern Pacific's annual reports show that it earned $24 million in
1970 from oil, gas and agricultural leases, including $15.4 million from
industrial and commercial rentals. In terms of monopoly, Southern
Pacific is an example of a modern American railroad receiving an indirect
subsidy from the U.S. government through its non-compliance with land
granting statutes, subsequent laws and Supreme Court decisions. This
situation has contributed to the shaky wheeler-dealer economics of the
American railroads in which several of the largest land-owning lines find
their earnings from rail services nearly matched by returns from land
development and the leasing of oil and mineral rights. Small wonder that
the general public cries in vain for decent rail passenger service! There is
less profit in passenger service and the railroad magnates know it.

The reasoning which originally justified the landgrab by the railroads is
attributed to "winning the West" and, of course, it had the inevitable
consequence of smashing Indian societies that held the lands. Today, for
example, with the Southern Pacific in California, the illegally-held lands
have a prior Indian title. S. P. owns, in Shasta County alone, 165,000
acres with an assessed valuation of $15 million. This includes land in the
Pit River Indian land claim, mentioned earlier.

> Throughout the West, S.P. holds nearly four million acres of other forest,
> grazing, agricultural and commercial land. As it eases out of the rail passenger
> business, its freight hauling goes up and this "railroad" is moving into related
> fields such as trucking and marine transport—and such unrelated ventures as
> non-rail real estate development, data processing and communications (*The
> Dispossessed* 1970:26).

Southern Pacific still owns more than two million acres in California and
is the largest private landowner in the state.

It is significant that the federal agency which has so far failed to
investigate the land still illegally held by the railroads is the Department
of the Interior, the same department which was given the trust responsibility for Native American land rights through its Bureau of Indian Affairs.

Other Means of Dispossession
Reservation lands continue to be taken under a variety of ruses and by
quasi-legal means ". . . During 1970 more than 200,000 acres of reservation lands passed from Indian ownership" (Meyer 1971:78). Edgar

Cahn (1969) documents many of these instances in *Our Brother's Keeper*, as does also Meyer (1971) in *Native Americans, The New Indian Resistance*. These include taking Native American land for public works.

It is said that power dams have displaced more Indian communities than did the U.S. Cavalry in the last century. Next to the Bureau of Indian Affairs, the U.S. Corps of Army Engineers is probably the bureaucracy most hated by Indians in the government's neo-colonial apparatus. The Corps of Engineers, in league with the Bureau of Reclamation and with the full cooperation of the Bureau of Indian Affairs, has repeatedly built dams in the name of reclamation which have flooded out viable Indian communities and destroyed valuable reservation lands.

Garrison Dam at Ft. Berthold, North Dakota, flooded one-fourth of the reservation (154,000 acres)—the richest land. It also caused the loss of substantial oil revenues. The Three Affiliated Tribes at Ft. Berthold (Mandan, Gros Ventre and Arickaree) were receiving only $5,000 a year for welfare prior to the dam; after its constructoin, 60 percent were found to be unemployed and welfare costs had risen to $573,000.

Garrison was one of three dams built by the Corps just after World War II on the upper Missouri River. The two others were also located on Indian reservations which, because of Indian powerlessness, are the easiest lands to appropriate or condemn. They are the Ft. Peck Dam in Montana (Assisniboin-Sioux) and the Oahe Dam at Ft. Yates, North Dakota (Cheyenne River Sioux). It is ironic that, in another case, on the Crow Reservation in Montana, the government named the dam after the Indian leader, Yellowtail, who had so steadfastly opposed its construction. The "Crow Indian reservation received no compensation for their rights either to land or water. There are 40 more cases just like this one" (Meyer 1971:48).

The practice of building dams on reservations has been going on for a long time. Old San Carlos, on the San Carlos Apache Reservation in Arizona, was destroyed by Coolidge Dam in 1929. The dam was built for the announced purpose of making water available for irrigation to the Pima Indians who are located downstream on the Gila River, but after its completion, the water allocation was given instead to white farmers. Said by the Bureau to be among the best Indian farmers in the country at the time, the San Carlos Apaches have never fully recovered economically from the loss of their farmlands which were flooded out.

Kinzua Dam in Pennsylvania broke the country's oldest Indian treaty. The treaty had been signed by George Washington with the Seneca

Nation (New York State) in 1794 and reaffirmed a number of times since then, never to claim Seneca land nor disturb their nation. "During the hearings on this dam, the Senecas hired their own engineers who proved that the dam could be built more cheaply and serve the same purpose if placed about 30 miles downstream. The Army Corps, which receives open-ending funding from the Congress, doesn't care about saving money. The dam was built. . ." (Meyer 1971:47). Since then, government officials have found the dam to be inadequate and now plan to build another in the near future.

More examples could be cited. In many instances, as in the Seneca case, feasible alternative plans which would not dislocate Indian communities were rejected by the government. No wonder Native Americans charge that dam construction is "Indian removal." Dam construction on reservations has served much the same racist purpose that urban renewal projects do in the cities—the forced removal of poor and non-white peoples for business expansion. Meyer (1971:46–47) indicates that much of dam construction is flawed on technological grounds as well:

> Perhaps few people are aware that a dam, though the actual structure is built to last for centuries, only functions to its full capacity for 50 years. Expensive and often impossible dredging operations extend their life only another 10 years. This is due to the tons of siltage and wastes which accumulate in the reservoir at a rate of one to six percent every year. With huge quantities of water gathered behind certain dams, there is the problem of evaporation. Lake Mead, to name only one, loses more water to evaporation every day than now flows into it, thus cancelling out one of its main purposes.

Robert Sherrill (1966:180), writing in *The Nation*, calls the Corps of Engineers "the Pork-barrel soldiers." In recent decades the Corps has become merely a political arm of Congress through which Congressmen can dole out largess back home in the form of public works money for private civilian contractors. The Corps justifies the projects and Congress appropriates the money. "During its 150-year life the Corps–Congress cornucopia has put, or is now putting, $22 billion into the contractors' pockets; another $35 billion is programmed for the next fifteen years." Said one Texas Congressman, "You never heard of an Army Engineer program that has not been criticized as pork barrel" (Sherrill 1966:180).

> It has pushed through dam projects on the west fork of a river when it was the east fork that presented the flood problem. It has scraped out harbors to give better access to tankers carrying fuel to utility plants that are converting to natural gas. It has proposed recreational reservoirs on rivers too polluted to

support fish life. It has built dams to protect less farm acreage than is flooded by the resulting reservoir.

Fearing that some day it may run out of projects, the Corps authorizes far more than it can handle. . . Discrepancies of 200 and 300 percent between original estimates and final costs are not uncommon (Sherrill 1966:181).

The crackdown on Indian hunting, fishing and gathering rights in the western states is another kind of dispossession. The abridgement of land-use rights has been under the guise of so-called Indian infringement of the public use of state and federal lands. In reality, the suppression serves the special interests of white "sportsmen" and commercial fishing concerns. Unfortunately, the conservationists have put special privileges of licensing, fish and game controls into the hands of the sportsmen's lobby (Meyer 1971:67). In 1975, for example, the National Wildlife Federation called for a "new national policy that would strip" American Indians of their hunting, fishing and timber rights (*Wassaja* 3(4):1). The book, *Uncommon Controversy* (American Friends Service Committee, 1970), documents the long and bitter fight by the Nisqually and other fishing peoples in the State of Washington to protect Indian fishing rights. One leader was arrested 75 times defending his fishing rights, supposedly treaty-protected. After many defeats at the hands of state interests, the Washington Indian nationalities secured a limited victory in the Boldt Decision, Judge Boldt ruling that Washington's Indian treaties gave the fishing tribes a right to take 50 percent of the annual salmon catch. For his courage and integrity in defense of Indian treaty rights, Judge Boldt was targeted by the Interstate Congress for Equal Rights and Responsibilities, a racist rightwing group.

The Indians' pursuit of traditional fishing, hunting and gathering rights is founded on historic treaties or, in some cases, on aboriginal land use rights. This pursuit is "ratified" by economic necessity. Native Americans need the food, if not the meagre income these activities sometimes provide. Indian unemployment rates and their general economic situation have critically worsened in the post-war decades. Subsistence food-getting activities, aside from their importance to the maintenance of the Indian heritage and identity, have become an economic necessity for many reservation and rural (non-reservation) Indian communities. Perhaps the non-Indian can now begin to appreciate this facet of contemporary Indian life. Rampant inflation and the rapidly rising cost of living are driving even employed white citizens in some cases to rustle cattle, hunt illegally, or shoplift in order to put food on the table for their families.

Land is continually taken for national monuments and parks even when the tourist-recreation development of the land in question is an Indian nationality's most valuable economic asset. In some cases, like the Sioux Badlands, the areas taken for this purpose constitute Native American holy-lands. In 1956 the Indian Claims Commission confirmed the right of Taos Pueblo in New Mexico to 130,000 acres of land, including their 48,000-acre Blue Lake shrine. But not until December of 1970, after many trials and tribulations, did the Taos people get their disputed lands returned.

Land was "temporarily" withdrawn from several reservations during World War II and not returned, even when increasing tribal populations desperately needed it. Used as gunnery ranges and bombing targets, the U.S. military is reluctant to give these areas up; or when given up, the land has been given to others, as in the case of the Pine Ridge Reservation, where the land was given to the National Park Service. Militant political protest on the Pine Ridge Reservation, the site of the Wounded Knee occupation, had its origin in this kind of land withdrawal.

At the beginning of World War II the government took over 3,000 acres of the Fort Hall Reservation in Idaho to make an airfield (Collier 1970:32). The Shoshone–Bannock received $10 per acre. After the war, instead of offering to give the land back, the government deeded it over to the city of Pocatello at $1.00 per acre for use as a municipal airport. By 1970 each acre was worth $500. If the Shoshone–Bannock had been allowed to retain title, the improved acreage could have been leased to the city at a sizeable commercial rate, bringing much needed income to this impoverished indigenous nationality.

A host of other bogus reasons have been used to deprive the Indian peoples of their remaining land base "for their own good." These include the use of allotted lands in some of the more racist states as a disposable resource in order to qualify for welfare. Lands are also slyly taken through the invalidation of wills, the appointment of white conservators of Indian-owned parcels (ruling the owners "incompetent"), and by forced sales and manipulation, usually with the open connivance of the Bureau of Indian Affairs. In Palm Springs, California, with its multi-million dollar real estate values, many an "incompetent" Indian has been bilked out of legitimate rights by court-appointed white conservators, some of them judges.

Although the remaining land base has continued to be diminished by these and other means, it is the expropriation of natural resources that has become the hallmark of the new dispossession. It is in this sense that we may continue to speak of an American Indian frontier in the last half of the 20th century. This theme is documented in the following chapter.

*The first order of business . . . must be the
development of a viable economic base for
the Indian communities.*

American Indian Policy
Review Commission

7

THE ECONOMIC
RIP-OFF

Shelton Davis (1973) has analyzed the expropriation of Native American natural resources by white-owned economic interests. Davis contends, like Jorgensen, that Indian reservations are fully integrated into the capitalist political economy. The nature of that integration, however, leaves reservations underdeveloped and superexploited. But measuring the "rip-off" is a difficult task, thanks primarily to the obscurantism practiced by the BIA and other government agencies in their statistical reports concerning Indian people. This problem can be overcome by the use of interpolations. Davis, for example, uses statistical information from the BIA, reproduced in Levitan and Hetrick (1971, Chapter 5), as the basis for his computations. To illustrate the nature and the extent of the expropriation, several of Davis' tables are reproduced below.

In Table 3 we have a breakdown of land use, but how much is used by Indians and how much by non-Indians? We already know, Davis tells us, that "since 1947, the Bureau has again been leasing Indian trust property to non-Indian agricultural, timber and mining entrepreneurs and firms. But, how much, and what is the relationship between the income which Indians get from such leasing, and the wealth, in the form of profits, which non-Indians expropriate?" This is the *key* question. To answer this question we must look at Table 4.

TABLE 3.

USES OF INDIAN LANDS

	Acres (thousands)	Percent of Total
Total	55,750	100
Open grazing	33,971	61
Noncommercial timber	8,821	16
Commercial timber	5,475	10
Oil and gas	3,483	6
Dry farming	1,832	3
Other minerals	940	2
Irrigation	650	1
Other uses	479	1
Businesses	99	–

Given the way the Bureau reports its statistics, the type of information we are given is the amount of income Indians obtain from the leasing of their lands. We see immediately that a total of over $70 million was earned in 1969. This is an impressive figure. Yet, upon a closer look at the leasing of Indian property to non-Indian entrepreneurs (Table 5), we find some interesting hidden facts.

For one, we learn that *non-Indian operators* controlled about 7.5 million acres of Indian land in 1969, or *about one-fifth of all agricultural land* (open grazing and dry farming in Table 3), in use for that year. If we

TABLE 4.

CASH REVENUE FROM PROPERTY LEASES
TO NON-INDIANS, 1969

	Revenue (thousands)
Total	$ 70,439
Forestry	23,074
Oil and gas	22,445
Farm and pasture	13,826
Other minerals	3,992
Business	3,493
Grazing	1,967
Outdoor recreation	728
Other Surface	914

TABLE 5.

AGRICULTURAL PRODUCTION BY NON-INDIAN
OPERATORS ON INDIAN LANDS, 1969

	Acreage (thousands)	Value (thousands)
Cultivated row crops	281.0	$ 53,826.7
Small grains	638.8	27,511.0
Forage hay	301.3	15,162.5
Horticulture & garden	16.8	12,324.4
Grazing	6,283.5	36,496.6
Totals:	7,521.4	145,321.1

take grazing land as an example, we find, according to Table 4, that this brought a revenue to Indians of $1,967,000; and yet, the value of production on this grazing land (from Table 5) totaled $36,496,000. In other words, *Indians received about 1/18th of the value produced on their grazing lands.*

The picture concerning agricultural lands which are used for purposes other than grazing is even more revealing. Dry farming made up 1,832,000 acres used in 1969, of which 1,237,900 acres or about 66 percent were leased to non-Indian operators. For farm and pasturage (see Table 4), Indian revenues from leasing amounted to $13,826,000. Yet non-Indian production value (all items in Table 5 except grazing) amounted to $108,824,000 or a difference of $94,988,600.

In summary:

Indian peoples received $14,793,000 for over seven million acres of land which produced $145,321,200. Given the low costs of land rental, and the availability of a cheap Indian seasonal labor force, this represents (even if exact costs cannot be calculated) a significant profit for non-Indian agricultural operators on Indian lands (Davis 1973:29).

The American Indian Policy Review Commission (1977:314) found that Native Americans in 1975 received less than one-third of the total value of range and farm products grown on Indian lands—$123 million in contrast to $271 million received by non-Indians. Indians hold approximately 44 million acres of pasture and rangeland, or about 5 percent of that in the nation. Furthermore:

In 1973, 17,910 Indian ranching operatio.is accounted for livestock products valued at $64.3 million. The remainder of the rangeland was used by 779 non-Indian ranchers who provided livestock products valued at $33.9 million (The Comptroller General 1975:30).

Thus about one-third of the income derived from ranching in 1973 was obtained by only a few hundred non-Indians at a much greater rate of profit than was true for the thousands of Indian operators.

An analysis of Indian commercial timber land bears out a similar trend of super-profits for the non-Indian entrepreneur. A recent government report (The Comptroller General 1975) states that Native American Indians hold 5.3 million acres of commerical forest land, or about 1 percent of the national total. Although the amount of surplus expropriation cannot be gained from Davis' tables, we see that in 1969, 5,475,000 acres of Indian timber lands (Table 3) created a revenue of $23,074,000 (Table 4) for the leasing of stumpage to non-Indian timber companies. This seems a sizeable amount, but it is actually quite misleading and obscures the relative inequalities between Indian income and the surplus expropriated by non-Indian timber companies. Davis (1973:29) is able to supply us with information from which to draw a correct inference, if not the actual dollar value in question:

> In 1967, for example, over 803,000 MBF (million board feet) of timber were cut on reservation lands, of which only 10,000 MBF or about 12 percent, were processed in tribally-owned mills. The remaining 700,000 MBF were processed and sold by white companies, bringing them high profits, and leaving Indians with a small increment to their tribal treasuries. The Bureau has consistently followed a policy of selling Indian timber to these companies while showing little interest in tribally-controlled mills.

Three reservations—Yakima, Colville, and Fort Apache—contain one-third of all Indian forest land, but on the first two reservations, private mills and loggers do most of the cutting. Only Fort Apache in Arizona has developed tribally-owned mills. Yet, according to the American Indian Policy Review Commission (1977:324), "the economic potential of the timber industry, if properly managed, is extremely significant. It is estimated that tribes with medium to large stands can become economically self-sufficient based on their timber resources alone, and timber unlike minerals, is a renewable resource." It is for this reason that the AIPRC recommended in its 1977 report that the tribes develop a timber industry, and not just a logging operation.

The surplus expropriated from oil, gas and other mineral leases is easier to estimate.

Beginning in the early 1950s, the BIA began to provide leases to large mining corporations for the expropriation of oil, uranium, sand, gravel, phosphate, natural gas, gilsonite, gypsum, coal, limestone, copper, lead, zinc, and other minerals. . . . Until recent years, the royalties on production from these leases, which supposedly accrued to the tribes, were based at a normal rate of 12.5 percent by Federal Law, except in individually negotiated instances (Davis 1973:30).

If, instead of the 12.5 percent figure, we use a liberal estimate of 20 percent royalties on production, a relative comparison of major oil and gas royalty tribal recipients (with estimated production value of the non-Indian firms) would give us the amounts found in Table 6.

TABLE 6.

MAJOR RECIPIENTS OF OIL AND GAS ROYALTIES AND
ESTIMATED PRODUCTION VALUE, 1969
(thousands)

	Royalties	Estimated Value of Production at 20% Royalty Rate
Navajo	$ 8,566	$ 42,830
Osage	7,013	35,065
Wind River	2,925	14,625
Five Civilized Tribes	1,802	9,010
Cononcity	1,696	8,480
Uintah-Ouray	1,590	7,950
Jicarillo Apache	1,428	7,140
Kiowa, Comanche, Apache, Oklahoma	1,159	5,795
Northern Cheyenne	1,098	5,490
Totals	27,277	136,385

Bear in mind that the twenty percent royalty rate is a high one. Therefore, the estimated value of production, as contrasted to the actual royalties received by the respective tribes, is a conservative estimate. The actual amount of surplus expropriation may be higher in some cases. As Davis (1973:30) concludes, "in other words, *tribal treasuries received $27 million of an estimated production value on oil and gas leases of $136 million.* Since 1950, an estimated $2 to $4 billion have been expropriated by large mining companies from Indian lands" [emphasis is ours].

From the above facts, measuring the "rip-off" or surplus expropriation, we see that Indian tribes lose tens of millions of dollars each year because they do not own the means of production on their reservations. They neither own, nor control, the mines, timber companies, or agricultural concerns which exploit their economic resources.

Agribusiness

Today, agriculture is a big business and is denoted by the term agribusiness. Since much of Native American land is agricultural, it is pertinent to ask what is the Native American's role in agribusiness?

Jorgensen (1978:49) has described the tremendous changes in U.S. agriculture over the last few decades. The farm population in the country had decreased from 32 million in 1920 to 8.2 million in 1977. The number of farms has also declined, but the total acreage farmed has increased by 125 million acres, and the size of the average farm has increased from 147 acres in 1920 to 393 acres today. In the Mountain and Pacific states where the bulk of the reservation Indians reside, the average size is now 2,262 and 567 acres respectively. Technology has reduced labor needs, the average farm having 2.6 tractors. The large air conditioned kind used for grain fields costs over $50,000, and machinery generally has become very expensive, to say nothing of soaring energy costs.

Technological advances and their capital requirements have therefore favored the growth of large operations over middle-size operations. Informal cartels and large food-processing trusts are increasingly dominating agriculture through vertical integration. "Supermarket chains are purchasing packing plants and feeder lots" to dominate beef production (Jorgensen 1978:46). Kroger, Safeway, and the principal energy corporations are among the 130 giant corporations, worth $1 trillion in assets, which influence Western agribusiness. There are 12,000 indirect interlocks among these 130 corporations, even though interlocking directorates are unlawful if they eliminate competition (Jorgensen, Davis and Mathews 1978).

While small operators are being liquidated, large corporations are receiving massive federal aid. "In 1967, 65 percent of all farm subsidies went to the top 10 percent of earners in the agricultural industry, and most of them were large corporations and food-processing trusts. On the other hand, the 43 percent of United States farmers with incomes of less than $2,500 per year received 4.5 percent of all federal subsidies" (Jorgensen 1978:49).

It is under these changing circumstances that it has become increasingly impossible for small Indian landowners to compete. To survive, Native Americans lease land to large, non-Indian operators.

> These people, in turn, receive special tax advantages for using Indian land, and have access to capital from local banks to conduct their businesses. The Indian is paid a modest fee for the use of the land—the fee being negotiated by the BIA—and the producer avoids paying land ownership taxes. The Indian land, therefore, is used when market and subsidy prospects are good, and remains fallow when prospects are not so good. Indian labor, too, was once exploited in these arrangements, but Indian labor is seldom required on modern farms (Jorgensen 1978:49).

There are 50 million acres of Indian trust lands. Of these about seven million are leased out to non-Indian farmers, or used under permit by non-Indian ranchers for grazing. An additional eight million are under mineral leases. A considerable amount of the remaining acreage is either severely eroded or it is desert and mountain land. The best agricultural lands are commonly under lease to whites.

A documented case (*Akwesasne Notes* 1974:17) of Indian leased land is that of Hildegard Catches who, against her will, was forced in 1970 by the government to rent her land on the Pine Ridge Reservation.

Ms. Catches inherited her land from her Sioux forbears. She owns interests along with many other "owners" in seven parcels of land, originally allotted under the 1887 Allotment Act. Through the years the allotted lands have been rendered useless economically to its Indian owners (but not to its non-Indian users) through fractionalization caused by BIA-enforced heirship rules and regulations. Ms. Catches is a 2/15ths owners of three parcels, a 1/15th owner of another, and a 1/90th owner of yet another. She owns nothing outright and her total interests add up to a meager 159.87 acres. On one of her properties she receives a mere $11.29 per year in grazing fees. On another she gets $70.53. Six of her seven parcels are under grazing permits. The seventh is leased. The leases are binding contracts and are for five years, whereas the grazing permits can be revoked at the end of the year.

All of the technical or business matters concerning the leasing and grazing rights to Ms. Catches' parcels are handled by the BIA Agency Land Office at Pine Ridge. There are now about 820,000 acres of allotted land on the reservation. This land has about 7,000 owners, but 45,000 separate ownership interests. "Most of the landowners are Oglala Sioux. The renters are [white] cattle ranchers, some of them millionaires" (*Akwesasne Notes* 1974b:17).

Not only has Ms. Catches been rendered a pauper landlord by this peculiar land tenure system, but her land is rented entirely without her permission. In fact, 75 percent of the landowners on the Pine Ridge Reservation have not given their permission to the government to rent land in which they hold interests, in spite of the fact that the government is supposed to get their permission according to its own regulations.

> Ms. Catches is listed as an "o" in the computer code which designates whether she gave authority for grazing permits. The "o" means she could not be located, which, if true, would legally give the BIA the right to grant the permits without her specific authority. But Ms. Catches is easy to locate. She lives on the reservation. She teaches at the Holy Rosary Mission, only a few miles from BIA offices in the village of Pine Ridge. In January, she ran for public office, and was the third highest vote-getter in her district (*Akwesasne Notes* 1974b:16).

The BIA's own records show that such land transactions happen all the time at Pine Ridge. These illegal transactions, which serve only to defraud Native American landowners, involve hundreds of thousands of acres and dollars. The stituation at Pine Ridge, however, is not dissimilar to many other reservations and Indian areas where there are allotted lands. In fact, unauthorized land transactions are commonplace. Therefore, grazing permits and the leasing of Native American lands to whites are a major source of economic expropriation leading to pauperism.

The exploitation described above could not exist were it not for the heirship problem.

The source of heirship and land fractionalization lay in the 1887 Indian Allotment Act which, until 1934, created individual allotments totalling almost 41 million acres. Today, almost 13 million acres of the remaining Native American land base remains allotted, half in single ownership, and the other half in heirship status. That in heirship status continues to grow with every new generation, thereby increasing the magnitude of the problem. Lagone (1969b:525) explains the situation:

> Since the General Allotment Act provided that title would be held in trust by the Federal government for 25 years—and this period was continued by congressional and presidential action—the death of an Indian owning such a tract required that, as his estate, it be divided among his heirs. Obviously, since the title was held in trust—and the heirs were considered "incompetent" to handle their own affairs—there could be no physical partition but only a division of interests on paper. For the non-Indian the same situation would be met by sale of the land and a division of the proceeds or by physically dividing the land among the heirs, each parcel thereafter being a separate estate. But the Federal Government, in attempting to protect the Indian, brought about the Indian heirship land problem we are facing today. Through the 80-odd years since the General Allotment Act the same tract of land may have been divided several times—on paper—and the number of heirs to one tract of land, in many

cases, exceeds 100. . . . The problem has snowballed to the extent that it is overwhelming in its complexity today.

Half the heirship lands are in the northern Plains reservations, and it is among Cheyenne River and other Sioux, the Blackfeet, Crow, etc., that the problem is extremely severe.

Water Rights

Water in itself is extremely valuable, aside from its value in the development process. Irrigated farming, for example, is the basic industry for many Indian communities, and water is worth at least $25 per acre-foot during the 6-month irrigation season (American Indian Policy Review Commission (1977:329). Yet a third of all Indian land stands idle because of a lack of water. All too often, water is available but is denied the Indian peoples because of state and corporate water interests. Deloria (1969b:92) writes that "attached to every major Interior Department appropriation bill is a litte rider stating that no federal funds can go to develop the water rights of the tribes of California, Oregon, and Nevada."

In a 1908 Supreme Court decision, *Winters v. United States,* Indian water rights were given priority over any other rights on streams or lakes which arise upon, border, traverse or underlie reservations. But this ruling has been enforced infrequently by the government; the BIA does not adequately watchdog Indian interests. Pyramid Lake, California, a lake which originally surpassed Lake Tahoe in size and beauty, is an example. Under the terms of the Supreme Court ruling, the Paiute Indians, who were deeded the lake in 1859, should have first priority in water rights. Instead, the states of California and Nevada have conspired to lower the water level, in order to appropriate the waters of the Truckee River, which flows out of the lake, for non-Indian interests.

Pyramid Lake is an extremely beautiful lake, home of the prehistoric Chui-ui fish and nesting grounds for the white pelican. It is all that remains of ancient Lake Lahontan, which covered more than 8,000 square miles of what is now western Nevada. Pyramid Lake, today, is approximately twenty-five miles long, four to eleven miles wide, and more than three hundred feet deep.

> As the lake comes into view, its unique and strange beauty is almost startling. The colors of its water, the clean barenness of its desert mountains, and its fantastic tufa formations glowing in the sunlight make it seem unreal. So often heard from Pyramid visitors that it may be a clue to the lake's attraction is the comment, "It seems like a place where time has stood still for thousands of years" (Wheeler 1969:89).

The lake has been the home of Native Americans for at least 11,000 years. The Pyramid Lake band of Northern Paiute are the "kuyuidokado," or "eaters of the Chui-ui fish." Numaga, their great chief in historic times, when forced by the invasion of hostile white miners, prospectors and adventurers into the Pyramid Lake area, successfully led his people into their first battle in 1860. Due to a clever strategem devised by the Indian defenders, more white men died in this battle than in any prior white-Indian engagement in the Far West.

Today, the lake has decreased approximately 87 feet from its depth of a hundred years ago. The Chui-ui face extinction; the trout fishery is exhausted; and the Pyramid Lake Paiute face the end of their economic livelihood, namely, fishing, the issuance of fishing licenses, and recreational use of their natural resource (Wheeler 1969). Their water rights to the lake have been stolen by dams, reclamation projects, and an interstate water compact. (See Veeder 1969).

Another interstate water agreement, the 1922 Colorado River Compact, apportioned the Colorado River water between the states of Colorado, Utah, Wyoming, New Mexico, Arizona, California, and Nevada. After a 1963 Supreme Court water decision involving the Lower Basin states, Arizona moved to utilize its water allotment for the Central Arizona Project. Because of Indian water rights being prior, in this case, the Navajo, Arizona's special interests in 1968 persuaded then Secretary Stewart Udall of the Interior Department to cause a resolution to be "slipped" through the Navajo Tribal Council which would relinquish Indian water rights to Arizona, the Council waiving virtually all rights to Colorado water in return for some minor governmental concessions, among which was $125,000 for the new Navajo Community College project. When the maneuver was later exposed, the Tribal Council rescinded its resolution (Collier 1970:36).

Indian farmers at Ak-Chin, south of Phoenix, Arizona, have seen their water table drop from 50 to 400 feet because of wealthy, off-reservation farmers pumping Indian water. Former Secretary of the Interior Cecil Andrus has explained the government's dilemma (*The Washington Post,* February 6, 1978): "The nation faces a conflict between the legitimate right of Indians to develop their resources and the impairment of enormous capital investments already made by non-Indians in the same water supply." The government's solution, in part, is to compensate Indians for their resource loss by building irrigation projects. Otherwise, Indians would bring suit in court. In one such settlement, Kennecott Corporation is paying Arizona's Pima Indians $1.5 million for past illegal use of the Gila River, and $50 per acre foot for future water. Compensation, however, does not allow Indians to use their precious resource for reservation development.

In a current case, the Papago Indians claim rights to the Santa Cruz Basin underlying Tucson, Arizona. Mining and agricultural interests, and the city, have over the years lowered the water table and caused tremendous erosion and ecological damage to reservation lands. An example of racism is the attitude expressed by the owner of a 5,000 acre pecan farm who pumps one-third of the Santa Cruz Basin water (*The Washington Post*, February 6, 1978): "The Indians are no more entitled to that water than they are to Manhattan Island. They once owned it, but they didn't develop it. The white men did." But to the contrary, the Papago who today live in poverty originally had extensive fields under cultivation using gravity flow irrigation. In fact, the Santa Cruz Basin was so developed that the invading Spaniards wrote glowingly of its lush promise to rival Mexico City.

The Central Arizona and San Juan Chama projects are inimical to Indian water rights in the Southwest. The main purpose of these projects is to divert water from Indian reservations for capitalist appropriation.

> Conceived by the United States Bureau of Reclamation under Department of Interior auspices, the project [CAP] entails the diversion of the waters of the Colorado River from their present route, for agricultural and domestic use in southern Arizona. The rechanneling will also involve the removal of one to two million acre-feet of water from Lake Havasu [on the Havasupai Reservation] . . . (Martone 1974:3).

Affected are the "dry" tribes of southern Arizona—the Yavapai Apache and Papago. Colombia River water is also contemplated for CAP, which would affect Native Americans in the Northwest, who even now have only limited access to their waters.

> The completion of the San Juan Chama Project will have an adverse impact on the Southern Utes, Mountain Utes, Jicarilla Apaches, and Navajos, from whose reservations 110,000 acre-feet of water has been diverted. The project will also affect the Fort Mohave, Chemehuevi, Colorado River Indians, and the Yuma Indian Reservation, all of whose waters are involved in CAP (Martone 1974:5).

Veeder (1969:493–497) cites the example of the Yakimas in the State of Washington where, illegally, 75 percent of the water from Ahtanum Creek has for over 50 years been given to non-Indian interests, thereby critically retarding Yakima economic development in the rich agricultural, Yakima Valley. The Yakimas only recently recovered their water rights, and for the first time have flourishing orchards, although it will be some years yet before orchards mature and are profit-making.

William H. Veeder (1969) testified before the Joint Economic Committee of Congress on the economic development of American Indian communities. Veeder, a BIA water expert, pointed out that Indian economic development is inseparable from Indian rights to land and water. Although the Supreme Court and other courts have always accorded to Native Americans the paramount and superior status to waters which arise upon, border, traverse, or underlie reservations, federal Indian policies have often negated these rights. The answer to this contradiction is to be found in the conflict of interest within the Interior Department. Its Bureaus of Reclamation and Land Management conflict with Indian water and land rights respectively, which are supposedly protected by the Bureau of Indian Affairs. Both the Interior and Justice Departments take antipodal positions in cases where Indian water rights conflict with Reclamation and other projects (Veeder 1969:492–493). Attorneys in the Department of Justice, for example, charged with bringing suits to *protect* Indian rights, must at the same time represent the United States *against* Indians seeking restitution for the violation of their rights by other agencies of government.

Furthermore, a loophole has been found in the Winters Doctrine and is being used by those interests opposed to Native American water rights. In *Arizona v. California* (1963) and the suit brought by Justice and Interior on behalf of the Pyramid Lake Paiutes, Indian water has been placed under control of the federal government. "The United States, therefore, under the guise of defending Indian rights, is actually trying to secure Indian waters for its own" (Martone 1974:7).

States have also made their intrusion into Indian water rights. The National Water Commission in 1968 recommended that rights to water should be determined in state, rather than federal, courts. But state courts have historically ruled in favor of non-Indian vested interests, such as big ranching outfits and subdivision speculators, rather than the Native American peoples and nationalities.

Water, more than any other single resource, illustrates the conspiracy against Native American economic rights. In addition to those cases mentioned above, Veeder (1969:513–518) documents other violations of Indian water rights: those Indian tribes along the Lower Colorado River

Basin; those in the Missouri River Basin (Ft. Peck and Crow Reservations); California Indians who have been "robbed of their rights to the use of water"; and other reservations, such as the Flathead and Gila River Indian Reservations. As Jorgensen (1978:61) contends, "It is clear that irreparable damage to the Indians in the United States has been caused by the expropriation of Indian resources by the federal government in service of the metropolis."

President Carter's energy program threatened Indian water rights under the Winters Doctrine, and thereby sought to deny Native Americans the possibility of developing their own industries. Indian water is, under law, private property, but the government seeks to bargain water rights away to corporate interests. (We have to see where the Reagan administration will stand on this question.)

The Case of Black Mesa

Inextricably linked with water is the extensive strip mining underway on the Navajo and Hopi reservations in Arizona. To support the continued growth of Los Angeles, to achieve a steady increase in energy consumption, and to allow the rich to become richer, a series of coal-fired, electrical generating stations are being constructed in New Mexico, Arizona, Utah and Colorado. The project is promoted by a group of 23 electric utilities from seven Western states. In the 1950s, West Associates started construction on seven of the largest electric power plants in the world, and the largest strip mine in the nation, which will burn 94 million tons of coal each year to produce electricity. These multi-megawatt, coal-burning plants will use vast amounts of Indian coal and fossil water—non-renewable resources—to carry electric power to Pheonix, Tucson, Albuquerque, Salt Lake City, San Diego and Los Angeles. Yet, according to *Akwesasne Notes* (1976:22), only one out of three Navajo homes has electric lights, and only one out of five has running water and inside plumbing. Among the non-Indian users of the electricity, furthermore, are the Bureau of Reclamation and two federally-funded water projects, the Salt River Project and the Central Arizona Project, which benefit large white- or corporation-owned farms. By 1978 two plants were already in operation, the Navajo and the Four Corners plants.

The pollution created by the project is hard to imagine. In 1966 Gemini 12 photographed from space an ash-laden plume 230 miles long from the Four Corners plant at Fruitland, New Mexico. Yet the air was once so clear that one could see for 100 miles. The plant began operations in 1963 and is now slated for expansion. During 1964 and since, there has been a marked increase in respiratory diseases among the local Indian population. Although emission control devices now remove much of the sulfur and dense smoke, pollution-related health problems persist.

Water is like gold in the arid Southwest. Besides polluting the air, the project will use tremendous amounts of scarce water. One plant alone uses 92 million gallons of water per day from the Colorado River, or more than the entire domestic water supply for San Francisco.

A leaflet, entitled "Suicide in the Southwest" and circulated in defense of Black Mesa, lists the diverse threats to the land and life posed by the strip mining operations and construction of the power plants. These include the withdrawal of billions of gallons of fossil water from beneath Black Mesa and the consequent threat to the springs and water tables on which the Hopi and Navajo depend; the further pollution of the Colorado River, its tributaries and Indian agricultural lands by the salts, clay and sulfur residues eroded down from the strip-mined areas of the mesa; and the several hundred tons of sulfur dioxide, oxides of nitrogen and particulate matter emitted into the air daily by the power plants. The document might have added that Black Mesa is a religious shrine.

An ecology leaflet in defense of the Grand Canyon asserts that "what we are faced with is a complete obliteration of the entire Southwest." Even the *Wall Street Journal* (Blundell, April 13, 1971) has admitted that the "area of fallout, as it were, may include six national parks, including The Grand Canyon; 28 national monuments; the big national recreation areas of Lake Mead and Lake Powell; and the historic Indian lands of the Southwest."

Black Mesa came to public attention in 1970. Black Mesa, the female mountain, is sacred to both Hopi and Navajo traditional Indians, but, today, it is being strip-mined for coal to supply the Mohave and Navajo plants. Two 30-year leases with Peabody Coal Company on Navajo and Hopi lands were made, one in 1964 for strip mining 40,000 acres in the Navajo Nation, and the other in 1966 for 25,000 acres in the Joint Use Area of the Hopi Reservation. A separate lease was signed for Indian water to carry the coal in a slurry line to the power plant at Lake Powell. Water for the slurry is drawn from five deep wells that tap a fossil acquifer millions of years old. The mesa will be almost totally destroyed, the run-off ruining agricultural lands, and the Indian inhabitants forced to relocate. A

Ford Foundation report found that it will take at least 300 years to reclaim the land at Black Mesa, if at all. *It is an environmental disaster!*

The leases were negotiated and signed before the Indian people knew what happened. As Clemmer (1978:17) states:

> There had been no open hearings, no community discussion, no administrative disclosures by either their own tribal government or the Bureau of Indian Affairs. . . Indians had lost control of 65,000 acres of land, and not more than a handful of people appeared to know anything about it.

Clemmer also reports that Peabody will make $750 million by selling coal to the two power plants. By the same token, the Hopi will receive only $14 million and the Navajo $58 million in royalty payments. This may seem like a lot of money, but one must consider that the Navajo Nation has an annual budget of $15-20 million. Thus the royalty money realized from the coal lease would amount to less than $2 million a year, a relatively small part of the modest tribal budget.

Peabody is the strip miner primarily responsible for the rape of Appalachia. The company is an example of the emergence of industrial conglomerates in post-World War II United States. In 1955 Peabody's profits were $9,430,000, a sizeable sum, but by 1963 its annual earnings had increased to $30,470,000. Since that date Peabody has become a subsidiary of Kennecott Copper. Reorganized in 1978, Kennecott Corporation's sales jumped from $1.9 billion to $2.4 billion by 1980. The Peabody affiliate helped contribute to the Kennecott success story. And Indian coal is part of the saga.

Industrial conglomerates not only victimize the public through escalating prices; they have also moved onto Indian reservations to maximize profits. In 1971, for the first time in U.S. history, strip mining produced more coal than underground mines. One reason for the change is technology, huge machines that take carload-sized bites out of Mother Earth. A related reason is higher profits, because strip mining is cheaper. Strip mining is now very much a part of the new U.S. Indian frontier.

The technology used in strip mining is almost inconceivable. Consider the ''Gem of Egypt,'' a giant earth-moving machine which weighs 7,000 tons and has a 125 cubic yard bucket capable of scooping 200 tons of earth at one bite. There is also ''Big Muskie,'' one of Ohio's tourist attractions and the pride of the Central Ohio Coal Company, which ''stands 20 stories high, lifts a boom 310 feet long operated by a five-

inch steel cable, and scrapes away 325 tons of overburden per scoop"
(Caudill 1973:88).

> We have created surface-mining tools of unbelievable size and power, and
> effectiveness: gigantic bulldozers, power shovels and drills, huge but agile
> "high-lifts," trucks that carry 60 tons per load, and cheap explosives com-
> pounded of petroleum and fertilizer. . . Mountains are taken apart layer by
> layer. Plains are plowed to shreds and reduced to formless chaos (Caudill
> 1973:88).

As for the Indian jobs created, Clemmer (1978:31–32) reports that
during construction in 1973, the Black mesa project employed only 440
Navajo out of a total work force of 2,200, that is, 20 percent of the
workers were Navajo. By 1977 the number was reduced to 300 Navajo
and two Hopi. Discrimination at the Page power plant led to unioniza-
tion. Savage (1972:14) states that the Four Corners plant had 240 employees, one-third of them Indians with an average monthly income of
$640. Hardly a high standard of living! Thus the supposed positive
aspects of reservation "development," the employment and tribal income created, hardly balance off the negatives. In fact, the loss of
traditional occupations like farming and herding, to say nothing of the
ecological destruction of Black Mesa, may far outweigh any minor gains.

The Indians must balance their "windfall" against the loss of their
most precious asset, water. Peabody pumps 2300 gallons a minute to
slurry the coal mined to the generating plants. The Navajo gave up rights
to Colorado River water for a bargain price, and Interior would not let the
Navajo Tribal Council renegotiate. Wells have been drilled 3500 feet into
the heart of Black Mesa. A total of 37 billion gallons of fossil water will
be pumped over the next thirty-five years (Loeffler 1972:14). The director of the Hopi Arts and Crafts Cooperative, Fred Kabotie, observed
sadly that "it's a crime to use so many acre-feet of that precious water to
slurry coal some two hundred seventy-five miles away. Money is all
right, but the contract is for thirty-five years and when there is no water
left there will be no life" (Jordan 1972:24).

Why did the Hopi and Navajo tribal councils so readily give their
consent in the first place? Both peoples were caught in a squeeze play
between two Bureaus within the Department of interior, Reclamation and
the BIA. The name of the game was the Central Arizona Project.

Several years ago the Sierra Club fought to save the Grand Canyon
from the dams of the Bureau of Reclamation. The plan to flood the
canyon was part of a monstrous irrigation scheme, the Central Arizona

Project. Environmentalists won out only because other states, notably Colorado and California, jealously feared Arizona's move to appropriate Colorado River water, and therefore came to oppose the measure. After the Grand Canyon plan was defeated in Congress, a new strategy was devised by Arizona interests to accomplish essentially the same ends. The strategy was born at the Interior Department, and it centered around Black Mesa instead of the Grand Canyon.

> Use the coal to fuel the plants, use the watts from the plant to pump the Colorado, use the water from the Colorado to cool the plant and to turn Arizona into a Southern California, complete with its own Los Angeles [i.e., Phoenix]. By using Black Mesa as the footstool for the Central Arizona Project, Interior could also establish a long-needed model for getting Indians into the system at an appropriate point of entry—the bottom. Cheap coal, cheap water, cheap power, cheap red labor (Linford 1972:26).

Planning for CAP goes as far back as 1947, and, although modified by political expediency from time to time, it was at last realized in Black Mesa through a circuitious strategy. Faced with the stigma and defeat of its earlier termination policy, the government shifted its game plan to that of an "economic partnership" between private business, the government, and the Indian nationalities of the Southwest. Under this plan the government uses its power over the corporate tribes which is vested in the Bureau of Indian Affairs. In February, 1967, Stewart Udall, Secretary of Interior under Kennedy, issued a report to Congress which shifted the administration's support from the Grand Canyon dams to a plan involving federal participation. A plant would be built at Page, the Navajo plant, and be fueled by coal from an obscure Indian shrine, Black Mesa. The environmentalists opposed to the Grand Canyon dams had not heard of Black Mesa. The strategy worked, the opposition lifted, and President Johnson signed a bill in September, 1968, which authorized CAP.

Udall was not the only political notable involved. According to Linford (1972), writing in *Clear Creek,* support for CAP came from two independent interest groups in Arizona: the irrigators and the politicians. The Bureau of Reclamation and the BIA worked hand-in-glove to smooth the way for CAP. A major part of their efforts, as related earlier, was the BIA pressure on the Navajo tribal council which forced through a resolution giving up the Navajo portion of Arizona's Colorado River water allotment to CAP, this despite the 1908 Winters' Doctrine which allows the Indian peoples "first rights" on all water touching their reservations. This was in exchange for expected royalties from Black Mesa, employment prospects, and funding for the Navajo Community College. In short, Reclamation and the BIA, both located in the Interior Department, collaborated in the interest of pushing through CAP, but at the expense of Native American land and water rights.

Reclamation is entitled to 24.3 percent of the electrical output from the Navajo Plant. This was in return for an equal share from federal funding sources and is part of Udall's program for an economic partnership between government, big business, and energy-rich Indian nationalities. The government's conflict of interest in this case is obvious:

> The Department [of Interior] is thus a buyer of the water and coal on the Indians' lands of Black Mesa. It is also trustee of the lands which it advised the Indians to lease and of those very resources it buys, clearly a conflict of interest (Savage 1972:19).

> Reclamation has as its constituency the lawyers, bankers, venture capitalists, industrialists, utilities, agribusinesses, construction combines and politicians who make money out of water and all the things that can be produced from it—including electricity. The Bureau of Indian Affairs, on the other hand, has a constituency made up of the most severely deprived economic group in the nation . . . (Linford 1972:28).

Thus both the Navajo and Hopi are caught in a political squeeze play between Interior's Reclamation and Indian Affairs. But Reclamation is not the only government agency which uses the BIA's trust responsibility for its own ends and to the detriment of Native Americans. One could also document cases involving Land Management, Outdoor Recreation, Mines, Sport Fisheries and Wildlife, the National Park Service, and the Forest Service.

There are two contrasting viewpoints among Indians toward energy development. There are those who favor mining, etc., but on the condition that the income is enough for Indians to develop alternate sources of productive income for the time when the energy resources are depleted. Then there are the traditionals who, for spiritual reasons, are opposed to mining altogether.

For those Indian leaders who favor development, but at fair royalty rates, it is an uphill fight. The Navajo, for example, receive only 15-20¢ per ton on coal mined, whereas the United Mine Workers of America, in comparison, levies an 80¢ per ton royalty for wage benefits. The capital and operating costs of the coal companies at Navajo have been estimated at $6.09 per ton. With sales at $8.35 per ton at the mine site, the immediate profit is $2.26 per ton compared to the pennies paid to the Navajo. The

Navajos receive only a 12-16 percent royalty on their crude oil compared to the Arab countries which receive 50-66 percent. Facts such as these have led critics to accuse the government of neocolonialism, of running a resource rather than a development economy in the Navajo Nation.

The Southwest is a major stronghold of traditional Indian peoples and nationalities. The most traditional are the Hopi, and it is they who have led the attack against Peabody. They, along with a coalition of Indians and a number of environmental groups, and represented by attorneys from the Native American Rights Fund, initiated a number of law suits in the 1970s. The Hopi and their supporters were up against the overwhelming financial and political power of both the federal government and the major utility companies. The utilities were represented by high-powered law firms with unlimited manpower and money, and the support of experts with impressive credentials, including even an archaeologist retained by the Tucson Gas and Electric Company.

> The power companies' economic clout allows them to wage expensive . . . public relations campaigns. The utilities use the prospect of an increased tax base and increased unemployment to cajole away the Indians' right to a clean environment. . . The utilities and the coal companies are pillars of the corporate state. Their skilled lobbyists have easy access to lawmakers, many of whom have been ex-employees.

> The power plants, strip mines, and transmission lines are located in some of the poorest and most underdeveloped sections of our country. Local residents, desperate for jobs, are forced to welcome development, regardless of the environmental price (Brecher 1972:62).

The history of Hopi opposition to Black Mesa and the current energy development started in 1951 when the BIA, with the support of "progressive" Hopi from Moenkopi, New Oraibi, and First Mesa, revived the Hopi Tribal Council. (See Clemmet, 1978, from whom the following information is drawn.) The Hopis were told that the corporate tribal council was their only hope to get land back which had been lost to the Navajos. Attorney John Boyden of Salt Lake City was hired to file a Hopi land claim, despite the fact that the traditional Hopis had refused to recognize the Indian Land Claims Commission altogether.

In 1961 the Secretary of the Interior, acting on a request by Boyden on behalf of the Tribal Council, authorized the Council to lease Hopi lands. Yet the Hopi Constitution, under Article VI, Section 1(c), expressly instructed the Council to "prevent the sale disposition, lease or encumbrance of tribal lands" (Clemmer 1978:27). By 1963 the Council had already let $3 million in oil and gas exploration leases. One million dollars were paid to Boyden for his work, and the remainder went down the "rabbit hole" of an industrial venture which failed. The Black Mesa leases were rationalized as a continuation of the Council's authority. Yet, when the second lease was signed in 1966, the Council's legality was still ambiguous.

By 1971 the political (traditional) leaders of five villages had retained John Echohawk, an Indian attorney, and the Native American Rights Fund to file a lawsuit against Peabody Coal and Secretary of the Interior Rogers Morton. The Hopi united against their own Tribal Council, and the Black Mesa issue hit the major media.

The activity of the Black Mesa Defense Fund in Santa Fe led to on-site hearings held by the Senate Committee on Interior and Insular Affairs to assess the environmental, social and economic impact of WEST's Southwest energy project. As a result, the largest of the projected plants at Kaiparowits, Utah, was cancelled. In 1972 the Committee to Save Black Mesa invited a delegation of Northern Cheyenne to view the Black Mesa strip mine firsthand. A year later their tribal council cancelled all energy leases on the reservation.

In 1975, however, the case against Black Mesa "development" was lost in court.

Energy Resources

Over one hundred years ago, the government forced Native Americans at gunpoint onto seemingly useless lands in the West. Today, however, it is known that these lands contain some of the nation's richest deposits of coal, oil, gas and uranium. According to the Council of Energy Resource Tribes (CERT), the 23 Indian nationalities in 10 western states, representing about two-thirds of the Native American population, have 33 percent of the country's low-sulfur, strippable coal, 80 percent of its uranium reserves, and 3 to 10 percent of all petroleum and gas. Alaska, alone, has inestimable wealth in energy resources, craddling hundreds of billions of dollars in oil, natural gas, coal, uranium and other minerals. It is already the number two oil-producing state and is fast becoming number one. And Alaska is a state where Native peoples have rights to 44 million acres of land.

Former President Nixon in November, 1973, established the goal of U.S. energy independence by 1980, and the doubling of coal production by 1985. These policies necessarily affect resource-rich tribes, since an estimated 70 billion tons of coal reserves, worth over $1,000 billion, and 16 percent of all U.S. energy resources are found on Indian lands (Raines 1979:21). The second keystone in former President Jimmy Carter's energy program, in addition to traditional fuels, was nuclear power. More than half the nation's uranium is found in the Grants Mineral Belt in New Mexico on Navajo and Pueblo Indian lands. The Reagan Administration is pledged to expanding traditional fuels.

Accordings to a 1975 report of the Federal Energy Commission, Indian lands have already produced over $2.7 billion in oil and gas, $187 million in coal, $349 million in uranium, and over $434 million in zinc, phosphate, copper and limestone. Yet, in the Navajo Nation, the coal companies are receiving an average net profit of $2.26 per ton while the Navajos receive only 15–20¢ per ton on their non-renewable resource. This is the Indian differential in terms of the resource "rip-off"!

Since World War II the production of coal and uranium has become increasingly monopolized. By 1972, fifteen large companies, many recently acquired by oil, steel, and electric utility corporations, accounted for over 50 percent of all U.S. coal production. By the early 1970s, more than one-third of coal produced came from open pit rather than underground mines. Furthermore, more than 90 percent of these low-sulfur coal reserves are located in western United States, much of it owned by either the federal government or Indian nationalities. The fifteen large corporations control 70 percent of the land under lease for coal extraction in the West. The largest coal company is Peabody, owned by Kennecott Corporation. Consolidation, owned by Continental Oil, is second. Both are tied to agribusiness.

In uranium, four firms now control 55 percent, and eight companies control 80 percent, of all production. Uranium extraction, already concentrated on Indian reservations, is expanding. Nafziger (1979:3) reports that "in New Mexico alone, by 1979, thirty-one companies are actively exploring and developing uranium on or around Indian reservations. Exploration efforts have nearly doubled since 1976, while the number of mines and mills has increased to seven mills and 43 mines. Current development efforts are expected to triple by 1986."

Parenthetically, there is an interesting relationship linking U.S. Indian reservations with the incredible monopolization internationally in the uranium field. Uranium production and reserves are controlled within five developed nations—USA, Canada, Australia, France and South Africa—and "are located either within internal colonies of those nations, such as

Indian reservations in the U.S. and Canada, and the aboriginee reserves in Australia, or in colonies and neocolonies. . ." (Nafziger 1979:3).

The Navajo Nation, equal in size to West Virginia, is energy rich. Its mineral wealth consists in 100 million barrels of oil, 25 billion cubic feet of natural gas, 5 billion tons of easily accessible coal, and 80 million pounds of uranium (Ruffing 1979:27). Yet, despite its proven resources, there is a tragic gap between the value of Navajo mineral wealth and the standard of living of Navajo people. Per capita income is $900, unemployment is 33.5 percent, underemployment is 44.7 percent, education level is five years, average age of death is 45 years, 14 percent of the children die before the age of five, and 80 percent of the homes are substandard. Clearly, energy "development" by the corporations is not bringing prosperity to the Navajo people.

Industrial energy developments on reservations characterize the 1970s. These developments centered on coal extraction and uranium mining, and were augmented by former President Carter's energy policies. Industrial energy projects, centered on the extraction and burning of Indian-owned coal, like the Black Mesa project, are being built to generate electricity for the urban centers of southern California, Arizona and Nevada. These plants will produce 5,000 megawatts of electrical power, or enough power for nearly five million American homes. The energy projects include the Four Corners plant at Fruitland, New Mexico; the Utah International Mine which supplies coal to the Four Corners plant; the Navajo Generating Station near Page, Arizona; two coal mines at Black Mesa; the Black Mesa and Lake Powell Railroad which conveys coal from the Black Mesa mines to the Navajo Generating Station; and the Black Mesa slurry line which conducts the coal to the Mohave plant near Bullhead City, Nevada. This vast network of coal extraction and related facilities are owned by utility and mining companies, not the corporate Indian tribes. Even the U.S. Bureau of Reclamation owns a piece of the action.

The U.S. government contends that mineral extraction by the energy corporations is a cure-all for reservation underdevelopment, but this is not true. "The Navajo Tribe has received crumbs and local residents have acquired only a few jobs while paying all of the environmental and psychological costs" (Robbins 1978a:48). Although more than $1 billion has already been invested in plant facilities in the Navajo Nation, only $17 million a year is realized in personal and tribal income from energy development. The Navajos estimate that it will take $380 million per year for 10 years to bring their standard of living up to the national average. Thus the amount of income realized from mineral extraction has a long way to go before it materially helps the Navajo people. Energy leases, royalities, rents and bonuses have contributed relatively little to the tribal treasury, and wages have added little to personal income.

Understandably, the Navajo are unhappy with the current situation. In 1978 angry citizens shut down reservation oil operations at Montezuma Creek, Utah, where Texaco, Continental, Superior and Phillips control most of the 800 wells which pump $100 million a year in oil. The underlying issue was the Navajo desire to control oil operations on their own land. Backed by the Navajo Tribal Council, complaints included dissatisfaction with the terms of the oil leases, ecological damage to traditional economic activities, harassment of local people, and failure by the oil companies to hire an appreciable number of Navajo workers (*Los Angeles Times,* April 13, 1978). The Navajos won all but the key demand, the oil leases, which the companies refused to renegotiate (Robbins 1978:47).

Facts such as the above led Ruffing (1979:25), an UNCTAD economist, to charge that the "Navajo Nation appears to be an internal colony of the U.S. in every conceivable sense. It is isolated geographically; it is discriminated against racially and culturally; it is dominated politically, economically and ideologically."

The Northern Cheyenne Reservation is a half-million acre area containing 3,000 Indians. It has a small sawmill and a cattle-raising industry. Even so, unemployment is high and per capita income is $1,700 a year. It has now been found that the reservation is atop 23 billion tons of coal. Thus, in the 1960s, the Northern Cheyenne leased out their mineral rights to more than half the reservation. Later, they sought to cancel their coal leases and develop their less polluting oil and gas resources. The Northern Cheyenne are the first local government in the United States to invoke the Clean Air Act, in order to preserve existing air quality (Gapay, 1978). But their valiant struggle to preserve their environment is an uphill one. Montana Power, and Pacific Power and Light Company plan two power plants at Colstrip 13 miles from the reservation. Montana Power already has two plants in operation and a strip mine there. There are surface coal mines planned in every direction around the reservation, including those planned by the Crow Indians on their nearby reservation.

Theoretically, energy-rich Native American tribes should be raking in the money through royalties. The Department of the Interior, in collaboration with the Department of Energy, however, sets royalties at a minimum. Indian peoples are receiving considerably less than the value of the minerals extracted. "The Navajos receive only 8.5 percent of the market value of their resources while bearing most of the social and environmental costs," reports Ruffing (1980:2). And the Jicarilla Apache received a mere $685,000 in bonus money for oil leases worth at least $80 million if fair market value were paid.

Royalty rates are usually too low. Being fixed in dollars per unit of production, the rates ignore the increase in value of the product. For example, "in four out of the five Navajo coal leases consummated between 1957 and 1968, the royalty was fixed between $0.15–$0.375 a ton. Since then, the average value per ton of coal rose from $4.67 (1968) to $18.75 (1975)" (American Indian Policy Review Commission 1977:339). The American Indian Policy Review Commission found that Native Americans have been unable to develop their own resources because of their lack of control over the resources, lack of technological expertise and skilled labor, and lack of capital. The AIPRC (1977:346) concluded:

> The BIA seldom attempted to assist the tribes in tribal development of their mineral and petrochemical resources. Rather, its involvement in resource exploitation has consisted largely of arranging leases of Indian land including the mineral contents to major petrochemical and mining companies at questionable rates.

> Indian people are losing valuable non-renewable resources to corporate developers. The return to Indian individuals and tribes is minimal. The most valuable development asset of many tribes is being wasted for them.

The reservation dilemma is this: Despite the fact that proven resources, particularly energy resources, are very considerable, Native Americans rank at the bottom of virtually every social statistic. There are energy-rich tribes where families live in poverty: 54.8 percent on Cheyenne River, South Dakota; 77.3 percent of Navajo and Hopi in Arizona. Pratt (1979:44), writing on Indian sovereignty, asks the fundamental question: "How do we explain this disparity between apparent resource holdings (and income potential) and the grim realities?" It is explained by the fact that although Indians own their resources, they do not control them! Native Americans own their lands only in the technical sense due to the federal "trust" status of reservation lands.

With "development," the Navajo have become dependent on mineral royalties rather than developing and controlling their own economy. In fact, theirs is a distorted economy because 70 percent of the tribal income comes from mineral royalties (Ruffing 1980:2–3). The energy corporations know that the Navajo cannot force renegotiations without critically disrupting services on the reservation, let alone halt the generation of electricity for millions of non-Indian consumers in western United States. The Navajo have been unsuccessful in getting Utah International and Peabody Coal to seriously consider renegotiating their coal leases. Consequently, the Navajo Nation has enacted a possessory interest tax to recapture some of the mineral wealth now being extracted under inequitable leases. The energy corporations, on the other hand, have initiated six lawsuits against the Navajo right to tax, and the issue is not yet decided.

Since 1975 a number of other Indian peoples, such as the Blackfeet in 1975, the Jicarilla Apaches in 1976, and the Colville in 1978, have been able to sign leases that contain significant improvements over the standard federal leases of the past. These tribes, according to Ruffing (1980:3), from whom this information is taken, have not yet developed dependence on mineral revenues. The Navajo and others, however, cannot realistically threaten cancellation because of their excessive dependence on existing leases and, concomitantly, their undiversified economies.

Ruffing (1980:3–5) points out that Native American entities do not have the bargaining power of Third World countries. They do not yet have the power to cancel leases unilaterally or to expropriate property through nationalization. In the Third World, on the other hand, 300 foreign mining and petroleum enterprises were nationalized between 1960 and 1976. In the U.S. case, the role of the government is paramount. The pro-corporation bias of the Department of Interior, plus the energy crisis, has led it to reject the notion of cancelling leases even after the mining corporations refuse to renegotiate. Interior maintains that the "public good," i.e., with respect to the energy crisis, must prevail over the Indians' interests.

CERT has been termed the "Indian OPEC." Yet it was not even consulted in the drafting of the Carter administration's 1979 national energy policy. Although CERT represents 20 percent of the nation's resources, its constituent tribes possess a variety of resources, not just one scarce resource; nor does CERT possess a monopoly on energy resources. Real sovereignty, as Ruffing points out, means not only complete ownership of mineral wealth, but also equitable compensation, Indian employment and training, diversification of the economy, protection of the environment, and the preservation of Indian culture.

Ruffing (1980) suggests that energy-rich tribes, while lacking the power of Third World countries, can nevertheless make more effective use of the media, pool information, develop greater negotiating skills, formulate a coherent mineral policy, implement the policy through regulations or codes, and form a mineral development corporation to ensure the regulations or codes. These are only half-way measures, however. Ultimately, an alliance must be forged with the working class, with progressive unions and mass organizations united in the struggle against monopoly, for racial equality and economic justice.

"Nuclear Indians"

By 1978, according to the Department of Energy (LaDuke 1979:5), 1,185,000 acres of Indian land were under lease for uranium exploration and development in New Mexico, Colorado, Wyoming and Washington. This acreage does not include Indian treaty land, such as the Black Hills, which is under Indian claim. If Indian treaty land were counted, it is estimated that Native Americans would own approximately 80 percent of the uranium in North America.

Uranium is the raw material used to fuel nuclear power plants and to make nuclear weapons. It has a half-life of five billion years. The problem with uranium mining is that it causes cancer. Mill tailings are the major and most difficult form of radioactive wastes that now exist. "Radon gas is one of the decay products of uranium. When inhaled it can cause lung cancer. According to officials from the United Mine Workers, 80-90 percent of uranium miners can expect to die of future lung cancer" (*Akwesasne Notes* 1979:13). When a small, oppressed minority faces odds like these, then uranium mining among Indians becomes a form of genocide.

Two hundred and fifty Navajo Indians worked in the Kerr–McGee mines above Red Rock near Cove, Arizona, from 1952 to 1963. Red Rock had a zero base rate of cancer, meaning that Navajos do not get lung cancer. Of the Navajo miners, however, 20 have died and 20 more are seriously ill. The company also left 71 acres of highly radioactive uranium mill tailings. The tailings pile was left totally exposed and 60 feet from the San Juan River, the major water source in the area. Nearby Shiprock is the largest population center in the Navajo Nation. Navajo workers have since testified that they were never told that uranium was dangerous. Dan T. Benally, who worked for 10 years as a driller and a blaster, told a news conference in Washington, DC, that "we ate lunch underground and drank the water which ran in the mine."

In 1979 an impoundment dam built of uranium mill tailings by United Nuclear Corporation failed and released 93 million gallons of radioactive and chemically dangerous materials into water running through Navajo grazing lands. The accident left contaminated residue over a distance of almost 100 miles. The dam's failure was not totally unexpected since cracks had appeared as far back as December, 1977.

At Laguna Pueblo in New Mexico, the Anaconda Corporation has been mining for 25 years and now has the largest uranium strip mine in the world (LaDuke 1979:6). Laguna water is today contaminated. People have unknowingly built their homes from material contaminated with the radioactive mine tailings.

The Black Hills uranium was discovered in the 1950s and mined principally by Union Carbide and the Tennessee Valley Authority until 1972, when mining became financially unprofitable. Now, however, it is profitable again due to the "energy shortage" and Carter's energy program, which projected 200 nuclear reactors for "peaceful purposes" and the neutron bomb. Nearly one million acres are currently under exploration in the Black Hills by Exxon, Union Carbide, and United Nuclear Homestake. Although one-fourth of all U.S. gold production comes from the Black Hills, uranium is now the most important resource. In fact, the Department of Energy estimates that 31 percent of our domestic uranium reserves lie in nearby Wyoming.

Much of the uranium is in coal. The coal will be strip-mined and probably burned to ash, which can then be milled for the uranium it contains. The burning process, however, produces radioactive gas and dust.

Another method for extracting uranium is solution mining or "earth enemas." This method utilizes great amounts of water. Chemicals are pumped into the aquafir, the uranium dissolved from the sandstone and pumped back out. But there are many unknowns about the effect of the chemicals and whether all the radioactive materials dissolved might not eventually get into water wells. The Tenessee Valley Authority plan calls for five major pit mines, three of which will use Cheyenne River water. How TVA plans to de-contaminate the water has yet to be explained. If the existing water tables are not contaminated, they will be depleted anyway by the projected coal-fired gasification plants planned for the Northern Plains. The entire region surrounding the Black Hills has been termed a "national sacrifice area." The various Sioux, Northern Cheyenne, and affected Indian peoples are necessarily extremely concerned.

Industrial Development

What about industrial development, acclaimed by government agencies only a few years ago as the final solution to Indian poverty? The BIA began in 1955 to encourage small industries to locate on or near reservations, supposedly to provide jobs for resident Indian workers, but nothing much came of the program until the Economic Development Administration (EDA), located in the Department of Commerce, entered the field in 1965. Millions of dollars have now been awarded, yet most of the funds are not directly capital-producing. Between 1962 and 1968, 10,000 jobs were created, but only 40 percent were Indians. This poor showing may be due to the fact that the government has favored non-Indian rather than Indian-owned and operated industries. By 1972 there were as many as 237 of these non-Indian-owned plants, but the ratio of white to Indian employment did not change.

An example of this so-called industrial development is the electronics plant which operated at Zuni in New Mexico from 1967 to 1973 (see Stoffle 1975).

The 5,000 Zuni were 77 percent unemployed and certainly merited being included in the EDA program. During the period of the plant's operation, between 200 and 300 Zuni and Navajo workers produced electrical parts for an aircraft component manufacturer. The Zuni, however, together with the BIA, had to supply the factory site, build the $100,000 plant, supply $50,000 worth of equipment, and provide cheap, government-subsidized labor, including worker pre-production training.

There was the matter of low wages. A condition attached to the contract with the Zuni and the BIA was that all Indian employees must qualify for the government's On-the Job Training (OJT) program. Under this arrangement the Indian employees could be paid the national minimum wage, at that time, $1.60 per hour. Stoffle (1975), from whom this information is taken, does not tell us whether any of the Indian workers were paid at a higher rate, and we conclude that the majority, at least, were not. Since the yearly average wage per worker at this pay scale would have been $3300 at the most, a family trying to live on a fulltime worker's wages would be living at the poverty line.

The story, however, does not end there. The OJT formula allowed the company to pocket half the miserable wages paid its Indian employees, because OJT permits a qualifying company to be reimbursed by the government by one-half the minimum wage rate. This could have netted the company as much as $353,325.65, or nearly $20,000 per month over the three years that the subsidy was given.

Thus we see clearly that the government's program of reservation industrial development utilizes the practice of an Indian wage differential. Wage differentials are low wages paid by companies which discriminate against workers on the basis of region of the country, sex, or race. The Southern differential, for example, discriminates against Black workers in the South, but depresses the wages of white workers as well, since northern Black operatives make 18 percent more than their white counterparts in the South (Hall 1976:10). Our concern here, however, is the government's condoning a wage differential paid to reservation Indians in the name of industrial development. Although we do not know the total amount of money lost to Indian workers through the Indian differential, Hall (1976:3) estimates that the differential paid to non-white workers as a whole is more than $100 billion. Based on this figure we would estimate that at least one billion dollars is lost to Indian workers because of the differential.

The EDA invested tens of millions of dollars in reservation development, much of it in the Navajo Nation, "primarily for the development of water resources and physical facilities to serve non-Indian industries, especially the enormous coal mines, slurry lines, and generating plants" (Jorgensen 1978:62). Over $185 million was funded, 77 percent for public works, such as water resources, sewer systems, and treatment plants. The theory behind the investments was that a reservation infrastructure is a prerequisite for attracting capitalist development. Yet, as Jorgensen (1978:62) points out, the pay-off to Native American peoples and nationalities has been minimal. "The optimistic theory that predicts growth from underdevelopment to development has not been proved on Indian reservations."

A small portion of the EDA loans were for Indian-controlled businesses. An example of "successful" reservation, small business development is the Rosebud Sioux. Located in central South Dakota, the Rosebud Sioux have a population of about 7,000. According to a government report (King 1969:73–74), Rosebud has been one of a limited number of reservations in which both the Office of Economic Opportunity and the EDA have concentrated their resources. One would suppose it would be a real success story. There were five "industries" listed as active in the 1960s. What were these "industrial enterprises," and how successful were they?

The Sioux Dairy Cooperative, initiated in 1965, had a difficult time of it. By 1969 it seemed to be financially marginal and was employing less than 20 people.

The Rosebud Manufacturing Company was initiated in 1965 through tribal financing and a private investor to make formica-topped kitchen counters. It originally employed 47 Sioux men, but by 1969 it had fewer than 20 employees. It was uncertain whether it would survive without the work contracted through a reservation housing program in progress at that time.

The Rosebud Jewelry Company, begun in 1967, lasted only a year.

Rosebud Electronics started in 1967 and was considered in 1969 to be the most successful of the five. It was employing 65 persons to assemble electronic components. While we have no current information, one wonders if it has been a repeat of the Zuni story outlined by Stoffle (1975).

Rosebud Sign Techniques employed five persons to make highway signs for the Bureau of Indian Affairs, and expansion was doubtful.

According to an article in *The Washington Post* (Richards and Peterson, May 30, 1978), the EDA has spent nearly $20 million to build 41 industrial parks on reservations. Occupancy rates, however, run around a dismal 5 percent. They are considered a failure, as are the several Indian shopping centers financed by another EDA program.

The most serious failure, according to a Ford Foundation study in 1977 (Richards and Peterson, 1978), has been the $61 million spent to finance Indian tourist projects. Recreation and tourist attractions are, of course, a potential asset for reservation economies. Examples of these developments include the Kah-Nee-Ta vacation resort on the Warm Springs Reservation in Oregon; the Flathead Tribe's Blue Bay Resort at Polson, Montana; the Havasupai Tourist Lodges at Supai, Arizona; and the Chickasaw Motor Inn at Sulphur, Oklahoma. But, as the Ford study found, while some of these developments might conceivably pay off in the future, they are not doing so at present. "Of the Indian-owned motels and hotels funded by the agency, two are closed and all are running in the red."

Part of the failure, it is charged, is due to EDA's policy of hiring poor or incompetent business consultants for the developments. Additionally, it has been found (Stoffle, Last and Evans, 1979), in a study of northern Arizona reservations, that tourists generally hold a negative impression of Indian reservations, although they appreciate their scenery and are otherwise interested in contemporary Indian culture. With current gasoline costs and the consequent cut-back in tourism, it is doubtful that reservation tourist development will improve the Indian economy in the foreseeable future.

Jorgensen (1978:62) sums up the government's policy of industrial development for reservations:

> . . . Private corporations have used Indian water, Indian capital, and other Indian resources, such as cheap labor, to expand, yet they have used the cheap Indian labor only when Indians possessed the skills deemed appropriate for the jobs. Indians do not maintain ownership or control, and the surplus white populations near the reservations—that is, the better educated groups in the shriveling satellites—have been sucking up most of the jobs that have been made available.

As for assistance to Indian small businesses, requests for government subsidy of Indian-owned and operated small businesses have been turned down on the grounds that Indians lack management skills or experience, and are poor credit risks. Instead, the government has provided poorly-run, white-controlled and unfairly-administered anti-poverty and welfare programs. Under the Reagan administration, it is questionable whether even these will be maintained.

*The responsibility of any nation, and the
particular responsibility of elected officials
of any nation, is not to justify what has
passed for legality, but to anticipate the
conditions and problems of tomorrow and
attempt to deal with them.*

Vine Deloria, Jr.

8

FRIENDS, ENEMIES
AND THE FUTURE

In the first chapter we critically examined the so-called Indian problem
and said that it is a political question arising out of the oppressed status of
Native Americans as indigenous peoples and nationalities, and not a
"problem" of cultural or ethnic differences. In the succeeding chapters
we documented this view by showing that dispossession and economic
exploitation under capitalist relations is the principal cause of powerlessness and underdevelopment. We contended that self-government, with
sovereignty over resources, will lessen this inequality. In conclusion, we
will show that the path to Native American liberation is an integral part of
the larger working-class struggle, and that it must have an anti-monopoly
strategy, including a united approach to electoral politics.

Friends and Allies
At the historic 1977 Geneva conference on discrimination against the
indigenous peoples of the Americas, Romesh Chandra, in his address to
the Final Plenary, highlighted four concepts that Native Americans had
brought to the attention of the international community. These were
NATION, LAND, GENOCIDE and SELF-DETERMINATION. To a

great extent these four key words illuminate the Native American struggle in the United States and comprise the thesis of the present volume.

The reader should by now understand that there is an important national component of the Indian question: not only Native American peoples, but peoples and nations!

Inextricably related to nationality is land—"Our land, our beautiful land, our Mother Earth," as Mr. Chandra, president of the World Peace Council, put it (International Indian Treaty Council 1977:31). Yet there are those who take Native American land, "rob and plunder it, to fill the pockets of a few people who are the enemies" of the land.

Genocide. This is the means by which the land and its wealth is taken. (A future volume will describe and analyze the history of U.S. genocide against the Indians.)

The solution concept is self-determination. Self-determination, said Chandra, means each "people has the right to decide its own destiny, what it wants to do with its own wealth, with its own land, its own life."

Finally, to plan strategy for self-determination, Chandra contended, indigenous peoples must carefully distinguish between friends and enemies. Here Chandra has raised a key question. Native Americans who constitute less than one percent of the total population and occupy only two percent of the U.S. land base, need friends and allies in their fight for self-determination.

Who are these friends and allies? Are they "anthropologists and other friends," the academic community, as Vine Deloria, Jr., wrote in his best-selling novel, *Custer Died For Your Sins* (1969a, Chap. 4)? Although Deloria strongly satirized anthropologists, he made it clear that he still considered them the Indians' friend. In a similar vein he criticized Congress and the church (1969:268–269). Yet we have demonstrated in the first chapter that anthropologists have largely contributed to the mystification of the Native American question rather than the illumination of it. Deloria (1969a:90–91), himself, understands the error of anthropological cultural determinism theory, as indicated in the following passage:

> Regardless of [biculturalism] theory, the Pyramid Lake Paiutes and the Gila River Maricopas are poor because they have been systematically cheated out of their water rights, and on desert reservations water is the most important single factor in life. No matter how many worlds Indians straddle, the Plains Indians have an inadequate land base that continues to shrink because of land sales. Straddling worlds is irrelevant to straddling small pieces of land and trying to make a living.

If one is either part of the solution or else part of the problem, then bourgeois anthropology would seem to be part of the problem. A similar case could be made for Congress and the church.

The point is that the academic community, Congress and the church as major social institutions cannot be considered reliable friends of the Native American movement because of their structural position in bourgeois society. All three have historically supported, and been supported by, the *status quo*. The goals of the oppressed, on the other hand, will be achieved only through radical social change, the restructuring of U.S. society, and in that process, the democratic transformation of the aforementioned institutions.

On the other hand, it is important to recognize that there are, and will always be, courageous scientists, elected officials, church leaders and organizations who speak out on behalf of the oppressed. The humanist anthropologist, Karl Schlesier, is a noteworthy example of Indian advocacy in anthropology (see Schlesier 1974, 1979 and 1980). The former Senator James Abourezk (Dem.–South Dakota), who headed up the American Indian Policy Review Commission, is an example of an Indian friend. And the Board of Church and Society of the United Methodist Church, which actively supported The Longest Walk in 1978, is yet another. Yet one must look beyond "anthropologists and other friends" to those who are oppressed and exploited as an entire class or people by the same monopoly and racist forces that victimize Native Americans.

In 1975 at the annual meeting of the Society for Applied Anthropology in Amsterdam, we attended a panel on action anthropology presented by the noted anthropologist, Sol Tax, and his students. During his presentation Tax suggested a new Chicago Conference for Native Americans like the one he organized in 1960, which issued the important "Declaration of Indian Purpose." Having recently read Deloria's *Behind the Trail of Broken Treaties* (1974), co-titled *An Indian Declaration of Independence*, he proposed that anthropologists again organize such a conference, invite the Indian peoples and assist them as specialists in deciding what their future relationship to the United States should be. We believed Tax's proposal incredibly patronizing and counterposed that anthropologists only fund the conference and assist with its publicity, but that the conference itself, including its agenda, must necessarily be under Indian control. We suggested further that the anthropologist's role should be to help build public support for the all-Indian conference and whatever program it chose to adopt, and that organized labor would be an important potential ally to mobilize in support of that program. Tax, however, took strong exception to our views and announced to the gathering that "Labor is the enemy of the Indian people!"

Is Labor the enemy of the Indian people? To begin with, asserting that Labor is the enemy presupposes that either Native American society is separate and apart from the capitalist political economy, a view we trust this work has convincingly disproved, or else that Native Americans occupy a non-working-class position within capitalism. Both views are incorrect, and one incontrovertible fact must be brought home here: Native Americans are largely working class. To say that Labor is the enemy is to say that Indians are the enemy, a contradiction in terms.

This point is so important that we will take the next few pages to document it and, furthermore, to detail the nature of the position Native Americans occupy in the U.S. working class.

The Native American Worker

Native Americans are "ripped off" not only through the exploitation of their lands and resources, but through their labor power as well. The vast majority are overwhelmingly in the working class: there are no capitalists, very few small business people, relatively few high income professionals and tribal officials, and a dwindling number of independent agriculturalists and herders. According to the 1970 Census, about 60 percent of all Native American men work as operatives, including transport; craftsmen, foremen and the like; and laborers, excluding farm labor. Seventy percent of all women are service workers, excluding private household workers; clerical workers, and operatives.

At the same time, vast sums are realized by the monopolies which, with the tacit, if not active, assistance of the BIA and the Interior Department, exploit native American lands and resources. Widespread unemployment in the Navajo Nation, for example, results in an estimated annual net loss to the Navajo economy of $600 million (Robbins 1977: 50). Yet the Navajo Nation is extremely rich in natural resources which, if properly developed, could provide employment. The Indian peoples have little real control over reservation development and do not own the means of production; in the resource "rip-off," relatively few jobs are generated for their own people. Thus the fight for self-government is an integral part of the struggle for full employment; national and working-class demands are related.

Ironically, because of underdevelopment, the federal government, through the BIA and the Public Health Service, is the single largest employer of Native American workers. According to the 1970 Census, twenty-four percent in the national work force and 32 percent on the reservations are government employees of one kind or another, mostly federal. As government workers they find themselves in the lower grades, receive the lowest wages, and are the first to be fired. This fact has been documented by the National Indian Youth Council (1973:2). In 1973 a coalition of Native American groups in the San Francisco Bay Area filed a class action civil rights complaint charging that federal agencies were discriminating in their employment policies. The complaint estimated that "the American Indian community would earn an additional $150 million per year, or $1.5 billion over the next decade" if given equal employment opportunities ("Bear Facts Newsletter" 1973:10). From this viewpoint, it can truly be said that the U.S. government is an exploiter of Native American labor.

Each racial and national section of the U.S. working class has special characteristics. It is therefore necessary to underline at the outset that most Indian workers are poor, unemployed or underemployed.

Poverty and Unemployment
Poverty is extremely severe for those on reservations where incomes are below the poverty line, with rates ranging from 20.3 percent at Laguna Pueblo in New Mexico, to 72.4 percent on the Navajo-Hopi joint use area in Arizona. The average for the 24 largest reservations listed in the 1970 Census (U.S. Dept. of Commerce, 1973:171–173) is 55.1 percent, and 46.8 percent for "all other identified reservations." On the two largest, federally-recognized Indian areas, the deficit family income (the amount needed to reach poverty level!) is $2,844 and $2,329 respectively. But even the figures for "tribes," which include members living off reservations, are extremely high, ranging in eastern United States from 22.2 percent for the Mohawk to 40.9 percent for the Lumbee, and in the West, 52.2 percent for the Ute, and 60.2 percent for the Navajo.

Due to astronomical rates of rural unemployment, Native Americans are forced into the cities in search of work. But in the urban areas, one out of four lives in poverty. Median income is low: $7,323 for "all families" and $3,695 for "female head" in 1970. The urban Indian worker faces racism and chauvinism, and is the poorest of the oppressed minorities. A study by Jorgensen (1971) of 1960 census data shows that, although Native Americans in California are probably the best trained and most highly motivated of any state's Indian work force, they had an unemployment rate four times the state's average, and generally held temporary or unskilled jobs.

Although city income is on the average higher, the urban worker, too, faces job discrimination. If, on the other hand, there were self-government and a strong reservation economy at home, an Indian member of such a powerful collective would stand a better chance of demanding fair working conditions and decent wages in the city. Thus self-determination for Native American peoples and nationalities is directly related to the improvement of the lot of the Indian worker generally, whether rural or urban.

The main reason for poverty, of course, is unemployment. The official unemployment rate for Native Americans in 1970, according to the Census, was 10.7 percent. For urban Indians it was 9.1 percent, and for rural, non-farm Indian people, 13.2 percent. The official rate, however, hides real unemployment because, for one reason, chronically unemployed workers do not show up in work force statistics. Only 63 percent were in the work force in 1970, compared to 75 percent for Blacks and 80 percent for whites. Tens of thousands of Indian and Alaska Native workers have become, as Marx termed it, part of the Lazarus layers of the permanently unemployed.

A BIA survey (1973) on Indian unemployment included Native Americans living on or near federal reservations, those living in the former reservation areas of Oklahoma, and those in Alaska. The BIA found an overall rate of 37 percent unemployed for the "resident Indian population," about 65 percent of the total U.S. Native American population. When temporary employment is added, however, the figure jumped to 55 percent. In the Indian states, and in order of size of the labor force, the unemployment-underemployment rate was 55 percent for Arizona, 52 percent for New Mexico, 42 percent for Oklahoma, 77 percent for Alaska, 57 percent for South Dakota, 48 percent for Montana, 58 percent for Washington, and 54 percent for North Dakota. When broken down by Indian agencies, the BIA found instances of rates higher than state levels. The Bethel Agency, for example, corresponding to a huge Eskimo area of southwest Alaska, had a rate of 91 percent!

Astronomical rates of poverty and unemployment therefore characterize the Native American working class. Excluding people from economic life is the structural basis for the social genocide practiced by capitalism against the indigenous peoples and nationalities and is the present-day extension of the genocide of the past.

Chronic reservation unemployment has been a dominant process since World War II. Able-bodied workers in an Apache community where the author worked in 1962 consisted of about 300 persons out of a total of 1500. The only steady jobs were those at the tribal store, the service station, the government school, the U.S. Public Health Service clinic, the tribal farm, and the police force—about 25 jobs in all! Others sought work off the reservation on nearby white-owned farms. A few steady jobs were filled by community people who commuted weekly to mines and lumber mills in other parts of the state.

For the reservation population as a whole, in an Apache work force of about 2,000 people, job opportunity was limited to roughly 150 slots. These consisted of jobs with the Bureau of Indian Affairs, the U.S. Public Health Service, the tribal office and its commercial enterprises (cattle, farm, gas stations, cafe). The only other avenues for fulltime employment meant leaving the reservation, either by joining the armed services or going on government relocation to far-away cities, such as Los Angeles, San Francisco and Denver.

A similar situation exists for most western reservations, but we must caution against those, such as Jorgensen (1978), who tend, even sympathetically, to consign Native Americans to a non-class position, i.e., consumers in the "satellite" sector of the national economy. The San Carlos Apaches, for example, were the backbone of the eastern Arizona labor force in the early decades of this century (see Talbot 1977). They built many of the railroads, dams and highways, and after World War I, they worked in Arizona's mines as well. The Depression drove them from the labor force, and they did not re-enter the job market until World War II. After the war the majority of Apache workers were again consigned to capitalism's reserve army of unemployed or underemployed labor.

Industries and Unions

Despite extremely high unemployment, most Native American workers, as stated earlier, are operatives. Because of their small numbers, Indian workers do not constitute a significant percentage nationally in any single industry. But in the Indian states it is another matter, such as mining in Alaska, construction and manufacturing in Oklahoma, mining and manufacturing in New Mexico, mining and manufacturing in Montana, and mining in Idaho. In these states Native America workers range from 4 to 11 percent of the industries specified. It is likely that mining will increasingly become important to Indian labor, since Carter's and now Reagan's energy policies emphasize exploiting traditional fuels like coal.

The question then arises, given Indian labor's significance in key industries in the Indian states, are Native Americans organized into unions to protect their job rights and working conditions? It is believed that a high proportion, especially in rural or reservation areas, are unorganized. Many tribes in the past, being under the thumb of the BIA, have barred unions from the reservations, but this is now beginning to change. The Navajo Nation, for example, which formerly outlawed unions, now has an estimated 6,600 union members, about 12 percent of the work force, an Office of Navajo Labor Relations, and its own hiring hall (Robbins 1978b). Mining and construction are the main unionized industries. About 300 Navajos join building trade unions each year.

Available data suggest that most Native Americans belong to craft rather than industrial unions. A 1974 survey of referral unions (unions with hiring halls and apprenticeship programs) by the Equal Employment Opportunity Commission (Libeau 1977) shows that Indians are better represented in the building trades than in the non-building trades unions. They are found mainly in the ironworkers international, roofers and laborers, although significant numbers are also members of plumbers, elevator constructors, asbestos workers, and plasterers. In the non-building trades, almost half of the Indian union members are Teamsters. Indian women, on the other hand, are found mainly in the Hotel and Restaurant Employees, and in the Teamsters. In Alaska, Montana, New Mexico, and Oklahoma, Native Americans form a significant percent of state referral union membership, ranging from 5 to 13 percent. Thus there is a good basis for building labor solidarity with the Native American struggle, and vice-versa. Labor, contrary to the anthropologist Tax, is hardly the enemy!

The importance of organized labor in the Indian struggle is seen also in the possibilities of its press which, generally speaking, is politically center to left-of-center on most issues. This is clearly not the case of the bourgeois or commercial press. Sixty million people, it is estimated, subscribe to the daily commercial newspapers, but tens of millions also receive a monthly or bi-weekly labor publication, such as the *International Teamster*, the *United Auto Workers Solidarity*, and the *United Mine Workers Journal*. There are 100 trade union affiliates of the AFL–

CIO alone, and most can be expected to take a better political line on Native American issues and problems than the corporate interests which own and control the commercial press.

For historical and cultural reasons, it would appear that most Native Americans identify along ethnic rather than class lines. Although this question begs serious study, surely the fact that Indians are channeled by the government into non-union shops, or else find themselves victims of racism and chauvinism even in unions, does not help them to develop strong feelings of class solidarity. Still, in structural terms, Native American workers occupy the same position with respect to the means of production as do other workers; *they have the same class enemy*.

Historically, as with other oppressed minorities, employers have used anti-Indian stereotypes and prejudice to weaken working class unity. This is most in evidence in regions where there are large concentrations of Native Americans. These are the regions of the country where racism against Native Americans has deep roots, the resident white population often being the descendants of the original settlers, those who were the shock troops for the railroads and the land companies on the old Indian frontier. (This has been described in Chapters Four and Five.) The region near Eureka, California, is such a place. Timber, in addition to fishing, is the main resource, and it is in this industry where whites and Indians most often work side by side.

In 1973 Redwood Construction's Hoopa division persuaded the drivers to vote out the Teamsters union by playing on anti-Indian prejudice and lying to the Hoopa Tribal Council and the National Labor Relations Board about the company's supposed concern to hire Indian workers. A report from Eureka (*Labor Today* 1973:2–3) explains the situation:

> Seniority is a trade union principle that was fought for in the 1930s. . . The idea behind seniority is to eliminate discrimination and favoritism. Yet, in this case, the company was able to utilize that principle against the union.

> The company succeeded in dividing the workers by telling Indian drivers that they could not hire them because of the union's demand for one seniority list located at Samoa [a non-Indian community]. Meanwhile the company was telling the Samoa drivers that "this bunch of Indians up in Hoopa want your job."

> Many white drivers did not see the company's game, which made it easier for the company to divide the men. However, it should now be clear to all Teamsters that the Hoopa division is rightfully entitled to its own seniority list, and that the union must begin to demand that Redwood Construction live up to its agreement with the Tribal Council (i.e., promised employment for local Indians).

This is the main reason why we have taken up the question of the class character of the Native American population, because it will take class unity to decisively win the Indian struggle.

Enemies

Carol Wright (1977:2), in her investigation of backlash groups for the National Indian Youth Council, has identified the elements most active in the racist Interstate Congress for Equal Rights and Responsibilities (ICERR). Formed in 1975, ostensibly "to halt a nationwide drive by professional Indians and attorney groups from taking over vast resources," the ICERR numbers among its most active and vocal supporters, according to Wright, environmentalists, sportsmen, local governments, corporations, ranchers, farmers and homeowners, and law-and-order types.

Are environmentalists the Indians' allies? Sometimes friends on specific issues, yes; class allies, no. Although they are an important part of the Great Basin MX Alliance opposing the MX missile, a coalition of groups ranging from businessmen and sportsmen to the Western Shoshone, they have at other times fought Native American treaty and land rights. In 1974 they actively opposed Havasupai land rights in the Grand Canyon, claiming the Indians would ruin the environment for the whiteman. In Alaska, too, environmentalists have marched to their own tune rather than support unequivocally aboriginal land rights.

The law-and-order individuals are those following the example of a right-wing vigilante group which emerged in opposition to the 1973 Indian action at Wounded Knee. "Originating from a group of 100 ranchers who own or lease 75 percent of the Pine Ridge Reservation . . . they call themselves the Civil Liberties for South Dakota Citizens" (Wright 1977:2). Having expanded to other states, they are assisted by the Minutemen and the John Birch Society.

The sportsmen's groups are against Native American fishing, hunting and gathering rights. Following the 1974 Boldt decision, Washington groups (mostly commercial fishermen) organized to end Indian fishing rights. These include Citizens United for Resources Emergencies, State Sportsmen's Council, the Northwest Steelhead–Salmon Council, and Trout Unlimited. Later, together with the National Wildlife Federation, they lobbied Congress to impose state game laws on American Indians.

Ranchers, farmers and homeowners in ICERR are those who lease or own lands within Indian reservations, many of which are checkerboarded with white ownership or land-use patterns. They have formed organizations in Washington state, such as the Quinault Land Owners Association, and the Lummi Property Owners.

Local or municipal governments opposed to Indian treaty rights are those "which have extended their city limits onto reservation lands [and] are now becoming aware that they may possibly lose some of their tax base if the tribes apply jurisdiction over lands legally still within their reservation boundaries" (Wright 1977:2). Examples are Roosevelt, Utah; New Town, North Dakota; Ronan and Polson, Montana; Espanola, Bernalillo and Albuquerque, New Mexico. There are also counties, such as Navajo and Apache Counties in Arizona, and Big Horn County in Montana. Finally, although Wright does not mention it, there are states, such as Washington which blatantly refused to carry out the Boldt decision, and New York which has threatened to mount a Wounded Knee-like attack on the Mohawks at Akwesasne.

Last, but not least, are the business corporations about which we have already written extensively.

On the surface it would appear from these facts that there has been an upsurge in anti-Indian activity from a wide cross-section of the non-Indian population. Stillwaggon (1980), an economist at Howard University however, convincingly demonstrates that it is the long-term economic aims of "certain individuals and corporations to wrest control over Indian resources" which is behind the funding for anti-Indian efforts. She analyzes the demogogic appeal to racism these forces have orchestrated among middle income and working folk (1980:3):

> Misinformation and prejudice have often led poor and working people to support causes which represent not their own interests but rather those of a wealthy elite which exploits both them and their supposed enemies in racial and ethnic minorities. Workers, sportsmen and other moderate-income whites have been spirited along behind a banner raised by a primarily bourgeois and petty-bourgeois leadership.

Stillwaggon makes a class analysis of the right-wing attack on Indian treaty rights, because Indian "advocacy and counter-offensive work has suffered as a result of the lack of economic analysis" (Stillwagon 1980: 21). Big money is behind ICERR, she explains. Montana, Washington and Oregon, for example, were each slated to raise $1 million in ICERR's 1978 national lobbying campaign. The First Vice President of ICERR is the mayor of Roosevelt, Utah, the largest town on the Ute Reservation. He is also a merchant and landowner opposed to Ute jurisdiction over Roosevelt's white business community.

Stillwaggon cites further evidence of her thesis in the case of the Maine land claims, filed in 1972 by the Penobscot and Passamaquoddy Indians. Although two-thirds of the state is under aboriginal title, the main target of the Indian suit was not small property owners, but 14 large paper companies. Yet with 43 percent of Maine's labor force employed in the paper industry, ICERR was able to portray the claim as menacing small homeowners and jeopardizing working-class jobs. ICERR "worked hard persuading goverment officials and union members to take the companies' side," which they eventually did (Stillwaggon 1980:13). The Great Northern Paper, which stood to lose the most acreage, threatened to leave the state, and ICERR garnered support among paperworkers. As a result, the case never went to court and is being settled in Congress for much less land than claimed, and with most of the money-part of the settlement coming out of the U.S. Treasury instead of the coffers of the paper companies.

A similar situation prevailed in the 1976 Mashpee-Wampanoag claim in Massachusetts. The Indian people sued primarily for underdeveloped town land in Mashpee, but the Mashpee Action Committee, controlled by local realtors and affiliated with ICERR, portrayed the claim as an attack on white property rights.

In the Pacific Northwest, the 1974 Boldt decision, awarding 50 percent of the off-reservation catch of salmon and steelhead trout to the Indians, is portrayed as injuring sportsmen and endangering environmental protection. In reality, the decision hurt only the commercial fishing industry. Stillwaggon sums up her thesis (1980:17):

> In the Pacific Northwest, as in Maine, while big corporate interests have a large stake in Indian resources, they have not needed to play a visible role in the political activity targeting Indian rights. They have been able to let others play the role of activist-protagonist, others whose image is more "down-home" and "regular".
>
> What could engender more sympathy than a paperworker in Maine or a sportsman in the Pacific Northwest? And these are the people doing the political work for the big canners and paper mills.

Anti-Monopoly Coalition

Despite the racist divisions created by ICERR, behind which corporate interests hide their attack on Indian lands and resources, there is a hopeful and necessary development in the formation of Indian/non-Indian coalitions opposing monopoly. In the summer of 1979, Sioux bearers of the sacred pipe led an anti-Nuke march in South Dakota, the Black Hills Alliance. The Sioux are opposed to a forced money settlement of their holy Black Hills, and they therefore joined with white ranchers and anti-nuclear activists to protest plans of the energy corporations "to mine uranium, use the meager water supply to process ore, and dispose of the water" in the Black Hills, which would threaten the way-of-life of both Indian and non-Indian in that region (Otterness 1979:3).

The Great Basin MX Alliance has already been mentioned and again proves that a wide grouping of people, representing different races and interests, can unite against a common foe, in this case, the U.S. Government and the military. The Alliance is comprised of ranchers, miners, farmers, local businessmen, sportsmen, recreationists, conservationists and Native Americans from the states of Nevada, Utah and Wyoming.

The Shoshone Nation claims 22 million acres of eastern Nevada under its 1863 Treaty of Ruby Valley. Today, however, the federal government controls 12 million of that claim, and another 10 million acres have already been given away to homesteaders, mining companies and railroads over the last century, the Shoshone retaining only four small reservations. The U.S. government is now attempting to use the 12 million acres of "public domain" under Indian claim for the MX missile system and a further give-away to corporate interests by offering the Shoshone $26 million for their land. This amounts to only $1.05 per acre for ancestral lands now valued at $200 per acre. The Shoshone are opposing this forced settlement and the danger the MX system poses for Nevada.

> The people of Nevada as a whole are concerned about the MX "race track" project because they feel it would make their state a "giant nuclear sponge" in the event of nuclear war. But they are also dismayed over the ruggedly beautiful state being torn up by roads, tracks and missile shelters (Karen Talbot 1980:40).

A resolution adopted by the Alliance in March, 1980, includes support for Native American rights in Nevada. Shoshone comment on the Coalition is instructive (Western Shoshone Sacred Land Association 1980:8):

> Our ranching and farming neighbors, for the first time, are beginning to understand what it means to be an Indian. They, too, see their way of life threatened by the military and the federal government. For once, perhaps, we can put aside our past differences and join hands with our non-Indian neighbors to fight this menace to our land.

Why fight the monopolies, which, these days, include the government as well? Today, in the Southwest and the northern Plains, as documented earlier, Native Americans are in danger of being strip-mined out of existence. The danger is highlighted by the following facts (*Indigena* 1974:4). The leasing of Indian lands is more profitable to large corporations than is the leasing of public lands. Aside from the fact that rental and royalty payments are lower, the average Indian lease is 15 times larger, thereby making reservation leases easier to mine, which increases productivity and therefore profits. This accounts for the fact that there is more current coal mining activity on the Indian leases, as opposed to public lands, despite the fact that the Indian leases are more recent. Finally, many of the strip-mining corporations, such as Peabody Coal, are multinationals, with international capital and power. Shields (1974:1) reports that "coal mines are owned by oil magnates, steel barons, copper interests, shipowners, utilities, etc." Behind Peabody, for instance, are Morgan bankers and the Guggenheim family. The second largest strip-miner is Consolidation Coal, a division of Continental Oil. In Consol, the Morgans share control with the Rockefeller interests. Consol is the main strip-miner which has tried to tie up the Northern Cheyenne Reservation with mining leases at rock-bottom prices.

The coal industry is highly concentrated. Fifteen companies produce more than half of the total U.S. coal output. The industry is interested in strip-mining in the western states, chiefly on Indian reservations, not only because of cheap land, resources and labor, but because it is easier to mine than underground coal. New technology has facilitated this development. With an unprecedented demand for coal at high prices, the monopolies want to extract coal at the lowest possible cost to maximize profits. There is also a tie-in with giant utility companies which are selling power to Los Angeles and other growing, western metropolitan areas. The government itself, through the Bureau of Reclamation, is a partner to these profit-making energy schemes.

Not only is western strippable coal cheaper to extract, but it is, by and large, unorganized (non-union). The coal industry therefore can cut corners by paying lower wages and fewer fringe benefits to workers, both Indian and non-Indian. The United Mine Workers Union has placed mine safety as its most urgent demand, because underground mining has the highest accident rate of any U.S. industry. (The key issue in the 1977 eastern coal strike was mine safety.) The cost of mine safety to the corporations may be another reason for the fact that half of all coal mined now comes from strip rather than underground mines, where the UMW is the collective bargaining agent.

The struggle against strip-mining by traditional Navajo, Hopi, Crow,

Ute and Northern Cheyenne Indians is a critical one for them much in the way that mine safety is for underground miners. On some reservations the tribal councils are carrying out a policy of collaboration with the coal companies for short-term gains, but the Northern Cheyenne Tribe has challenged the legality of the Interior Department's transaction on its Indian land leasing program.

For these reasons, the formation of a coalition uniting energy-rich tribes, the energy-consuming public, and mine workers is paramount. It is in the interest of ordinary energy consumers and organized labor to support Native American peoples and nationalities which call for mora-toriums, renegotiated leases, environmental controls, worker safety and the like. The Indian governing bodies, in turn, will have to support the right of their workers to organize, to form or belong to unions, and for the public to have reasonable (competitive) energy rates for heating and lighting homes. Hopefully, this consciousness is coming, but it behooves whites, members of the exploiter nation, if you will, to take the initiative.

To a considerable degree, Native Americans are conscious of the existence and role of the monopolies. Mickey Gimmell, former tribal chairperson of the Pit River Nation, made crystal clear the anti-monopoly nature of their struggle (*The Dispossessed* 1970:9):

> Therefore, let it be known by all concerned that the Pit River Tribe makes the following demands: number one, that the U.S. government and the large corporations including PG&E, PT&T, the Southern Pacific Railroad, Kim-berly Clark, Hearst Publications and the Los Angeles Times-Mirror corpora-tions, among others, return all of our land to us immediately. No amount of money can buy Mother Earth.

It is also worth quoting William Bennet, formerly of the California Public Utilities Commission, concerning the Pit River fight against PG&E, a private utility giant (*The Dispossessed* 1970:6):

> The plight of the Indians is symptomatic and typical of the manner in which a monopoly such as Pacific Gas & Electric Company treats people whether they be ratepayers or in some cases even small shareholders. . . What's going on at Pit River should illustrate to people how difficult the task toward achieving economic justice in the United States of America is in the year 1970. When I talk about the PG&E . . . I could do the same thing about U.S. Steel or General Motors or whatever. They're all basically the same: the same type of narrow corporate thinking—an almost calloused indifference to the spiritual nature of man as a beautiful creature and animal, the great preoccupation with profit for the sake of profit to the neglect of human values. But the important thing to know is you and I, in a sense, don't have the power to correct these except

through organization, union and numbers. Individually we can't do it, and that's what has to be done. And this is why people, whether they are black or brown or red or white, students, intellectuals, oppressed third-layer corporate utility executives, have something in common. They're being had. And unless they realize it they will continue to be had or exploited.

Another example of the anti-monopoly struggle is that waged by the Alaska Natives against the oil barons—British Petroleum, Atlantic–Richfield, Humble Oil, Phillips Petroleum, Union, Mobil and others. Estimated worth of the Prudhoe Bay deposits in the Arctic Ocean is $200 billion, yet the Native Peoples, and especially the North Slope Inuit (Eskimo), whose oil it is, have had to wage a tremendous effort against those oil capitalists and a host of "smaller fish" to get even a token settlement. Although the 1971 Alaska Native Claims Settlement Act has been represented as a great concession to indigenous rights—almost $1 billion plus 44 million acres of land (which has yet to be parcelled out)—the fact of the matter is that it is one of the greatest land and resource robberies yet perpetrated against Native Americans. Land rights to hundreds of millions of acres have been liquidated, subsistence hunting and fishing seriously curtailed, and it remains highly doubtful whether the grassroots Alaska Native will ever benefit from the government money, controlled as it is by 13 profit-making native corporations operating under federal regulations.

The struggle in Alaska continues. Deprived of the ownership and means of extracting their own oil, the Inuit won a tactical victory in the early 1970s when they legally formed their own borough. As the Barrow Borough, they are in a position to tax the oil giants. Thus 2800 Inuit are squared off against the oil companies. They know a little something about monopoly capitalism.

Other prominent Native Americans have made insightful comments respecting monopoly and the possibility of a coalition. Rupert Costo, Cahuilla, director of the American Indian Historical Society and co-editor of *Wassaja–The Indian Historian,* has written:

> The Indian economy is stifled and the corporations grow fat on the proceeds of Indian resources. Mining companies, railroads, and industrial concerns make their millions as a result of the expropriation of Indian land. Research documents exist in the hundreds bemoaning this situation, but today expropriation continues. From a previous condition of self-support, self-reliance, and self-government . . . the Native American has been forced into underdevelopment, is now locked in poverty, moves to urban areas only to find that he has extended his condition of impoverishment, and is trapped in the web of

American society's jungle of mismanagement, exploitation, and the super-structure of American big business interests (Davis 1973:30).

M. Magowan, editor-publisher of the *Cherokee Examiner* and publisher of *Rainbow People*, understands the link between Indian exploitation and the exploitation of non-Indian working folk. He told a non-Indian audience:

> Money runs the politics of your country; it has nothing to do with morality or anything else. . . Face reality: we the People have been aware for many moons that big business does not give a hoot about the people. This means YOU and US! Big business is interested ONLY in BIG money. People are of value only so long as they produce for big business. We, the Native People, are a dead-loss to big business, because we as a race are not on their money-trip. We are further a dead-weight because of our love of the land. We have reached the point that we are fighting to preserve this land. Big business views the land as something to strip! Look at what Crown Zellerbach has done right here; here they have stripmined the land, ravaged the vegetation, polluted rivers and reduced water tables to well below the danger point. This is big business, and unless things change, YOU will see this land ravaged into a total desert, and all for big business. In reality, our enemy is the same as yours. WE are not enemies (Council on Interracial Books for Children, 1971:321–322).

Richard Oakes, Mohawk, ex-iron worker and organizer of the Alcatraz occupation in 1969, also saw that the oppressed have a common enemy—big business. "It has to be remembered," he said, "that big business and government are almost synonymous terms. Big business and its pressures exert policies emanating out of the government and affect not only Indians, but poor whites, Blacks and other minorities."

An anti-monopoly struggle includes also unified action on the electoral level. Non-Indians should not discount the importance of the Indian vote in the country. Although a small minority nationally, Native Americans nonetheless form a significant voting block in several western states. As Wilfred Scott (*Wassaja, The Indian Historian,* 1980:17), Vice Chairperson of the Council of Energy Resource Tribes, analyzes it:

> . . . The "Indian vote" in absolute terms is relatively small. But in terms of its ability to swing the electoral result in selected states, its potential is large . . . in four states, Alaska, New Mexico, Oklahoma and South Dakota, the Indian voting-age population exceeds the margin of votes by which Gerald Ford beat Jimmy Carter in 1976.

Robbins (1978:17) reports that the AFL–CIO assisted the Navajo with a voter drive through COPE for the 1974 election, and the Navajo vote made the difference. A Democratic governor was elected in Arizona by only 4,000 votes, nearly equal to his margin of victory among the Navajo electorate. In other words, the link-up of organized labor and Navajo voters was of key importance.

The electoral political struggle for Native Americans, however, goes beyond the struggle for bourgeois democratic rights, as important as they are, and non-Indians must come to understand and support this principle. A real application of self-determination would mean full representation at all levels of government, thus giving Native American peoples and nationalities a voice in those bodies that make the laws and decide Indian policies. A way to achieve this goal might be to give each major reservation the right to elect a Congressman, and major nationalities the right to elect a Senator, with the same principle applying to state and county governments (CPUSA 1979). Non-Indians must also support the right of Native Americans to decisively control the Bureau of Indian Affairs. The Assistant Secretary of the Interior–Indian Affairs, for example, is an unelected office, yet the BIA controls the destiny of most ethnic Native Americans. The need to develop new forms of electoral struggle—for accountability by the government to the Indian and Alaska Native masses, and electoral coalitions of Indians and non-Indians around common causes—is vitally important.

A critical test for the Native American movement will be the challenge posed by President Ronald Reagan's 1982 economic program. It is in effect a declaration of class war against the people of the United States, and hardest hit will be the working-class poor and oppressed minorities. The rationale for cutting badly needed social programs is the so-called Soviet threat, and the Reagan administration, therefore, proposes to increase military spending to 33 percent of the total budget. The impact on Native American peoples and nations would be devastating. Spokespersons of the Native American Rights Fund and the National Tribal Chairman's Association, according to *The Washington Post* (March 14, 1981), estimate that spending for Indian communities would be reduced by 35 percent and reservation unemployment would rise to 60 percent or more. The elimination of the Economic Development Administration and cutbacks in the Indian housing program, general health care, reforestation, education, and welfare would pose an extremely serious crisis for Indian country.

Within this context, Native Americans must, in their political strategy, discriminate between friends and allies. In the fight-back against the Reagan military budget and administrative policies broad coalitions will have to be formed, possibly with those who have taken anti-Indian positions in the past, around areas of agreement to roll back Reagan's oppressive policies. The military build-up, for example, making operative the MX missile, would have a great impact on the land rights of Native Americans. It is therefore in the interests of all peoples struggling against the build-up to advocate Indian land rights, and vice-versa.

In the final analysis, however, there must be a decisive class content to the anti-monopoly coalition, and the role of the oppressed minorities— Black, Chicano, Puerto Rican, Asian, Native American—in that coalition must be a key one. The best and truest allies of Native American peoples and nationalities in the fight-back, in terms of their structural position in the U.S. political economy, will be the other oppressed minorities and the working class generally.

WORKS CITED

Akwesasne Notes
  1971   "Drums," *Akwesasne Notes* 3(8):16–17.
  1972   "Numbers Games, Anyone?," *Akwesasne Notes* 4(3):9.
  1973   "American Public Support for Independent Oglala Nation," *Akwesasne Notes* 5(3):6.
  1974a   "The Effects of Colonialism on Indian Life," *Akwesasne Notes* 6(4):40–42.
  1974b   "Real Estate at Pine Ridge," *Akwesasne Notes* 6(2):17.
  1976   "Gasification and the Death of the Land," *Akwesasne Notes* 8(1):22–23.
  1979   "Uranium in the Black Hills," *Akwesasne Notes* 11(1):13–14.

American Friends Service Committee
  1970   *Uncommon Controversy: Fishing Rights of the Mukleshoot, Puyallup, and Nisqually Indians.* Seattle: University of Washington Press.

American Indian Movement
  1973   Bulletins issued by the Lakota Coalition and other documents regarding the Wounded Knee occupation. Rapid City, South Dakota: Red Man's International Warrior Society.

American Indian Policy Review Commission
  1977   "The Economics of Indian Country" (Chapter Seven) *AIPRC Final Report.* Vol. 1:301–365. Washington, DC: U.S. Government Printing Office.

Aptheker, Herbert
  1975   "The Class Character of the American Revolution," *World Marxist Review* 18(7):40–42.

Ayres, Mary Ellen
  1978   "Federal Indian Policy and Labor Statistics," *Monthly Labor Review* (April): 22–27.

Bailin, Roxanne and Aubrey Grossman
  1971   *One of the Last Human Hunts of Civilization.* San Francisco: Image 3 Graphics. (Pamphlet).

Bear Facts Newsletter
  1973   *Bear Facts Newsletter* 2. Native American Studies Program, University of California, Berkeley.

Beard, Charles A.
  1956   *An Economic Interpretation of the Constitution of the United States.* New York: Macmillan.

Berkey, Curtis, Charles Chibitty, Kirke Kickingbird, and Lynn Kickingbird
  1977   *Indian Sovereignty.* Washington, DC: Institute for the Development of Indian Law. (Process).

Blundell, William E.
  1971   "Ecological Shootout at Black Mesa," *The Wall Street Journal,* April 13. (Reprint.)

Boyer, Richard O., and Herbert M. Morais
  1970   *Labor's Untold Story.* New York: United Electrical, Radio and Machine Workers of America. Third Edition.

Brandon, William
  1961   *The American Heritage Book of Indians.* New York: Dell.

Brecher, Joseph
  1972   "Black Mesa and the Law," *Clear Creek* 13 (June):62, 64.

Brown, Dee
  1970   *Bury My Heart at Wounded Knee.* New York: Bantam.

Bureau of Indian Affairs
1969   "Economic Development of Indian Communities," *Toward Economic Development for Native American Communities. Part II: Development Programs and Plans.* Subcommittee on Economy in Government of the Joint Economic Committee, Congress of the United States: 331–355. Washington, DC: U.S. Government Printing Office.
1973   *Estimates of Resident Indian Population and Labor Force Status; By State and Reservation: March 1973.* (Process.)

Burnette, Robert and John Koster
1974   *The Road to Wounded Knee.* New York: Bantam.

Cahn, Edgar S.
1969   *Our Brother's Keeper.* Washington, DC: New Community Press.

Caudill, Harry M.
1973   "Farming and Mining—There Is No Land to Spare," *Atlantic* 232(3):85–90.

Clark, Ira Granville, Jr.
1947   *The Railroads and the Tribal Lands. Indian Territory, 1830–1890.* Unpublished Ph.D. dissertation, University of California, Berkeley.

Clemmer, Richard O.
1973   *Culture Change and the Hopi Nation: The Impact of Federal Jurisdiction.* Binghamton: Department of Anthropology, State University of New York. (Process.)
1976   "Hopi Political Economy," *Southwest Economy & Society* 2(1):4–33.
1978   "Black Mesa and the Hopi," in *Native Americans and Energy Development.* Edited by Joseph G. Jorgensen et al:17–34. Cambridge, Mass.: Anthropology Resource Center.

Cohen, Felix S.
1971a   *Handbook of Federal Indian Law.* Albuquerque: University of New Mexico Press. (Originally published 1949).
1971b   "Indian Self-Government," in *Red Power.* Edited by Alvin M. Josephy, Jr.:17–29. New York: McGraw-Hill.
1973   "The Erosion of Indian Rights, 1950–1953: A Case Study in Bureaucracy," in *Who's the Savage?* Edited by David R. Wrone and Russell S. Nelson:531–539. Greenwich, Conn: Fawcett.

Collier, Peter
1970   "The Redman's Burden," *Ramparts* (February):26–38.

The Comptroller General of the United States
1975   *Indian Natural Resources—Opportunities for Improved Management and Increased Productivity. Part I: Forest Land, Rangeland, and Cropland.* Report to the Committee on Interior and Insular Affairs, U.S. Senate. Washington, DC: Department of the Interior.

Communist Party USA
1979   *The Path to Native American Liberation.* Resolution of the 22nd Convention, August 23–26. (Pamphlet.)

Congressional Record, U.S. Senate
1972   *Congressional Record,* September 19, and November 8.

Coulter, Robert
1977   *The Denial of Legal Remedies to Indian Nations Under United States Law.* Washington, DC: Institute for the Development of Indian Law. (Process.)

Council on Interracial Books for Children
1971   *Chronicles of American Indian Protest.* Greenwich, Conn.: Fawcett Premier.

Davis, Shelton
1973   "Surplus Expropriation on American Indian Reservations," in *The American Indian in the Contemporary United States.* A Syllabus, with documents, for Social Sciences 152, Spring Term, Harvard University. (Process.)

Day, Robert C.
1972   "The Emergence of Activism as a Social Movement," in *Native Americans Today: Sociological Perspectives*. Edited by Howard M. Barh, Bruce A. Chadwick, and Robert C. Day:506–532. New York: Harper and Row.

Deloria, Vine, Jr.
1969a   *Custer Died For Your Sins*. New York: Avon.
1969b   "The War Between the Redskins and the Feds," *New York Times Magazine*, December 7.
1971   "This Country Was a Lot Better Off When the Indians Were Running It," in *Red Power*. Edited by Alvin M. Josephy, Jr., New York: McGraw–Hill, pp. 235–247.
1973   *God is Red*. New York: Grosset & Dunlap.
1974a   "The Question of the 1868 Sioux Treaty . . . a Critical Element in the Wounded Knee Trials," *Akwesasne Notes* 6(1):12.
1974b   *Behind the Trail of Broken Treaties*. New York: Dell.

The Dispossessed
1970   *The Dispossessed*. A discussion manual accompanying a 16mm documentary film on the Pit River Indians' struggle to regain their lands. Canyon Cinema Cooperative, Sausalito, California. (Process.)

Dobyns, Henry F.
1966   "Estimating Aboriginal American Populations," *Current Anthropology* 7(4): 395–416 and seq.

Economic Development Adminstration, Department of Commerce
1969   "Indian Development Program," *Toward Economic Development for Native American Communities*. Vol. 2:356–369. Subcommittee on Economy in Government of the Joint Economic Committee, Congress of the United States. Washington, DC: U.S. Government Printing Office.

Engels, Frederick
1942   *The Origin of the Family, Private Property, and the State*. New York: International Publishers.

Erdoes, Richard
1972   *The Sun Dance People*. New York: Random House.

Ewers, John C.
1939   *The Role of the Indian in National Expansion. Part II. Removing the Indian Barrier*. Washington, DC: National Park Service, U.S. Department of Agriculture.

Faherty, Robert L.
1974   "The American Indian: An Overview," *Current History* 67(400):241–244.

Fedoseyev, P. N.
1977   *Leninism and the National Question*. Moscow: Progress Publishers.

Forbes, Jack D.
1965   "The 'Indian Domain' of Nevada and Its Relationship to Indian Property Rights," *Nevada State Bar Journal* 30(3):16–47.
1972   "The New Resistance," *Akwesasne Notes* 4(3):20–22.
1979   "Is Carter Reviving Georgia's Indian Policy at the National Level?," *Wassaja* 7(5):16.

Foster, William Z.
1951   *Outline Political History of the Americas*. New York: International Publishers.

Gapay, Les
1978   "Fighting to Keep Montana's Skies Blue," *The Washington Post*, March 30.

Garbus, Martin
1974   "General Haig of Wounded Knee," *The Nation*, November 9.

Grossman, Aubrey
1970   *Memorandum in Support of Motion to Dismiss Charges*, filed in Burney District

198 WORKS CITED

Court by Grossman, Ackerman, Peters, and fifteen other attorneys. Reprinted in *The Dispossessed* 1970:11–15.

Hall, Gus
1974   *The Energy Rip-Off, Cause and Cure.* New York: International Publishers.
1976   *World Magazine,* October 16.

Hertzberg, Hazel W.
1971   *The Search for an American Indian Identity.* Syracuse: Syracuse University Press.

Hess, Bill
1980   "Seeking the Best of Two Worlds," *National Geographic* 157(2):273–290.

Indigena
1974   *Indigena* (Summer).

International Indian Treaty Council
1977   *The Geneva Conference* 1(7). New York: IITC.

Iowa Law Review
1966   "The American Indian: Tribal Sovereignty and Civil Rights," *Iowa Law Review* 51:654–669.

Jackson, Helen Hunt
1965   *A Century of Dishonor.* Edited by Andrew F. Rolle. New York: Harper & Row. (Originally published 1881.)

Jacobs, Wilbur, R.
1972   *Dispossessing the American Indian.* New York: Charles Scribner's Sons.

Jordan, Gil
1972   "Street Scenes from the Electric Fiefdom," *Clear Creek* 13 (June):20–24.

Jorgensen, Joseph G.
1971   "Indians and the Metropolis," in *The American Indian in Urban Society.* Edited by Jack O. Waddell and O. Michael Watson:67–113. Boston: Little, Brown & Co.
1978   "A Century of Political Effects on American Indian Society, 1880–1980," *The Journal of Ethnic Studies* 6(3):1–82.

Jorgensen, Joseph G., Shelton H. Davis, and Robert O. Mathews
1978   "Energy, Agriculture, and Social Science in the American West," in *Native Americans and Energy Development.* Edited by Jorgensen *et al*:3–16. Cambridge, Mass.: Anthropology Resource Center.

Josephy, Alvin M. Jr. (editor)
1971   *Red Power.* New York: McGraw-Hill.

Kane, Albert E.
1965   "Jurisdiction Over Indians and Indian Reservations," *Arizona Law Review* 6:237–255.

Katz, William Loren
1977   "Black and Indian Cooperation and Resistance to Slavery," *Freedomways* 17(3):164–174.

King, Bill
1969   "Some Thoughts on Reservation Economic Development," Appendix, *Toward Economic Development for Native American Communities. Vol. 2:*73–74. Subcommittee on Economy in Government of the Joint Economic Committee, Congress of the United States. Washington, DC: U.S. Government Printing Office.

Labor Today
1973   "From the 'Rank and File Reporter,'" *Labor Today* 2 (September).

La Duke, Winona
1979   "How Much Development?," *Akwesasne Notes* 11(1):5–8.

La France, Joan.
n.d. *The Unwritten Chapters*. Olympia, Washington: Superintendent of Public Instruction. (Process.)

Lagone, Stephen A.
1969a "A Statistical Profile of the Indian: The Lack of Numbers," *Toward Economic Development for Native American Communities*. Vol. 2:1–18. Subcommittee on Economy in Government of the Joint Economic Committee, Congress of the United States. Washington, DC: U.S. Government Printing Office.

1969b "The Heirship Land Problem and Its Effect on the Indian, Tribe, and Effective Utilization," *Toward Economic Development for Native American Communities*. Vol. 2:519–548. Etc.

Levitan, Sar and Barbara Hetrick
1971 *Big Brother's Indian Programs—With Reservations*. New York: McGraw–Hill.

Libeau, Vera A.
1977 *Minority and Female Membership in Referral Unions, 1974*. Research Report No. 55, Equal Employment Opportunity Commission. Washington, DC: U.S. Government Printing Office.

Linford, Lloyd
1972 "A Little Closer to God, the Central Arizona Project," *Clear Creek* 13 (June): 25–29, 68.

Loeffler, Jack
1972 "A Crystal of Many Windows: The Southwest as Symbol," *Clear Creek* 13 (June):10–12.

Los Angeles Times
1978 "Indians and Oil: Bitterness Runs Deep," *Los Angeles Times*, April 13.

Lumer, Hyman
1975 "Some Features of U.S. Capitalist Development," *World Marxist Review* 18(12):24–27.

Lurie, Nancy O.
1971a "The Contemporary American Indian Scene," in *North American Indians in Perspective*. Edited by Eleanor Leacock and Nancy O. Lurie:418–480. New York: Random House.

1971b "Menominee Termination: or Can the White Man Ever Overcome a Cultural Lag and Learn to Progress with the Indians?," *Indian Historian* 4(4):32–45.

MacLeod, William Christie
1928 *The American Indian Frontier*. New York: Alfred A. Knopf.

McNickle, D'Arcy
1973 *Native American Tribalism*. New York: Oxford University Press.

Martone, Rosalie
1974 "The United States and the Betrayal of Indian Water Rights," *The Indian Historian* 7(3):3–11.

Maruskin, Boris
1975 *The American Tradition, What Remains?* Moscow: Novosti Press Agency.

Marx, Karl
1954 *Capital*. Translated by S. Moore and E. M. Aveling. London: Lawrence & Wishert. (Originally published in 1867).

Meyer, William
1971 *Native Americans: The New Indian Resistance*. New York: International Publishers.

Morgan, Lewis Hunt
1965 *Houses and House–Life of the American Aborigines*. Chicago: Chicago University Press. (Originally published 1881.)

Nafziger, Richard
1979   *Transnational Energy Corporations and American Indian Development*. Occasional Paper, Development Series. Native American Studies Center, The University of New Mexico. (Process.)

Nagel, Gerald S.
1974   "Economics of the Reservations: Origins of the Indians' Plight," *Current History* 67(400):245–249.

The National Lawyers Guild
1977   *The Proper Status of Native Americans Under International Law*. The National Lawyers Guild, USA (September). (Process.)

National Indian Youth Council
1973   "Preference," *Americans Before Columbus* 6(2):1, 2, 3, 8.

Nickeson, Steve
1973   "On the Road to Wounded Knee," *Race Relations Reporter* 4(13):21–28.

Novack, George
1970   *Genocide Against the Indians: Its Role in the Rise of Capitalism*. New York: Pathfinder. (Pamphlet.)

Oswalt, Wendell H.
1973   *This Land Was Theirs*. New York: John Wiley & Sons. Second Edition.

Otterness, Eleanor and William
1979   "Anti-Nuke March in the Black Hills," *Peace & Freedom* 39(7):3.

People's World
1955   *People's World*, December 5.
1974   "To Our Brothers," *People's World*, February 23.

Perlo, Victor
1973   "South Dakota's Piincipal Victims," *Daily World*, March 6.
1975   *Economics of Racism USA*, New York: International Publishers.

Petrakis, Peter L.
1970   "PG&E, Squatter on the Public Domain," *San Francisco Bay Guardian*. (Reprinted in *The Dispossessed*, 1970:28–33.)

Philip, Kenneth R.
1977   *John Collier's Crusade for Indian Reform, 1920–1954*. Tucson, Arizona: University of Arizona Press.

Pittman, John
1973a   *Daily World*, March 9.
1973b   "Wounded Knee and the Indian Future," *Political Affairs* 52(7):66–74.

Pratt, Raymond B.
1979   "Tribal Sovereignty and Resource Exploitation," *Southwest Economy & Society* 4(3):38–74.

Raines, Howell
1979   "Struggling for Power and Identity," *New York Times Magazine*, February 11.

Richards, Bill and Bill Peterson
1978   "The Indian Tourism Bust," *The Washington Post*, May 30.

Robbins, Lynn
1977   "The Navajo Nation and Industrial Developments," *Southwest Economy & Society* 2(3):47–70.
1978a   "Energy Developments and the Navajo Nation," in *Native Americans and Energy Development*. Edited by Joseph G. Jorgensen *et al*: 35–48. Cambridge, Mass: Anthropology Resource Center.
1978b   "Navajo Workers and Labor Unions," *Southwest Economy & Society* 3(3):4–23.

Rogin, Michael
1972   "And Then There Were None," *New York Times* book review, June 24.

Ruffing, Lorraine Turner
1979   "The Navajo Nation: A History of Dependence and Underdevelopment," *The Review of Radical Political Economics* 11(2):25–37.
1980   *The Role of Policy in American Indian Mineral Development.* Occasional Paper, Development Series. Native American Studies Center: University of New Mexico. (Process.)

San Francisco Sunday Examiner and Chronicle
1973   "For Indians It's a Life with Built-in Failure," *San Francisco Sunday Examiner and Chronicle*, March 18.

Savage, Melissa
1972   "Black Mesa Mainline: Tracks on the Earth," *Clear Creek* 13 (June):13–19.

Schlesier, Karl H.
1974   "Action Anthropology and the Southern Cheyenne," *Current Anthropology* 15(3):277–283.
1979   "Of Indians and Anthropologists," *American Anthropologist* 81(2):325–330.
1980   "Reply to Deloria, Demaille, Hill and Washburn," *American Anthropologist* 83(3):561–563.

Schusky, Ernest
1969   "The Right to Be Indian," *Hearings Before the Special Subcommittee on Indian Education,* Committee on Labor and Public Welfare, 90th Congress. Washington, DC: U.S. Government Printing Office.

Sclar, Lee
1972   "Participation by Off-Reservation Indians in Programs of the Bureau of Indian Affairs and the Indian Health Service," *Montana Law Review* 33:194–195.

Sherill, Robert G.
1966   "Corps of Engineers: The Pork-Barrel Soldiers," *The Nation* 202(7):180–183.

Steiner, Stan
1968   *The New Indians.* New York: Dell.

Stillwaggon, Eileen M.
1980   "Anti-Indian Agitation and Economic Interests in the 1970s." (Manuscript.)

Spicer, Edward H.
1969   *A Short History of the Indians of the United States.* New York: Van Nostrand Reinhold.

Stoffle, Richard W.
1975   "Reservation-Based Industry: A Case from Zuni, New Mexico," *Human Organization* 34(3):217–226.

Stoffle, Richard W., Cheryl A. Last, and Michael J. Evans.
1979   "Reservation-Based Tourism: Implications of Tourist Attitudes for Native American Economic Development," *Human Organization* 38(3):300–306.

Sutton, Imre
1975   *Indian Land Tenure.* New York: Clearwater.

Talbot, Karen
1980   "Struggle of American Indians Against Genocide," *New Perspectives* 3(4):40–41.

Talbot, Steve
1977   "The Myth of Indian Economic and Political Incompetence: The San Carlos Case," *Southwest Economy & Society* 2(3):3–46.

Taylor, Theodore W.
1974   "American Indians and Their Governments," *Current History* 67(400):254–258, 275–277.

Trail of Broken Treaties
1973   *Trail of Broken Treaties.* Mohawk Nation via Rooseveltown: Akwesasne Notes.

Trout, Richard
  1973   "Railroad Land Grants and Indian Lands." Term paper for Native American
               Studies 175c, Winter Term, University of California, Berkeley.
United States Code, Congressional and Administrative News
  1974   *U.S. Code, Congressional and Administrative News*. 93rd Congress, Second
               Session 4:7775–7804. St. Paul, Minn.: West Publishing Co.
U.S. Department of Commerce, Bureau of Census
  1973   *Subject Report, American Indians*. 1970 Census of Population PC(2)–1F.
               Washington, DC: U.S. Government Printing Office.
U.S. Senate, Kennedy Report on Indian Education
  1969   *Indian Education: A National Tragedy—A National Challenge*. U.S. Senate,
               Committee on Labor and Public Welfare, Special Subcommittee on Indian
               Education. Report No. 91–501, 91st Congress, 1st Session. Washington, DC:
               U.S. Government Printing Office.
Veeder, William H.
  1969   "Federal Encroachment on Indian Water Rights and the Impairment of Reser-
               vation Development," *Toward Economic Development for Native American
               Communities*, Vol. 2:460–518. Subcommittee on Economy in Government of
               the Joint Economic Committee, Congress of the United States. Washington,
               DC: U.S. Government Printing Office.
Voices From Wounded Knee
  1974   *Voices From Wounded Knee*. Rooseveltown, NY: Akwesasne Notes.
Vogel, Virgil J. (editor)
  1972   *This Country Was Ours: A Documentary History of the American Indian*. New
               York: Harper and Row.
Warren, John S.
  1972   "An Analysis of the Indian Bill of Rights," *Montana Law Review* 33:255–265.
Washburn, Wilcomb E.
  1971   *Redman's Land/White Man's Law*. New York: Charles Scribner's Sons.
The Washington Post
  1978   "Indian Tribes Are Asserting Water Rights," *The Washington Post*, February 6.
Wassaja **(The American Indian Historical Society)**
  1973   "Fraud, Injustice, Trickery Shown in California Land Claims Settlement,"
               Wassaja 1(1):9–22.
  1974   "American Indian Historical Society," *Wassaja* 2(11):14.
  1975   "Angry Indian Reaction to Wildlife Federation Position," *Wassaja* 3(4):1.
Wassaja, The Indian Historian **(The American Indian Historical Society)**
  1980   "The Indian Vote," *Wassaja, The Indian Historian* 13(3):17.
Wax, Murray L.
  1971   *Indian-Americans, Unity and Diversity*. Englewood Cliffs, N.Y.: Prentice–Hall.
Western Shoshone Sacred Land Association
  1980   "Land is the Only Issue," WSSLA 1(1):1, 8.
Wheeler, Sessions S.
  1969   *The Desert Lake, The Story of Nevada's Pyramid Lake*. Caldwell, Idaho: The
               Caxton Printer, Ltd.
Williams, William Appleman
  1961   *The Contours of American History*. Cleveland, Ohio: The World Publishing Co.
Wissler, Clark
  1966   *Indians of the United States*. New York: Doubleday. Revised Edition.
Woddis, Jack
  1967   *Introduction to Neo-colonialism*. New York: International Publishers.
Wright, Carol
  1977   "What People Have Formed Backlash Groups?," *Yakima Nation Review* (To-
               penish, Washington). Special Autumn Supplement.

INDEX